MAKING DECISIONS IN COMPULSORY MENTAL HEALTH WORK
Boundaries, Frames and Perspectives

Edited by
Jill Hemmington and Sarah Vicary

First published in Great Britain in 2023 by

Policy Press, an imprint of
Bristol University Press
University of Bristol
1–9 Old Park Hill
Bristol
BS2 8BB
UK
t: +44 (0)117 374 6645
e: bup-info@bristol.ac.uk

Details of international sales and distribution partners are available at
policy.bristoluniversitypress.co.uk

© Bristol University Press 2023

British Library Cataloguing in Publication Data
A catalogue record for this book is available from the British Library

ISBN 978-1-4473-6288-3 hardcover
ISBN 978-1-4473-6289-0 paperback
ISBN 978-1-4473-6290-6 ePub
ISBN 978-1-4473-6291-3 ePdf

The right of Jill Hemmington and Sarah Vicary to be identified as editors of this work has been
asserted by them in accordance with the Copyright, Designs and Patents Act 1988.

Cover design: Nicky Borowiec
Front cover image: Adobe Stock/lawrence gill salgado/EyeEm
Bristol University Press and Policy Press use environmentally responsible
print partners.
Printed in Great Britain by CPI Group (UK) Ltd, Croydon, CR0 4YY

Contents

Notes on contributors vii
Acknowledgements xi

1 **Introduction** 1
Jill Hemmington and Sarah Vicary
Boundaries 4
Framing 5
Outline of the book 6

2 **Lived experience and the boundaries between professionals and others** 13
Neil Caton and Jen Kilyon
Introduction 13
Neil's experiences 13
Jen's experiences 18
Conclusion 21

3 **Frames and boundaries of race and ethnicity in Mental Health Act assessments** 25
Hári Sewell
Introduction 25
Race and ethnicity 26
Racial inequalities and institutional racism 27
Race and ethnicity in compulsory mental health work 29
Conclusion 36

4 **Gender and forensic services** 41
Rebecca Fish
Introduction 41
Gendered preconceptions 41
Restrictive practices 44
Progression 46
Power disparity 46
Eliminating restrictive practices 47
Flattening the hierarchy 48
Conclusion 50

5 **Boundaries of risks and rights and personality disorder** 55
Andy Brammer
Introduction 55
Personality disorder and contested narratives 55
The practice and the principles 57
Weighing up rights and risks 59
Pressures on the decision makers 61

Experiencing alienation 62
Some suggestions for practice 63
Conclusion 63

6   **Reflective supervision, emotional containment and the framing** 67
     of self and others
     Gill Robinson
     Introduction 67
     Why is reflective practice of value? 69
     Methodology 69
     Why a case? 70
     Firmly managed boundaries encourage free expression 70
     How does the RPG work? 71
     Psychosocial researchers' observations of the work of the group 72
     Theorised sense-making 72
     Organisational defences? 74
     Impact on Sarah 75
     Role of senior managers 75
     Conclusion 76

7   **Reflective practice, truth-telling and safe spaces** 81
     Kevin Stone
     Introduction 81
     Context 81
     Lack of AMHP supervision 82
     Personal liability 83
     Complexity of the AMHP role 84
     Organisational impact 86
     Accountability in practice 87
     Safe spaces for reflection 90
     Conclusion 92

8   **Practice education: boundaries of knowledge, theory and practice** 97
     Che McGarvey-Gill
     Introduction 97
     Preparation of self and context 98
     Supporting trainees remotely 99
     Learning processes 100
     Modelling good practice 101
     Direct observation 102
     Decision making under mental health legislation 104
     Supervision of trainees 105
     Placement outcomes: pass or fail? 107
     Factors that impact practice educators' decisions 107
     Conclusion 108

Contents

9   Compulsory mental health work and multi-professional   115
frames: occupational therapy in AMHP work
Rachel Bloodworth-Strong
Introduction   115
The value of occupational therapy   116
Health enablers   117
Alternatives to hospital   119
Independence   119
Occupational therapy skills   120
Occupation therapy and AMHPs: the research   121
The case for occupational therapy   124
Conclusion   125

10   Nurses as AMHPs: from 'unclean' to 'honorary social worker'   131
Sarah Vicary
Introduction   131
Background   131
Methods   132
Findings   133
Discussion   140
Conclusion   141

11   Who do you think you are? Hybrid professionals, boundaries and   145
the context of AMHP practice
Caroline Leah
Introduction   145
The context of AMHP practice   145
Hybridity definitions   147
Professional role(s) and boundaries of practice   148
Boundary working   150
Hybrid Identities Project: a case study of the AMHP role   152
Conclusion   156

12   Framing mental capacity and mental health legislation in   161
decision making
Matthew Graham
Introduction   161
The freedom to make decisions   162
The establishment of the Mental Capacity Act   162
Mental capacity, consent and compulsory treatment   163
Knowing what law requires of professionals   165
Balancing people's wishes and feelings against a need for care or   167
treatment
Conclusion   169

13	Navigating communication boundaries: statutory assessments as places for shared decision making	173
	Jill Hemmington	
	Introduction	173
	Statutory contexts, policy contexts and principles	173
	Shared decision making	174
	Paternalism, values and attitudes in mental health services	177
	What is important to service users?	178
	Developing and enabling reciprocity and decision sharing in practice	179
	Communication: attitudes, styles and skills	180
	Repair	182
	Barriers to SDM	182
	Taking the power elsewhere? The kitchen conversation	183
	Incorporating principles of Open Dialogue	184
	Conclusion	185
14	Compulsory mental health work: framing the future	191
	Jill Hemmington and Sarah Vicary	
	Index	197

Notes on contributors

Rachel Bloodworth-Strong has a BSc (Hons) in occupational therapy and a master's degree in advanced mental health practice, on which her chapter is based. Rachel worked for five years for third-sector organisations including the Stroke Association and the Shaftesbury Society. She has been an English for speakers of other languages (ESOL) teacher in adult learning and a lecturer in occupational therapy for Oxford Brookes University. Rachel has been an occupational therapist for 20 years, working in a variety of fields including trauma, older adult acute mental health, recovery-based supported mental health housing and adult social care. Rachel has been a qualified and practising Approved Mental Health Professional (AMHP) for three years.

Andy Brammer is a registered social worker, AMHP and Best Interests Assessor (BIA). He has worked in social care for 40 years and mental health social work for the past 20 years. He has recently taken on the role of Mental Health Act/Mental Capacity Act Practice Lead for a local authority in the north of England and was previously AMHP lead there for eight years. Andy has been a registered Living Works suicide prevention trainer for over 12 years.

Andy is an associate lecturer at Sheffield Hallam University and also teaches at Leeds Beckett University. Andy mainly teaches on postgraduate programmes, including AMHP, BIA and adult safeguarding. In addition, he supervises master's students undertaking research into child and adolescent mental health. His main research interests involve the decision making of mental health practitioners, risk assessment in mental health and the professional identity of mental health social workers.

Neil Caton has lived experience of a range of mental health services and he has been assessed and detained under the Mental Health Act in England. He works as a service user researcher in Lancashire and South Cumbria NHS Trust, where he contributes a lived experience perspective to a wide range of projects. He is a long-standing trustee of the International Society for Psychological and Social Approaches to Psychosis (ISPS) UK, where he helps promote rights-based and person-centred alternatives to mainstream psychiatric care for people who experience psychosis. Neil has done a wide range of involvement work within mental health services in research, teaching and service provision. He has run a hearing voices and paranoia group in Chorley and Blackburn for around ten years. Neil has worked in health and social care as a support worker for 19 years, with different client groups but mainly people with learning difficulties.

Rebecca Fish has been researching mental health services since 1997. Her early research explored service responses to self-harm and aggression from the perspectives of service users and staff. The research filled a gap in knowledge in this area and features in National Institute for Health and Care Excellence (NICE) systematic reviews of evidence. More recently, her work has investigated the experiences and perspectives of women detained on locked wards, using an ethnographic approach informed by feminist disability studies. Rebecca has presented her work in Norway, Sweden and Denmark, and was a keynote speaker at the 2019 UK Restraint Reduction Network conference.

Matthew Graham is a registered social worker who has been an academic in social work since 2007. Matthew has extensive experience of working in local authority mental health services and academia. He has a passion for teaching, writing and researching on mental health, mental capacity and associated legislation. Matthew specialises in delivering continuing professional development to a range of social work and healthcare professionals in practice, as well as publishing on the subjects of mental capacity and the Mental Capacity Act 2005. Matthew is co-author of *A Practical Guide to the Mental Capacity Act 2005: Putting the Principles of the Act into Practice* (Jessica Kingsley Publishers, 2015).

Matthew is also interested in adult safeguarding and risk analysis, and supports social workers in practice to develop their knowledge on these subjects through delivering a wide variety of training, teaching and consultancy. Matthew is a tutor at the University of Central Lancashire (UCLan) on the AMHP programme and leads the BIA qualifying module.

Jill Hemmington is a registered social worker, practising AMHP and course leader for UCLan's AMHP qualifying and post-qualifying (CPD) training and education, both of which are delivered nationally. Prior to this Jill worked in and managed a community mental health team, acted as an Approved Social Worker (ASW) and ASW practice educator. Jill continues to practice as an AMHP. She has completed a PhD in AMHP (shared) decision making, communication and power in Mental Health Act assessments. Jill has a keen interest in supporting practitioner-led research and the relationship between research and practice. She also has a particular interest in stress and burnout in the AMHP role.

Jill represents the AMHP Research Group, as well as acting as a higher education institution (HEI) representative, supporting national AMHP workforce development and education. Jill is keen to develop and support relationships between mental health services and education, particularly in relation to AMHP programmes. She is an education quality assurance inspector (registrant AMHP and BIA) for Social Work England and a specialist lay member to the Mental Health Tribunal.

Jen Kilyon became a campaigner for more compassionate and family-friendly approaches to psychosis many years ago, when her son first became entangled in the mental health system. She is a trustee of ISPS UK and the Soteria Network and helped set up the first UK Soteria House. She has been promoting Open Dialogue since she first learnt about it in 2005. Jen is the co-editor of *A Straight*

Talking Introduction to Caring for Someone with Mental Health Problems (PCCS Books, 2010).

Caroline Leah is an experienced academic and a registered social worker with a background in working with adults with mental health problems and managing community mental health services. She is driven by values connected to social justice, inclusion and social cohesion, and her work places an emphasis on promoting meaningful change through working alongside people who experience mental health distress.

Caroline's primary research interests are in the professional role and identities of AMHPs and in development of practice-based interventions that can lead to better outcomes for people with lived experience of mental distress and illness. She favours approaches that are coproduced with people with lived experiences, that respect people's diverse needs and value their human rights.

Che McGarvey-Gill is a registered social worker and practising AMHP. She joined UCLan in 2020 where she works as a lecturer. Her previous areas of work include domestic abuse, homelessness and older adults. Che has a particular interest in practice learning and has worked with AMHP trainees, social work students and social work apprentices. Che contributes to UCLan's AMHP programme, offering support to practice educators.

Gill Robinson qualified as a social worker in 1992, motivated by her own life experience and a desire to make a difference to people's lives. She was particularly interested in working in mental health and began practising as an ASW in 1997. She continues to practise as an AMHP and manages an AMHP service in an outer London borough.

On behalf of the University of Hertfordshire AMHP programme, Gill jointly initiated and taught on the AMHP practice educators' course, run twice annually for the past few years, and now runs a twice-monthly reflective practice session for practice educators. She is also currently a visiting lecturer at the Tavistock and Portman NHS Trust, teaching on the master's social work course. As an accredited Balint leader and active member of the Balint Society, she currently runs a monthly reflective thinking space for AMHPs, AMHP leads (London region) and jointly facilitates a Balint group for psychiatrists and general practitioners (GPs) based in southern Ireland. Gill successfully completed her doctoral studies at the Tavistock and Portman (University of Essex) in 2022, which were based on research involving qualitative exploration of a bounded reflective group for AMHP practitioners working on the front line.

Hári Sewell is founder and director of HS Consultancy and a former executive director of health and social care for the National Health Service (NHS) in the UK. He has worked for the Department of Health in regulation and policy. He is a writer and speaker in his specialist area of social justice, equality, race and culture in mental health. Hári is an honorary senior visiting fellow at UCLan, specialist guest lecturer at the University of Bradford, visiting lecturer at Christ Church Canterbury University and a member of the Scientific Board of the Economic and Social Research Council (ESRC) Centre for Society and Mental Health. Hári is a proud member of the council (board of trustees) at the British Association of Social Workers. He has had various books, articles and book chapters published, with new material emerging regularly.

Hári worked with another local campaigner to secure services for survivors of sexual violence and currently runs the campaigns 'Men Supporting Women's Rights' including 'Men Against Rape'. He is increasingly studying forms of masculinity and the possibilities in practice and employee relations to recognise the intersections between masculinity and other aspects of identity.

Kevin Stone is an associate professor of social work, director of social work at the University of Warwick and an honorary associate professor at the University of Plymouth. He has worked in health and social care for nearly 30 years. During this time, he has worked in both voluntary and statutory mental health agencies. He was an ASW and has worked as a mental health team manager and later as an emergency duty team officer. He has worked as an academic in social work education for several universities, leading social work and law programmes (pre-registration and continuing professional practice), managing academic teams and developing academic programmes. Kevin remains in practice on a part-time basis as an AMHP, and also sits as a Justice of the Peace in the south-west of England. Kevin has published widely in the field of mental health law (domestic and international), focusing on the socio-legal impact of mental health legislation on families and carers, as well as considering mental health social work practice across Europe. He teaches law, social policy and mental health practice to undergraduate and master's students and supervises doctoral students. Latterly Kevin has been the lead for inter-professional practice within the School of Health Professions at the University of Plymouth. He is also a registrant education quality assurance (EQA) inspector and education and training associate for Social Work England.

Sarah Vicary is a professor of social work and mental health. She is a a qualified registered social worker who has worked primarily in mental health services, including as a front-line practitioner, an ASW, manager of a multidisciplinary mental health crisis service and a senior manager for inner-city emergency mental health services. Sarah was also a Mental Health Act commissioner for nine years. Since moving into academia, Sarah has led qualifying programmes for social work and mental health and is widely published in these fields. Her latest research concerns interpreter-mediated Mental Health Act assessments, a project funded by the National Institute for Health and Care Research (NIHR) (School for Social Care). She is co-author of *The Approved Mental Health Professional Practice Handbook* (Bristol University Press, 2020).

Acknowledgements

Several chapters in this book are written by colleagues who are practitioners in mental health settings. The editors would like to acknowledge the value of research and writing by those with daily experience of work in mental health settings, not least since the work is exceptionally demanding. We hope that this will serve to generate interest and encourage practitioner colleagues to consider writing for publication and sharing their wisdom.

We also acknowledge that for people with lived experience it can be challenging in many different ways to revisit and write about difficult circumstances and we are very grateful to colleagues who took the time to share this.

1

Introduction

Jill Hemmington and Sarah Vicary

This book has a wide lens focusing on compulsion and coercion within mental health settings, but it deliberately applies a more specific, narrow frame to the process of assessment and decision making that can result in detention. With breadth and depth, it aims to evaluate the variables surrounding decisions on compulsory detention and the impact this type of intervention has on both practitioners and people with lived experience.

Compulsion and aspects of coercion in mental health settings are ubiquitous and go beyond the boundaries of the statutory assessment and detention process. Many professionals, practitioners, students, academics, researchers, people with lived experience and perhaps others will be involved with the prospect of compulsory legal interventions. This book enables the reader to develop critical analytical skills and an understanding of their own self and particular viewpoint within this. Each chapter encourages the reader to begin to consider the many complex variables that surround compulsory decision making.

Statutory detention is sanctioned in a range of countries and under various Mental Health Acts. Within the constituent parts of the United Kingdom (UK) statute differs, although not radically, and there are overlapping statutory duties and key roles. One key role is that of the Approved Mental Health Professional (AMHP) in England and Wales where, following the 2007 revisions to the Mental Health Act 1983 (MHA), a range of professionals (social workers, mental health nurses, psychologists and occupational therapists) can undertake the role. The AMHP replaced the Approved Social Worker (ASW) role, which, as the name suggests, was an exclusively social work role. In Northern Ireland and Scotland, the AMHP role continues to be undertaken by social workers as an ASW and as a Mental Health Officer (MHO), respectively. In all nations in the UK, the core responsibilities of MHO, ASW and AMHP are the same: to undertake an assessment of a person with a mental disorder, taking into account social circumstances, and considering the need for an application for formal admission to a mental health hospital by simultaneously exploring alternatives to admission and considering the least restrictive approach.

The fundamental themes of the book have relevance for all four countries of the UK, as well as having international application. At every juncture, readers are invited to critically reflect on the many complex variables surrounding statutory assessments and decision making. Yet, while the approach is to deliberately address commonalities across jurisdictions, the book is timely in that it is developed in parallel with statutory and professional reforms in England and Wales, and it

1

supports the development of these. England and Wales are currently seeing a reform of the MHA and there is, at the time of writing, a new Draft Mental Health Bill (DHSC and Ministry of Justice, 2022), so it is an opportune moment to look at the nature of coercion and compulsion in mental health settings. The Independent Review of the Mental Health Act (DHSC, 2018, p 20) spoke of 'modernising', 'improving choice and decision making', and recognised the structural factors that engender racism, stigma and stereotyping, which increase the risk of differential experiences in 'ethnic minority communities'. It is of concern that there has been an ongoing, increased use of detention across the board and, additionally, people from racialised backgrounds are over four times more likely to be detained under mental health legislation (NHS Digital, 2021), which was one clear rationale for beginning a reform of the current MHA (DoH, 2015, p 7). There is an urgent need to begin to reflect on what lies beneath this.

England and Wales now have in place the first national Workforce Development Plan for AMHPs (DHSC, 2019), although, arguably, its themes apply to all UK jurisdictions and all aspects of statutory assessment and compulsory detention internationally. The plan recognises that 'AMHPs need to have the tools and organisational structure to do the job', that AMHP services should be seen as 'open-learning environments in order to promote social models' and that 'supervision should be viewed as the cornerstone of quality AMHP practice' (DHSC, 2019, p 33). These are familiar themes within many chapters of this book, including the high level of stress and burnout and the need for professionals to address their 'personal, professional, physical and psychological safety' (DHSC, 2019, para 4.1). Exploring aspects of coercion, compulsion and decision making that have relevance for this book, the plan also recognises that there are organisational and environmental contexts, that decision making is values-based but should be oriented to a human rights approach, and that there are affective and relational issues attached to the work. The plan considers the experiences of people who have experienced AMHP services, and it speaks of the need to promote their dignity, human and civil rights (DHSC, 2019, para 6.1), to reduce stigma and, in particular, to tackle racial and cultural disparity (DHSC, 2019, para 6.2). More broadly, AMHP services should seek to embed the principles of coproduction (DHSC, 2019, para 6.3), to 'ensure the patient experience and perspective is captured and harnessed' and to identify ways in which service users are 'able to engage and influence the development of AMHP services and AMHP practice' (DHSC, 2019, para 6.3).

Readers of this book may have other specific statutory roles (including Responsible Clinician, Section 12 Doctor, Approved Clinician in England and Wales or other clinical and medical roles), or they may be otherwise working with, experiencing or writing about these types of interventions. However, the book is not about the statutory roles, although many of the chapters use some specific role, relevant to their jurisdiction, as a starting point upon which to highlight and further explore the salient themes of the book. A significant and fundamental premise of this book is that these roles are much more than simply legalistic, and that decision making is not straightforward. This book therefore aims to support the reflection and engagement of all professionals involved with mental health interventions, students and trainees from all professional backgrounds and people who have lived experience of coercion and compulsion – people whose experience should continue to inform practice and statutory reforms.

Decision makers are required to act autonomously and make independent decisions, free from the influence of others, while working in complex and changing systems. Yet there is little understanding, research or guidance available within this area. Decisions about detention are subjective, are value judgements, and yet there is, currently, no clear theory or evidence base underpinning practice and decision making. Yet outcomes of MHA assessments are understood to be inconsistent, variable and influenced by many factors; further, as outlined earlier, detention decisions are known to disproportionately affect some groups or to indirectly discriminate. Arguably, then, reforms and practice more broadly must draw more robustly from research exploring subjective positions, values (personal and professional) and experiences, and to deliberately recognise and critically evaluate aspects of a role that is far greater than just a legalistic one.

Despite expectations of critical reflection in training and education around the statutory roles, a lot of education and practice materials focus on the legalistic aspects of the role only and there remains a need for students, practitioners and others to develop critical reflection skills in relation to their values, principles, social perspective and independence. Legislation, policy, resourcing, the sociopolitical agenda, formal mental health roles and the nature of the work are all changing, and this needs interrogating further. There is an immediate need for all involved to pause and reflect on assessments and to consider decision-making points as micro-encounters. Assimilating these encounters into practice and understanding how they influence decision making can be one of the most challenging aspects of making decisions in compulsory mental health work and of professional development.

There are several viewpoints and domains that influence compulsion, coercion and decision making: the work is practical and processual, for example coordinating MHA assessments and attempting to find alternatives to admission; it is a statutory and legalistic role, requiring expert knowledge of relevant statutes; there are professional aspects of the role that involve the need to assert a social perspective, anti-oppressive and anti-discriminatory practice, and the requirement to maximise service users' self-determination; moral and ethical dimensions arise from the independence of the role and the need to balance state paternalism; and, finally, the work is relational, interpersonal and involves a critical awareness of the use of self in practice. These five dimensions of influence are illustrated in Figure 1.1.

By extension, the influence these dimensions have ultimately impacts the service user in their lived experience of a statutory assessment. Consequently, as decisions arise in the communication space between service users and AMHPs the relational and interpersonal aspects of the work become of crucial importance. As

Figure 1.1: Five dimensions of assessment and decision making

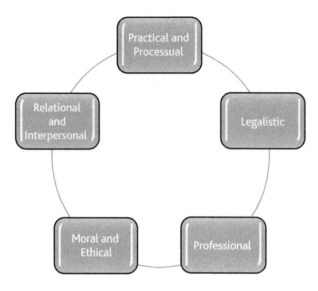

highlighted earlier, outcomes of assessments are understood to be disproportionate and variable and subject to biases (DoH, 2015). It is therefore crucial to view assessments, and their interpersonal exchanges, as 'micro-encounters' (Staley, 2009) in which we can explore the dynamics and frames for decision making with people from a range of different backgrounds and identities. To support and encourage this multifaceted way of thinking, in this book we encourage the application of the themes of frames and boundaries when considering the nuanced aspects of coercive practice.

Boundaries

Common metaphors have evolved to describe the violation of professional boundaries, such as 'crossing the line' or 'blurring the boundaries'. There are also suggestions that mental health professionals must put a boundary between themselves and the service user, and yet, arguably, this traditional representation of professional boundaries reinforces power imbalances and undervalues communication and engagement at a distressing time (O'Leary et al, 2013).

Boundaries can be subjective, objective, sharp or blurry, natural or artificial. Whether theoretical, organisational, professional or cultural it is an entry point to discussion and reflection on social distinctions and emotional separations. All of these shape experiences, outcomes and decisions in different ways. They rest on the use of critical reflection and developing the ability to understand and 'hold' different approaches at the same time, and it is this that underpins good practice.

All relationships contain inherent boundaries around knowledge and power. In mental health settings boundaries represent rules (formal or informal), possibly containment and safety, or they are an objective, real divide. As the individual chapters reveal, boundaries are also theoretical, professional and organisational. There is a need to deconstruct our binary approaches – whereby a thing either is or isn't – and go beyond viewing scenarios in terms of lawful or not lawful; ethical or not ethical; ill or healthy; powerful or powerless; medical or social models; us or them; rational or irrational; health or social organisations; mad or bad; self-determination or social control – all ideas that are ubiquitous within psychiatry. We see boundary work as the different positions competing for authority in the statutory mental health and compulsory decision-making field (Staley, 2009).

Framing

Frames, in the current context, are understood to be conceptual tools. Framing involves embedding events in a context that gives them meaning. It is an 'ongoing story' giving coherence to our experience, without which everything would appear random or unrelated (Beach and Connolly, 2005). Wong (2007, p 401) describe the ways in which we use information about our environments to make decisions, but the 'pictures in our heads' do not always resemble government administrative units and policy contexts). This can lead to difficulty in decision making.

Schön and Rein (1994), both organisational theorists and policy analysts, illustrate the ways in which, depending upon our views on an issue, we will differ as to what facts are relevant: we focus on the same facts but give them different interpretations (Schön and Rein, 1994, p 4); we have a remarkable ability, when we are embroiled in controversy, to dismiss the evidence of others and construct our view of social reality through a process of naming and framing (that is, we selectively attend to some 'facts' and name them in such a way as to fit the frame we have constructed for the situation) (Schön and Rein, 1994, p 26). Institutions hold particular beliefs, values and perspectives (institutional frames) and policy positions are derived from these. Organisational and societal cultures, thinking and actions are developed from these (metacultural frames). Based on the contents of the following chapters we can also add personal, professional, gendered, racialised and many other frames. Consequently, differences that seem insoluble can sometimes be resolved pragmatically by 'reframing' the issues and understanding the taken-for-granted assumptions around policy, statements of fact and value judgements (Schön and Rein, 1994).

We invite the reader to adopt Schön and Rein's (1994) 'double vision', or the ability to act from one perspective, while in the back of our minds holding awareness of other possible perspectives. Understanding framing is understanding how we give events particular, subjective meaning and the impact these have on our decisions. People who work within – or experience – compulsory mental health work can enhance their understanding of their own and others' critical frames of reference. This is critical reflection on, and in, practice.

Outline of the book

A core strength of this book is that it brings together a range of viewpoints and draws on the working experience and knowledge of individuals who are directly involved with, or subject to, compulsion in mental health work. Chapters include new material drawn from research, scholarship and practice. The chapter authors have expertise in experiencing, understanding, practising, researching or writing about compulsory mental health work.

The individual authors introduce their position and discussion drawing on theory, research and practice. Individual authors are those with lived experience, practitioners, practice leads, academics and researchers, but chapters are not necessarily practical guides; they are invitations to begin, or to deepen, reflection on compulsion, coercion and decision making in mental health settings. Throughout, readers are invited to focus on the ways in which decision making can be improved by understanding the framing and boundaries of each critical practice scenario. The critical reflections within each chapter illustrate the ways in which decision making goes beyond any narrow professional, legal or national boundaries and the reader is invited to be part of an active dialogue and to reflect on their own framing of the chapter contents.

As highlighted earlier, there is limited research and understanding of the subjective, lived experience of people who have experienced MHA assessments and detention. Furthermore, within research and academic literature the voice of people with lived experience of statutory assessments has been limited, if not almost completely lacking (Akther et al, 2019). There is a lack of research around the process of the MHA assessment generally and only a very small body of research exploring service users' experiences of statutory assessments specifically (Barnes et al, 2000; Blakley, 2021; Hemmington et al, 2021). Generally, the literature conflates hospital detention and the assessment process. All of this could be said to be indicative of the comparative value assigned to different types of evidence and research priorities (Barnes et al, 2000). Chapter 2, by Caton and Kilyon, is written from the perspective of two people who have experienced statutory assessment and it provides powerful personal perspectives upon which the remaining chapters rest. One author writes from the perspective of their experience of statutory assessment and compulsory detention. The other chapter author has had significant experience of being a family member and Nearest Relative (a statutory role under the England and Wales MHA that carries specific roles and responsibilities). The chapter highlights the ways in which mental health professionals and service users have not always navigated the boundaries and crossed the bridge between them to develop shared ways of working with psychosis or extreme states. The chapter authors use their experiences to suggest ways in which all parties might be better able to use an open approach where experience and meaning is respected and shared. They highlight the ways in which mental health professionals could give deep thought to their own professional, ethical and moral frames, including the ways in which they communicate; crucially, that they consider whether their role might lend itself to one resembling advocate and ally. It provides a powerful message throughout the book, inviting the reader to step into the shoes of another and offering a meaningful, personal, emotional frame that can often be missed. The chapter is food for thought in relation to the true meaning of policy rhetoric around 'recovery', 'coproduction' or 'relationship-based practice'. Readers are invited to take a fresh look at their decisions and to consider ways in which they can decide whether or not conventional approaches are always in people's best interests and whether hospital is always the best place for people to be.

There is also a lack of research focusing specifically on the experiences of people from racialised backgrounds who have experienced statutory assessment or detention, which is of particular concern given the greater likelihood of their being detained. In Chapter 3, Sewell invites the reader to engage critically with the issues at the boundaries of racism and mental health in order to understand how this discourse shapes systems, institutions and practice. Rather than aiming to be instructive, it invites the reader to engage critically with these issues and suggests that critical thinking requires the reader to consider what has been normalised in relation to race. Introducing the concept of 'racist processing', Sewell argues that as citizens, mental health professionals are socialised to see and experience the world in racist ways: cognitively, emotionally and as embodied racism. The chapter suggests that decision making in compulsory detention needs to be trauma informed and attention needs to be paid to the forces outside of the person, as these have relevance for the problems that lead to the person having contact with mental health services. Moreover, the person being assessed will also experience the consequences of racism as thoughts and feelings in an embodied way. Later chapters also return to this notion of attending to feelings.

In a similar vein, while not directly about statutory assessment, in Chapter 4 Fish offers a powerful overview of the significance of gender and perceptions of power in forensic settings for women. The chapter evaluates the experiences of coercion using the example of a mental health inpatient unit. It looks at the use of seclusion and organisational responses to self-harm and aggression using a gendered analysis. The author considers reputation, where women are referred to as being 'difficult to manage' and their conflicts and 'dramas' are interpreted within a framework that values a masculine type of conflict resolution, in a predominantly male environment. There is very little in the way of research and literature in this area and the reader will be further enabled to reflect on the relevance and framing of gender and power as part of their own assessments and interventions.

In Chapter 5, Brammer continues with a focus on challenging perceptions as part of statutory assessment. Using the example of AMHPs in England, and based on findings from a recent research study, this chapter explores aspects of decision making in relation to people who hold suicidal ideas, self-injure or present with other high-risk actions when distressed (people sometimes referred to as having a personality disorder). The chapter explores the complexities of the decision-making process arising from boundaries between statute and the less visible subjective narratives, including the dominance of the medical model and associated narratives of risk management, as well as the imperative to uphold people's rights in independent decision making. Brammer attends to the ways in which this impacts the AMHP's emotional responses and, consequently, interpersonal interactions. The concept of alienation is used to explain the negative cycles that develop when working within a medical and risk-based environment and it is argued that understanding these dynamics, as well as the fears and frustrations of the AMHP, enables a more open and honest reflection on the use of self and the emotions of the decision maker.

The reader is invited into discussion on the need for reflective spaces and supervision when involved with compulsion and coercion. In Chapter 6, Robinson frames the need to create space at policy and practice level to accommodate the emotional needs of mental health professionals, particularly where compulsion is involved. The chapter begins to attend to the ways in which distress and trauma can also be experienced by mental health professionals and that effective models of supervision can offer support with this. It highlights the crucial need to understand the personal and professional self within practice and, as with other chapters in this book, it acknowledges that decision making on compulsion is deeply relational. Having the support and time to engage in deep reflection is a crucial aspect of the work if we are to maintain high standards of practice and avoid stress and burnout.

With a similar focus on reflection and reflective practice, in Chapter 7 Stone frames the tensions that can exist for professionals when making decisions about compulsion. The tensions from undertaking this work can make authentic reflective practice challenging to achieve, thereby preventing and denying the benefit to practice that reflective processes can offer. Decisions to detain carry a significant amount of responsibility, some of which is shared with other professionals, but the AMHP, the focus of this chapter, is the only professional with the power to make an application (or to not do so) – a significant act with specific boundaries. As such, this chapter suggests that to enable safe and effective AMHP practice, reflective safe spaces need to be created and facilitated, either for self, one-to-one or group reflection to occur. This chapter also draws on the author's own experiences of using techniques in education and practice to encourage openness and truth-telling, through maintaining anonymity and encouraging participation.

Critical reflection is an essential aspect of professional qualification and continued professional development, and again, using AMHP practice as an illustration, in Chapter 8 McGarvey-Gill focuses this specifically on practice education. Practice placements are embedded within university-led academic programmes for the qualifying AMHP role, and practice learning can present a challenge for trainees to understand, and evidence, applied knowledge, the theory–practice relationship (and boundaries) and general practice 'competence'. Trainees come to this vocational qualification as experienced mental health professionals who also need to navigate a transition to 'student' or 'adult learner' status. This chapter explores the unique challenges of these placements for practice education. The author critically examines practice education frameworks and discusses their applicability to the specialised statutory mental health practice educator role. In focusing on the tensions around statutory decision making, the chapter highlights the need for creating a culture within practice education of knowing oneself, of critical, honest reflection and of the importance of supervision. The learning environment, potential boundaries around diversity and more subtle aspects of support are discussed, and suggestions for preparing for, and framing, placements as successful, immersive learning experiences are considered.

In a turn towards reflection on the influence of professional backgrounds and identities on practice, in Chapter 9 Bloodworth-Strong (a practising occupational therapist and AMHP) acknowledges and responds to the structural barriers and professional boundaries relating to occupational therapists (OTs) undertaking the AMHP role in England and Wales. Specific professional frames are presented and the suitability and convergence of OTs' practice and values as part of compulsory decision making is outlined. The case for OT AMHPs is made creatively and with profession-specific detail. The chapter sets out how OTs can continue their health enabler role into their AMHP practice in the ways in which they consider alternatives to hospital and how they promote people's independence through their clinical reasoning, decision making and communication skills. Overall, the chapter raises awareness about OT values and skills and how these relate to human rights work in a mental health context and, in so doing, could be a vehicle to promote the OT profession and inspire therapists to train in these roles and, in a much-needed move, improve AMHP recruitment. An opportune chapter, given the structural and organisational barriers to professions other than social work being able to access AMHP education and approval (DHSC, 2019), the author makes a creative case for the suitability of occupational therapy for AMHP practice.

In Chapter 10, Vicary continues the discussion around statutory assessment and decision making having a multidisciplinary viewpoint. This chapter seeks to address professional identity boundaries in considering the opening up of the AMHP role to mental health nurses. It critically examines whether any of the doubts expressed about doing so have been realised. Drawing on data from a wider study of AMHPs, the author discusses the relationship between role fulfilment and professional identity from the perspective of mental health nurse AMHPs. In a creative application of the concept of framing, fulfilling the role of an AMHP is interpreted in four stages. During the first two stages, a transition from 'unclean' to 'honorary social workers' is shown; in this perception of mental health nurses as AMHPs, it is claimed that the ascription of the professional role as honorary, or special, denotes a change in professional identity and, also, acceptance into it. In an extension of the metaphor, the third and fourth stages indicate that, once clean, mental health nurses go on to use this shift in professional identity to challenge hitherto accepted professional boundaries and, also, to begin to challenge how the AMHP role itself is fulfilled.

Chapter 11 extends the focus on professional identities, where Leah examines decision making through the lens of hybrid professionalism. Again, the AMHP role is used to facilitate discussion around communication and mediation among mental health professionals. The author addresses how hybridity intersects dynamically with boundary working in a number of interrelated ways: through professional knowledge (apparent via AMHPs' application of a biopsychosocial model of mental health); as professionals drawn from different backgrounds (social work, nursing and occupational therapy); and, finally, as professionals who straddle multiple roles. The author concludes that although hybridity can be embedded and straddle boundaries of professional knowledge and practice, it is a concept that confronts and problematises boundaries but does not erase them. As such, hybridity implies an unsettling of identities and asks the reader to consider the difficulties of working with cultural and professional differences.

Chapter 12 sees a refined and deepened focus, wherein Graham considers the interface between mental capacity and mental health legislation as an exemplar for the need for a depth of thinking and a viewpoint that, as with all else, goes beyond a legalistic one. The reader is invited to reflect on the spirit of the legislation and on their own position and interpretations. There is an emphasis on emancipatory, values-based practice and a focus on choice. The author uses this practice example to suggest that practitioners need to strike a balance between enabling and sanctioning people, and that balance sits on a very fine line. The chapter therefore asks the reader to be aware of professional, organisational and legal boundaries and frames, and to acknowledge and understand the complexities and nuances of decision making. Historical, contemporary and, finally, future frames are addressed. The reader is invited to reflect on the spirit of the legislation and the ways in which their own frames and values accord with this to enable 'bottom-up' rather than 'top-down' legalistic approaches.

In Chapter 13, Hemmington returns to the opening philosophy and revisits principles brought by Caton and Kilyon in Chapter 2. Within assessments, people have reported little discussion around options and alternatives to hospital admission, leaving them to believe that the only outcome could be admission (Barnes et al, 2000; Blakley et al, 2021). More broadly, this chapter asks the reader to consider communication needs at the point of decision making during statutory assessments. It focuses on participation of the person, framed here as shared decision making. Providing first the policy context and principles as to why this should happen, the chapter explores ways in which shared decision making can be supported for those who are deemed to have capacity and also for those who may not. Discussing concepts such as insight and the use of jargon, the author explores the paternalism that can affect decision making, which in turn leads to a person not being meaningfully included in decisions made about them. Given the seriousness of the outcome of an MHA assessment, such participation is key. It is argued that developing and enabling reciprocity is fundamental to shared decision making, and that the navigation of these boundaries are underpinned by attitudes, styles and skills. Concluding with a discussion of their own research and developments such as Open Dialogue, the author looks ahead to the emerging shifts that may be seen in forthcoming changes suggested for mental health legislation in England and Wales.

The final, concluding chapter, by Hemmington and Vicary, revisits, synthesises and reconciles the ideas raised in the introductory chapter and throughout the book. It summarises how the different frames connect and reviews how to practise across boundaries. It illustrates how there are alternatives to rigid thinking – perhaps there is a middle ground and blurring of the boundaries – and suggestions are made for ongoing development of professionalism and practice wisdom in keeping with policy and statutory reforms. A clear message is that power resides in interpersonal relationships and is constructed through professional practice and organisational cultures (Sheldon, 2011). As the reader begins reading, we ask them to consider Peattie's (Schön and Rein, 1994) 'double vision' and focus on our ability to act from one perspective while, in the back of our minds, we hold on to an awareness of other perspectives. Decision making on compulsion and coercion is beyond legalistic; perception is a prism, and an understanding of frames and boundaries is fundamental to critical reflection.

This book invites the reader to deconstruct practice scenarios and prisms. The chapters evaluate the impact of the sociopolitical environment on decision making, and draw attention to the nature of relationships with their inherent boundaries around knowledge and power. They consider a number of implications for decision making with people from a diversity of backgrounds and in a variety of professional roles. The book enables the reader to develop critical analytical skills and an understanding of the self within practice, aiming for a panorama of thought. Decisions are influenced by many variables, including legal, political, interpersonal, organisational, professional (including identities), those relating to resources, the self, stress, power, language, status, knowledge, aspects of race, gender, age and culture. The editors are aware that this book only begins to cover the essential areas for practice. Due to changes in personal circumstances, we were unable to include a chapter on assessing children and young people, as planned. As yet, there are no publications on this area of practice. We hope to address this in future. We hope that this book stimulates discussion and highlights gaps in our knowledge and that, collectively, we may all go on to refine our focus on all aspects of compulsion and coercion with people and all their diversity.

References

Akther, S.F., Molyneaux, E., Stuart, R., Johnson, S., Simpson, A. and Oram, S. (2019) Patients' experiences of assessment and detention under mental health legislation: systematic review and qualitative meta-synthesis. *BJPsych Open*, 5(3), E37.

Barnes, M., Davis, A. and Tew, J. (2000) Valuing experience: users' experiences of compulsion under the Mental Health Act 1983. *Mental Health Review Journal*, 5(3), 11–14.

Beach, L.R. and Connolly, T. (2005) *The psychology of decision making: people in organizations*. Thousand Oaks, CA: Sage Publications, Inc.

Blakley, L., Asher, C., Etherington, A., Maher, J., Wadey, E., Walsh, V. et al (2021) 'Waiting for the verdict': the experience of being assessed under the Mental Health Act. *Journal of Mental Health*, 31(2), 212–19.

Department of Health (DoH) (2015) *Reform of the Mental Health Act: summary of consultation responses*. London: DoH.

Department of Health and Social Care (DHSC) (2018) *Independent review of the Mental Health Act*. London: DHSC. Available at https://www.gov.uk/governm ent/publications/modernising-the-mental-health-act-final-report-from-the-independent-review.

Department of Health and Social Care (DHSC) (2019) *National workforce plan for Approved Mental Health Professionals (AMHPs)*. London: DHSC. Available at https://assets.publishing.service.gov.uk/government/uploads/system/uplo ads/attachment_data/file/843539/AMHP_Workforce_Plan_Oct19__3_.pdf.

Department of Health and Social Care (DHSC) and Ministry of Justice (2022) Draft Mental Health Bill. Available at https://www.gov.uk/government/publi cations/draft-mental-health-bill-2022.

Hemmington, J., Graham, M., Marshall, A., Brammer, A., Stone, K. and Vicary, S. (2021) *Approved Mental Health Professionals, Best Interests Assessors and people with lived experience: an exploration of professional identities and practice: a report prepared for Social Work England*. Sheffield: Social Work England.

NHS Digital (2021) Mental Health Act statistics: annual figures – 2020–21. Available at https://digital.nhs.uk/data-and-information/publications/statisti cal/mental-health-act-statistics-annual-figures/2020-21-annual-figures.

O'Leary, P., Tsui, M.S. and Ruch, G. (2013) The boundaries of the social work relationship revisited: towards a connected, inclusive and dynamic conceptualisation. *British Journal of Social Work*, 43(1), 135–53.

Schön, D. and Rein, M. (1994) *Frame reflection: toward the resolution of intractable policy controversies*. New York: Basic Books.

Sheldon, B. (2011) *Cognitive-behavioural therapy: research and practice in health and social care*. London: Routledge.

Staley, T.W. (2009) Keeping philosophy in 'mind': Shadworth H. Hodgson's articulation of the boundaries of philosophy and science. *Journal of the History of Ideas*, 70(2), 289–315.

Wong, C.J. (2007) 'Little' and 'big' pictures in our heads: race, local context, and innumeracy about racial groups in the United States. *Public Opinion Quarterly*, 71(3), 392–412.

2

Lived experience and the boundaries between professionals and others

Neil Caton and Jen Kilyon

Introduction

We believe it is crucial to hear lived experience perspectives and we rarely get the chance to explore with professionals, in detail, the pertinent factors that affect our journeys with the mental health system. This writing process has given us the opportunity to collaborate and hear each other's perspectives. Neil has experienced statutory detention within the mental health system and Jen is a family member of someone who became 'tangled up' in the system of compulsory detention. We talk about life before and after experiencing our difficulties. We do this because we think it is important to draw out what affects us when we end up in the position of having been subjected to decision making about compulsion. Our experiences have significant differences, but we have tried to draw out similar themes. Neil draws out some positives of using the system, but also some damaging aspects. Jen highlights the dangerous consequences of the long-term use of mental health legislation and how this impacts the whole family. She also draws on wider experiences of other family members and carers. We talk about life before mental health services and our wider experiences as this gives the context of how people who find themselves using the mental health system, including family members, relate to professionals when they consider using coercion. We also look at other systemic responses, such as diagnosis and medication, and how this impacted our recovery journeys. We expose the power imbalances that exist between mental health professionals and those on the receiving end of services. We draw out the injustices we have experienced at the hands of the mental health system and the effect this has had on our lives. We identify the need for informed choice within the mental health system and alternatives to the mainstream.

Neil's experiences

Life before the mental health system

My primary and secondary schooling was dominated by bullying. As far back as I can remember I was always struggling to find friends. As the years went on, I became increasingly withdrawn and socially anxious and by my teenage years I was often unable to engage with people in the most basic everyday conversations. My life became one where I was constantly on guard, waiting for the next time I would be ridiculed by my peers. I dreaded lunchtime, where I would wander the school yard, hoping no one would notice me. I always felt that when my peers matured, they would start to accept me, each year going back to school hoping things would change. I remember in my last year of secondary school, when we were preparing to leave school, I started to sense people were more accepting of me, but to my surprise this only made me more nervous and I just didn't know how to react. This was a reality that followed me into adulthood.

Experiences of the mental health system

I was referred to the Early Intervention Team (EIT) after developing paranoid ideas about the people closest to me. Medication kept my paranoia under control, but I was still severely depressed during my first year with the EIT and unable to perform basic everyday tasks. EIT worked with my family and gave me therapy, and after a year I had a breakthrough and was liberated from my more severe issues. I still felt quite socially anxious and dissatisfied with life, but nothing like life pre-EIT. The team told me it was only a matter of time before I dealt with these residual issues and discharged me.

After failing my social work master's qualification due to issues with social anxiety, I became hopeless. Things weren't as bad as pre-EIT, but I still felt that I wasn't properly living. I was referred to the Community Mental Health Team (CMHT) and worked with a care coordinator who I had a good relationship with, but there was still very little meaningful change. I was given dialectical behavioural therapy, which taught me strategies such as radical acceptance, self-soothing and mindfulness, but this didn't seem to make much of a difference either. More years of turmoil passed and eventually I started to experience psychosis again. I agreed to go to an inpatient ward. Reacting to my parents' relief that I had agreed to be admitted, I went into the ward, head held high, and was immediately teased by the other patients. I misread the things they said and believed they were actors who had been put on the ward to teach me a lesson about recovery. I went to one of the nurses furious about this and said I would smash up the ward, but she showed me no compassion and simply said if I did that, she would call the police and let them deal with me because I was a voluntary patient. This set the tone for my stay at the ward and my relationship with the other patients who I thought were ridiculing me. They discharged me in a worse state than when I arrived.

I was referred to the crisis team soon after my release; I believed that MI6 were responsible for the fake psychiatric ward and that I must be an undiscovered genius and as a result I reviewed all the relationships I had in my life, questioning who I could trust. I was quite attached to the idea that MI6 were trying to get me to recover, as this assured me that I would make a full recovery. I wanted the crisis team to help me learn to trust the people around me in this new world. I saw many different clinicians, most of whom I felt I could not trust, and they tried to pull all the beliefs about MI6 from me, telling me I could have no say in the way I was treated due to my 'condition'.

After about a year of working with the crisis team and understandably refusing to go back to hospital, a Mental Health Act (MHA) assessment team entered my flat and I was detained. I did have a better stay in the hospital and managed to tune into the staff, who were more understanding. My psychiatrist, who I had worked with in my job as an involvement worker at EIT, reached out to me, making it clear that he wanted me back as a colleague. I also experienced some of the staff being more assertive, while also responding with compassion, when I was challenging towards them. All this made me feel I could trust the people around me and any beliefs relating to MI6 collapsed.

Problems with the construct of 'mental illness'

When I attended college, I started to develop friendships and the bullying finally almost completely ceased. However, unable to shake off the past I was crippled by social anxiety and feelings of worthlessness. I struggled to engage with people in the most basic social interactions. I found myself silent and miserable in most group conversations. In the summer break I went to volunteer at a hotel for disabled people, and although I was initially nervous, I came out of myself and had the time of my life, connecting and bonding with the clients and other volunteers who were all around my age. I felt a euphoria I'd never felt before, leaving me with a sense of how life could be. When I returned to college, I went with a certainty that at last I had dealt with the issues that had held me back for so long. For a while my confidence remained, and I saw nothing but potential for the year ahead. However, it didn't last very long, and I slumped back into being my socially anxious former self, this time feeling all the lower and seeing suicide as a possible way out.

It was then that I decided I must be mentally ill and have depression, unknowingly colluding with the sense the bullying had left me with that I was somehow defective, but this time with the caveat that I could be cured. The mental health system, for all the good things it has done for me over the years, has also reinforced and colluded with this sense of defectiveness by pathologising my experiences, creating another barrier to recovery. Admittedly, I actively colluded with the process, seeing my experiences through the lens of mental illness as it offered me the possibility of eventually being the person I'd always thought I was; refusing to accept as legitimate the person I was, something I still struggle with today. For many years I was angry at the situation I found myself in, above and beyond the bullying I had experienced at school, but was unsure why. It was only when I was exposed to survivor narratives that I realised why I felt like this. They talked about their experiences in terms of distress, not illness, and their extreme states were a response to life events, not a chemical imbalance.

It is clear that the narrative of mental illness that society gave me when I first experienced severe depression had a hugely destructive effect on my life. It is this realisation that has equipped me with the insight to unpick the feelings of shame and defectiveness, allowing me at the age of 36 to start to rediscover that confidence I last encountered as a 17-year-old. I have looked back with self-blame at that 17-year-old who started on such a destructive path, but concluded that I did fulfil all the criteria of having a severe mental illness and was simply being a responsible citizen by giving myself this status.

Problems with medication

In my recovery journey my psychotic experiences have often been breakthroughs in dealing with difficult emotions. This first happened when I was working with EIT and ended up being hospitalised with a lot of persecutory beliefs. For the duration of my stay, I was overwhelmed by intense emotions that, after being put on slowly increasing doses of antipsychotics, began to subside. Being able to experience these difficult emotions emancipated me from the most severe difficulties I was experiencing prior to this. I have never had a return to the problems I had in my late teens and early twenties. It was after this that I began to stagnate in my recovery, still experiencing some lesser, albeit significant difficulties. A similar thing happened in my last psychotic episode when, after I was detained, I broke down in floods of tears believing that my life was over. After being reassured by my uncle that this was not the case, I again passed through some intense, previously unreachable emotions. Again, I began to stagnate when I was medicated. It seems to me that instead of working with these experiences and their emancipatory potential, the mental health system always seems to suppress them and extinguish their potential. It is not surprising, then, that I have had such difficulty in dealing with emotion ever since, when the mental health system, perhaps unintentionally, teaches me that I have to continue to suppress my emotions – something I felt I had to do when I was being bullied at school, thus colluding and adding to this unresolved trauma. It is knowing this that has allowed me to start to experience difficult emotions without losing touch with consensus reality.

I'm not saying there are any easy answers to supporting people in a psychotic state. I have worked with others who experience intense paranoid ideas and finding a way to reach them and gain their trust is no easy process. For this reason, I am not against the use of medication if it provides significant relief that allows you to gain the trust of those trying to help. I speculate that if EIT had slowly brought me off my medication it would have unlocked more potential to recover, but this proved impossible in the crisis I endured after failing my social work master's qualification. However, in my experience, professionals seem to know little about the withdrawal effects that happen when people try and come off these medications; they often do it as recommended by the doctors, who in my view always try to do it too quickly over a few months, in which I have always experienced unmanageable withdrawal effects. The only way I see a chance of me reducing my medication successfully is through the literature I have found in the lay person withdrawal community. This advocates reducing over a year or more and making lifestyle changes to equip you with the best chance (Farmer, 2021). This is beginning to be picked up by some psychiatrists, who are adopting a similar approach. Horowitz et al (2021) advocate a slow tapering off of antipsychotics, outlining the withdrawal effects of coming off these medications too quickly. Mainstream psychiatry is yet to catch up with this.

Least restrictive alternative

The reason I tell this story here is that it explains what met the MHA assessment team when, as strangers, they entered my flat one summer evening and were faced with my hostility, mocking the speech impediment of one of the psychiatrists because I thought he was ridiculing me by the way he was speaking. It didn't help that he was suggesting Clozaril as the only medication that would be appropriate for me; fortunately the Approved Mental Health Professional (AMHP) said I had the capacity to make that decision. I'm not sure what happened behind the scenes, but I didn't end up being prescribed it. I share my experience with those involved in other research, where people being assessed do not know the roles of the assessors and do not share decision making (Blakley et al, 2021). AMHPs see themselves as advocates (Hemmington et al, 2021), and possibly my experience supports this, but I was not involved with this decision making.

I find it hard to imagine that on that day there could have been any other conclusion but to detain me. I would have liked to have a pre-existing relationship with the AMHP so that they might pay special attention to my history in the mental health system, as well as the concerns I had at that time. A mediative relationship with the crisis team would have helped them to elicit and take seriously my plan to find a way to trust the people around me. This would not be an easy task, given my understanding of what was happening at the time was fundamentally different from the people trying to help me, but there was still a path to recovery that I was trying to follow. If we can see past the medical model interpretation of what I was experiencing this can be seen more easily. It would have been good if they had taken a meditative position about my beliefs at the time, for instance my fixed belief that I had been in an inpatient unit made up of actors. They could have respected my right to my beliefs and tried to find a way of working together, despite the differences in our beliefs. We could have then talked about my wider conspiratorial beliefs, which at the time I knew were speculative, but I could have found a way of understanding why people around me were behaving the way they were and that was keeping my speculative conspiratorial thinking alive. It felt like the professionals were *doing to me* instead of *working alongside me* to achieve a shared goal. It so happens that when I was able to trust the people around me, any ideas about MI6 controlling my life fell away. While I appreciate that the National Health Service (NHS) isn't structured in such a way where AMHPs can work with service users who face the possibility of being detained, I do think it is important that they raise with their managers that doing so would allow them to do their job more effectively, truly allowing them to advocate for people being assessed for compulsory detention.

Jen's experiences

Life before the mental health system

My family member,[1] who has been given the pseudonym Joe in this chapter, always tells me and others that he had a very happy childhood. He still speaks very fondly of his school years and keeps in touch with old family friends regularly. When he was 13, he had a very traumatic experience when he was playing the lead role in the school production of *Oliver Twist*: he had to go into a coffin with the lid closed for five nights onstage. That was the week his very dear nanna died in our house and was taken away in a coffin. Ten years later, when he was locked away in a dreadful semi-secure unit, miles away from home, he called me one evening and asked if I remembered when he used to sleep in a coffin. When I replied yes, he told me that he really did meet death in there and now everyone was wearing a death mask and they all smelt of death. It was then that it dawned on me that we were not just dealing with a chemical imbalance of the brain, which could be corrected by more chemicals. I realised that what Joe was thinking and believing had its roots in reality. It was only because I understood the background to what he was now saying that I realised the link between trauma and psychosis was so important. Until then I had accepted the advice I was given by so-called professionals not to 'engage' with the 'delusions' because I would just be encouraging him to stay in his own tortured world. Sadly, no one with responsibility for Joe wanted to open this Pandora's Box.

Problems with coercion

If I'd known many years ago what I now know about the MHA in England and Wales and how it can compel people, against their will, to stay behind locked doors, seemingly indefinitely, I would certainly never have made an appointment, in the year 2000, with our general practitioner (GP) to discuss things. I felt that I needed to talk to her about what was happening to Joe when we had to bring him home in his second year at university. It was clear to me that he was terrified about many things – some of these I understood, others I was unsure about. I believe if we'd had more options then he wouldn't have been detained under the MHA on a section 3 (a treatment order) for almost 20 years, as well as 7 years on a Community Treatment Order (CTO). This resulted in huge damage to him physically, emotionally and cognitively, and caused huge rifts in the family for a long time. It also broke the trust between us and for many years he would be so angry and shout, "Why did you let them do this to me?" or "Why did you put me in prison?" I would often cry myself to sleep at night knowing there was nothing I could do about it.

If the powers of the MHA didn't allow him to be on a CTO, where he could have more easily been recalled to hospital if he didn't comply with certain conditions, he would not have felt like a prisoner in his own home for seven long years. He would not have been terrified when strangers came to his house with notebooks. He would not have been so frightened by the thought that the bullies might come back to his house and take him away, which often brought on persecutory voices. Those 'episodes' often caused the psychiatrists to be called to his house, which again caused more extreme states. The whole scenario was a vicious, rather than a virtuous circle.

When the decision was recently made to remove Joe from the power of the CTO – which meant that he was able to make his own decisions about taking medication, where he went and who he allowed into his house (although no mental health professional explained this to him) – he said to me, "I'm a free man and I can say what I want, do what I want and even think what I want!" I would ask all mental health professionals to think long and hard about these words when making decisions about CTOs. They should consider, very carefully, the possible consequences of their actions before subjecting someone to any section of the MHA.

Working with families

There has been ample evidence for many years that working with families and supporters from the start of a person's involvement with mental health services has the best outcomes for everyone involved, including staff (Jankovic et al, 2011; Laing et al, 2018; Shaw et al, 2018; Hemmington et al, 2021). So why is it that I still hear from so many relatives that they are consistently ignored, excluded and sometimes vilified for trying to get help, suggest different ways of working or express their concerns when things are going drastically wrong for their loved ones? Very often it can feel like our very existence as family members, next of kin or a Nearest Relative (a nominated person according to strict criteria under the MHA in England and Wales, who has certain rights and responsibilities and is formally consulted as part of a MHA assessment) is seen as a hindrance or afterthought to the work of care coordinators, psychiatrists and AMHPs.

Each time a decision about compulsory detention was made about my family member all I got was a phone call to tell me what was happening. There was a pretence that I was being consulted and asked to agree to the decision that was being made, but in reality we both knew there was no viable alternative. The first time this happened I had no idea what I was agreeing to, as I had no knowledge of the law or what it would be like on the other side of locked doors in a psychiatric ward. Even less could I imagine what could happen when very vulnerable people couldn't escape and weren't believed when they said that serious abuse had happened. I have written about some things that happened in the early years of our experiences (Kilyon, 2015), but I had no idea then how dire the future for our whole family was going to be. Some things that happened are still too raw and traumatic for me to write about and they are even now having serious consequences for me and my own mental health. I believe that families need accessible information about their rights and those of their loved ones before there is any referral to secondary mental health services; this includes available support and less restrictive alternatives to hospitalisation.

One family member told me the following:

> My son has been detained so many times I have lost count. On a few occasions I was not even informed that the assessment had taken place and at no time was I ever consulted for my views nor involved in decision making, just informed and asked if I was in agreement after the assessment and decision-making process were over.
>
> Had I been involved in thinking through alternatives, for example my son returning to live with me with appropriate community support, there is a good chance that hospital admissions may have been avoided.
>
> On two separate occasions, my concerns about my son's mental state were ignored by the community team until after the crises I predicted had occurred, with dire consequences. Then he was detained. If my concerns had been taken seriously and treated with more respect the serious consequences of the delays would have been avoided.

The Code of Practice for the MHA in England states that families and carers should be consulted and involved in decision making, especially when the individual may be living with the family (DoH, 2015, para 14.66). I recognise that sadly there are circumstances where people have been abused by families, in which case it may be impossible to work with them in any way, but they will hopefully be a small minority. It may be that family and friends don't always understand what is helpful for their loved ones, but ignoring it is not going to improve the situation.

I would hope that by now most AMHPs will have heard of Open Dialogue (OD) and may be fortunate enough to be working in a care trust where teams may be either part of the ODDESSI trials,[2] or at least have members within them who are trained in using OD or dialogical approaches. In parts of England, this is starting to be used in statutory assessments (see also Chapter 13 for an overview of OD approaches).

One family told me the following about their experience of an OD approach:

> Having Open Dialogue as part of my daughter's current recovery plan has been transformative. It continues to help us all as a family heal properly (as opposed to a sticking plaster) and will continue to support us as she comes off her medication over the next few years. If

we had had Open Dialogue available to us when she was hospitalised the first time, we might have avoided a further five years of extreme pain, distress, hospitalisations and trauma.

I have written about our own family's experiences of using OD (Kilyon, 2015), and although I knew that it was too late for our family, I was writing about its importance because I didn't want others to go through similar deep, dark years. It was then that we were offered some network meetings, even though the CMHT didn't take up the opportunity to work with our family as a whole. My family member's psychiatrist and the care coordinator did join us for some meetings, and I believe if they'd been able to continue over a longer period of time then we could all have worked together to have a better understanding of each other and developed stronger and more trusting relationships. It did make a real difference to us, however, as we were able to trust and understand each other better and say and bear difficult things. In our case it was especially helpful, because we were able to use drama therapy at the beginning to find ways of expressing ourselves often in a playful way. My family member told me that it helped him feel that what he was thinking and feeling was important to others and that it enabled him to find his own voice. The power imbalance between families, those experiencing extreme states and mental health professionals needs to be addressed before any real changes can be made to how responsive and helpful mental health services can be.

Conclusion

For Neil, the main driver behind a refusal to go to hospital voluntarily was that the environment there may be worse than the chaos he faced at home. If there had been a prior relationship with the AMHP it may not have been so overwhelming on that day to be met with strangers from the MHA assessment team, who he had no idea were coming, and when he was already in a paranoid state.

For both of us, campaigning and working for complete changes to the mental health system have led to a discovery of the many healing, respectful and non-compulsive ways of working that could help people and their families make sense of what was happening. Resources such as a Soteria House[3] do not force people to stay behind locked doors. They don't give people labels that can mark them for life, make people judge, make assumptions about what is going on or think they could fix things by telling people what to do while taking away their liberty and forcing people to take damaging drugs for many years without any choice or informed consent. It could have been possible for a peer respite, where people would not challenge our beliefs. We could have had a choice about medication, been free to leave at any time in the context of having therapeutic relationships with the staff. At the same time, if hospital inpatient environments were less distressing then maybe they would be an environment that people might choose to be in.

Hearing Voices Groups[4] could have enabled Jen's family member to share his experiences of hearing voices or having unusual beliefs in a non-judgemental way. These groups are often facilitated by someone who also hears voices or may have a peer support worker. Rufus May, a group facilitator and psychologist,[5] has been through similar experiences to Joe. He would have been listened to by someone he knew who 'got it', rather than being talked at by someone whose training had taught them that he had a life-long brain disease caused by a chemical imbalance that needed to be 'corrected' and/or managed by more chemicals. These 'chemicals' would after many years of compulsory 'treatment' be almost impossible to withdraw from safely, and we now know they are likely to cause diabetes, stroke, heart disease and other chronic problems and may take up to 20 years off his life.

Joe's family members wouldn't have been in a situation where they had no real power to change the appalling situation he was in for almost 20 years in eight different institutions. Where the power imbalance and the rules, structures and attitudes of most staff were so rigid they didn't allow for any individuality. Where in many places Joe couldn't see a flower, a leaf, the sky or hear the birds singing for year after year. Where he had no choice who he was with, where he could go or what he could do. Where, for what he said felt like a prison sentence, the only thing he had to look forward to was his next cigarette – now he is so hooked on nicotine that his GP has told him if he doesn't quit smoking he may not be with us in three years' time.

Our narratives have challenged our world view and made us aware that the experiences of vulnerable people in society are often different to the perceptions of professionals and wider society. Our activism within mental health settings has empowered us to challenge conventional ways of understanding and working with those experiencing extreme distress. We've also learnt how damaging the system can be and how different this can be from the understanding of well-intended professionals. We have tried to promote a rights-based understanding of our experiences – a lens we think is central for the recovery journeys of people who seek help from or are drawn to the attention of mental health services. We think our activism has enabled us to do this in a congruent way.

We need to elicit meaning from others' experiences – especially those who may sense injustice and experience anger – but still see their reasons for using mental health services as being due to a personal defect where the reason for their anger could have been seen as a rational response. They are taken down a path of diagnosis and medication that has made their life measurably worse than it would otherwise have been.

We both started with a deficit-based perspective, and it was a journey to get to the point where we see our experiences as a human response to a complex world and where we had to meet the right people along the way to see this. Some may never get to do this in a meaningful way. This is something our society, and in particular the mental health system, teaches us. Some may not know there is an alternative or may think that having a diagnosis is the only way they can justify their distress and financially support themselves through much-needed benefits. This can often have the unintended consequence of starting a war with the part of themselves that is hurting, instead of seeking to empathise and justify why it is hurting. In a system that promotes these realities it is not surprising that mental health professionals feel the need to coerce vulnerable people with the intention of keeping them safe and yet, in our experience, placing them in often physically and emotionally unsafe environments where they do not know how long they will be detained – something that cannot be said for the penal system.

Notes

[1] Jen's family member has provided consent for this information to be shared.
[2] See https://www.ucl.ac.uk/pals/research/clinical-educational-and-health-psychology/research-groups/oddessi/oddessi-trial.
[3] See www.soterianetwork.org.uk.
[4] See www.hearing-voices.org.
[5] See www.openmindedonline.com.

References

Blakley, L., Asher, C., Etherington, A., Maher, J., Wadey, E., Walsh, V. and Walker, S. (2021) 'Waiting for the verdict': the experience of being assessed under the Mental Health Act, *Journal of Mental Health*, DOI: 10.1080/09638237.2021.1922624.

Department of Health (DoH) (2015) *Mental Health Act 1983: Code of Practice*. London: DoH.

Farmer, A. (2021) What I have learnt from helping thousands of people taper off antidepressants and other psychotropic medications. *Therapeutic Advances in Psychopharmacology*, 11, 1–18.

Hemmington, J., Graham, M., Marshall, A., Brammer, A., Stone, K. and Vicary, S. (2021) *Approved Mental Health Professionals, Best Interests Assessors and people with lived experience: an exploration of professional identities and practice a report prepared for Social Work England*. Sheffield: Social Work England.

Horowitz, M., Jauhar, S., Natesan, S., Murray, R. and Taylor, D. (2021) A method for tapering antipsychotic treatment that may minimize the risk of relapse. *Schizophrenia Bulletin*, 47(4), 1116–29.

Jankovic, J., Yeeles, K. and Katsakou, C. (2011) Family caregivers' experiences of involuntary psychiatric hospital admissions of their relatives: a qualitative study. *PLoS ONE*, 6(1), e25425.

Kilyon, J. (2015) Open Dialogue: a family perspective. *Context*, 138, 7.

Laing, J., Dixon, J., Stone, K. and Wilkinson-Tough, M. (2018). The Nearest Relative in the Mental Health Act 2007: still an illusionary and inconsistent safeguard? *Journal of Social Welfare and Family Law*, 40(1), 37–56.

Shaw, E.H., Nunns, M.P., Briscoe, S., Anderson, R. and Thompson Coon, J. (2018) Experiences of the 'Nearest Relative' provisions in the compulsory detention of people under the Mental Health Act: rapid systematic review. *Health Services and Delivery Research*, 6(39), np. Available at https://doi.org/10.3310/hsdr06390.

3

Frames and boundaries of race and ethnicity in Mental Health Act assessments

Hári Sewell

Introduction

The subject of race inequality in mental health has been scrutinised by policy makers and researchers for decades. Despite government initiatives such as 'Delivering Race Equality in Mental Health Care' (DoH, 2005) there seems to be an intractability in relation to the closing of equality gaps. Amid this, mental health professionals are at the sharp end of the data that attracts the sternest criticism: the higher-than-average rates of detentions of racialised minorities. Though solutions may be found in attending to socio-economic obstacles to equality in mental health, mental health practitioners need to have the skills to critique and amend their own practice so that they can take account of the antecedents of poorer mental health in the lives of racialised people whom they assess, and to mitigate against the impact of their own unconscious bias and prejudices as well as those of colleagues within the mental health system. Rather than being instructive, this chapter invites the reader to engage critically with the issues at the boundaries of racism and mental health as they pertain to one type of decision maker in compulsory mental health – the Approved Mental Health Professional (AMHP). Critical thinking requires that consideration is given to what has been normalised in relation to race and to understand how discourse shapes systems, institutions and practice.

This chapter first explores the meanings of race and ethnicity. Next, the data in relation to ethnic inequality in referrals, pathways and outcomes for racialised minorities is reviewed. Drawing on the latest research, five key decision-making points are analysed to identify where biases may be affecting practice. Attention is given to unconscious bias and individual skills in challenging models, practice and policies that institutionalise the disadvantage of racialised minorities. Overall, boundaries are considered in racialised terms and framed in terms of awareness and communication.

The chapter introduces the concept of 'racist processing', which speaks to the way in which AMHPs, as citizens, are socialised to see and experience the world in racist ways: cognitively, emotionally and as embodied racism. The latter includes a heightened sense of threat in relation to someone from a black background,[1] which is not just about racist stereotyping as a way of thinking, since emotions and physiological sensations are also at play. Trauma-informed practice supports approaches that pay attention to the forces outside of the person, which are relevant to the problems that lead to contact with mental health services; the person being assessed will experience the consequences of racism as thoughts and feelings, and in an embodied way.

Engaging with the influence of the unconscious encourages insight into the ways that AMHPs may perceive racialised people and their role in challenging their own self and others. Direct challenges are often met with defensiveness and one technique for making visible the invisible forms of bias is curious questioning. Biases may occur through stereotypes and prejudice, but may also emerge through non-validation of people's experiences of racism. This chapter introduces toxic interaction theory as a framework for understanding the potential harm caused to racialised people by the non-validation of the relevance of racism in their lives. This theory relates to everyday racism (Sue, 2015), as well as more visible and obviously offensive incidents. The harm may be caused relationally and because of category fallacy, where responses to racialised traumas are reframed as signs of a biological mental illness. Linked to this reframing is the impact of seeing the overrepresentation of black people in mental health services, which can lead to a bias due to the availability heuristic, wherein exposure to a pattern is interpreted as an indicator of reality (for example, 'black people are overrepresented in mental health so therefore black people must be more ill').

Attending to the impact of racism in the lives of racialised people is not purely an altruistic act. The chapter demonstrates that racism has negative consequences for the whole population. At the very basic level, resources and effort are spent on interventions that could have been ameliorated by a more just society. AMHPs are encouraged to think intersectionally about inequalities. The inequalities in mental health faced by racialised people are in part derived from the individualised paradigms of psychiatry. Rather than thinking of the professional response through a *rescuer* lens, AMHPs can begin to recognise that there is scope for coalitions to be built with all those with whom they interact.

Race and ethnicity

The issue of race is present in all interactions. When a white AMHP is assessing a white person the perceived absence of the need to take account of race arises precisely because there is often a view that race is not an issue because there are no apparent racial differences between them. This invisibility of whiteness is as much a key indicator of the salience of race as is the case when race is more obviously 'in the room'.

Assumptions about a person's own racialised identity based purely on observed features are unreliable. These characteristics indicate little more than where they sit in a racial hierarchy. In terms of meaning, a racialised identity observed from outside the person cannot communicate anything about that person's own relationship with their racialised identity. It can only speak of the preconceptions or biases of the outside observer.

It is a paradox that race is real and salient as an influential characteristic in human relations, but is unreliable as a system of categorising people. It is scientifically unsound. Across regions and nation states there are different notions of which racial categories exist. Inaccurate assumptions are made about people's racial background, for example a person of Black Caribbean and white dual heritage may be mistaken for being South Asian. This is the kind of error that happens regularly in social interactions. Further, the categories that are used to group people racially rely on observational criteria, which are then imbued with meaning about biological similarity or difference and about character. The reality, however, is that racial categorisation is a very bad proxy for genetic similarity or difference (Rutherford, 2020).

There was a time when the characteristics that are considered to be indicators of someone's racial identity did not carry the same social significance as they do now (Shah, 2020). Pieterse (1995) documented European depictions of Africans that changed over time, from around 2500 BC when images showed them mixing and intermarrying, up to the colonial period that became dominated by racist subhuman depictions. The concept of race as a way of subdividing the world population emerged from racism, rather than racism emerging from race (Shah, 2020).

Race was developed by white colonialists, not based on scientific examination of people, but rather an ideology that sought not only to categorise humans but also to establish a hierarchy (Kendi, 2016; Grandison, 2020). One of the key figures in the movement was Carl Linnaeus (1707–78), who developed categories including groups that he had only heard about at second hand (Shah, 2020). An understanding of the origins of race is important because the history illustrates that we have all been racialised; made to live with identities that are not scientifically real, but that are social constructions.

Ethnicity brings together geographical origins, faith, language, culture and a sense of belonging (Fernando, 2010). The concept of ethnicity is often conflated with race, partly because these concepts are both open to interpretation. A key feature of ethnicity is *belonging*; the literal translation from the original Greek word is 'tribe'. Self-identified ethnicity is changeable (Fernando, 2010). The external world has the potential to change which components of an ethnicity are most salient in a sense of identity.

Racial inequalities and institutional racism

The racial hierarchy is evident in dominant narratives about different racialised groups, as well as in their attainments in many aspects of civil life (Sarpong, 2017; Eddo-Lodge, 2018). In mental health services, in particular, there is an irrefutable relationship between being from darker-skinned racialised groups and poorer outcomes. Racial inequalities are present in the most common metrics such as detentions rates, lengths of stay, repeat admissions, contact with secure mental health services and exposure to interventions such as Community Treatment Orders (CTOs) (Fernando, 2017; Sewell, 2019).

The specifics of racial and ethnic variations are well documented, for example:

- Rates of diagnosis of psychosis for men of African Caribbean backgrounds in the United Kingdom (UK) are 3.2 per cent compared with 1.3 per cent for South Asian men and 0.3 per cent for white men (McManus et al, 2016).
- People from black backgrounds are ten times more likely to be on CTOs (NHS Digital, 2022).
- Detention rates per 100,000 in 2018/19 were 306.8 for the broad category of 'black' and for 'white' it was 72.9 (NHS Digital, 2022).
- A higher proportion of black men who die by suicide were known to services compared with the average (Vernon, 2020).

An annual report based on a snapshot data capture study (ADASS and NHSBN, 2018) found that in England, of the people assessed after arrest by the police, only 37 per cent of men were White British as compared with the remainder who were of other racial origin.

Morgan et al (2017) identified that African Caribbean and African patients experienced more social disadvantage at baseline and throughout the course of their typically longer and unbroken contact with mental health services. They hypothesised that there is potential to gain improvements in outcomes for this demographic through investment in social support. Institutional racism was cited as one of the explanatory paradigms for what was referred to as alarming and persistent disadvantages. Institutional racism, a term coined in 1967 by Ture and Hamilton (1992) and popularised by MacPherson (1999), includes three elements: unwitting prejudice, collective action and poorer outcomes. Walker (2020) contests the use of the term institutional racism on the basis that the MacPherson (1999) definition includes the notion of unconscious ('unwitting') rather than conscious bias.

The Commission on Race and Ethnic Disparities (CRED) (2021) rejected the notion on account of their assertion that the system is not rigged against racialised people. This argued that racial inequalities in mental health cannot be explained by institutional racism, along similar lines to Gajwani et al (2016), who also argued that variations can be explained by higher levels of pathology in populations groups, albeit with potential links to social inequality. This opinion is diametrically opposite to the arguments of Fernando (2017) and Sewell (2022)in the UK, and is the primary theme of the book from the United States, *Racism without Racists* (Bonilla-Silva, 2018). Bonilla-Silva (2018) examined a range of data in the social sector that showed significant and persistent racial disparities, while at the same time no individual or organisation would identify as being racist. Explanatory models that refute institutional racism as a cause are rooted in the belief that racism appears as visible and intentional acts to cause harm. Central to this chapter is the critique of such a perspective.

Each AMHP is faced with a responsibility to be clear about their ideological position in relation to the function of racism in race disparities in mental health. This is clearly not an individual choice and will be shaped by personal experiences and knowledge, as well as the approach of the organisation within which they work. The possible orientations can be summarised as seeing a deficit in the biology and/or culture of racialised groups; seeing racism and discrimination as something that occurs as antecedents of poor mental health; or seeing the mental health system, including their AMHP role, as contributing to racial inequalities. This latter perspective would include unconscious biases in decision making and racism in systems and policies. A key determinant of the various orientations is the definition of racism being applied.

Racism was pluralised as 'racisms' by Garner (2010) to draw attention to the fact that there are various manifestations. Sue (2015) listed racisms that include microaggressions and non-validations, as well as the overt and easily identifiable forms of racism such as race hate crimes and the use of tropes and blatant stereotyping. Racism is often defined as an ideology (Grandison, 2020), while Kendi (2019) asserted the importance of distinguishing between people's character and their words and behaviours, which may be racist. People who live in a society that gives explicit and implicit messages about the superiority of white people will inevitably lead to behaviours that stem from this and are consistent with studies in unconscious bias (Banaji and Greenwald, 2013). It is possible for people to have the right values and yet do and say racist things.

Race and ethnicity in compulsory mental health work

Five key decision-making points for one mental health professional – the AMHP – are worthy of attention, each of which will be discussed in turn:

- personal development to engage critically with race and ethnicity;
- Mental Health Act 1983 (MHA) referral;
- toxic interaction theory;
- risks and the racialised patient;
- recording.

Personal development to engage critically with race and ethnicity

The preparation for professional tasks such as MHA assessments undertaken by AMHPs in England and Wales commences long before contact with the person being assessed. Training and other ongoing personal development (OPD), including identifying and maintaining learning networks, are all part of the preparation. This OPD supports confidence and competence in practice.

The circumstances of an AMHP's personal and work life will have an impact on the amount of time and the nature of development that can be undertaken to support them in their role. Notwithstanding this caveat, it is important for AMHPs to recognise the importance of underpinning their approach to race equality with clear theoretical understandings. AMHPs are attuned to the need for legal compliance across relevant legislations and policies, and practice is shaped with this being centre stage. It is contended here that addressing race equality is worthy of the same rigour.

Perhaps the most critical delineation in relation to racial justice is between being non-racist and being anti-racist in AMHP practice. Being non-racist is the equivalent of keeping one's head down and not getting involved in politics, while trying to be fair. As Kendi (2019) stated, in the face of the overwhelming deficit narrative of non-white identities and the racial inequalities that are systematised and normalised, there is no neutral positive. The call to mental health professionals is to be anti-racist; to 'combat' the narratives and structures that lead to inequality based on racialised identities, where it is imperative that they 'evaluate their roles and (moral and regulatory) responsibilities. Current race relations require [professionals] to be proactive and do our homework to stay contemporarily astute as allies to Black and ethnic minority colleagues and service users' (Reid, 2021, p 249).

Engaging critically with race and ethnicity means actively investigating the sources of dominant ideas of race and the benefits to any system in maintaining these. Transformation occurs from the inside. As AMHPs, this work begins with self. There is overwhelming evidence from the field of social psychology that it is impossible to live in a society and not be invaded by the persistent associations between particular racialised identities and sets of characteristics and traits (Kahneman, 2011; Banaji and Greenwald, 2013). One way of exploring these associations is for AMHPs to examine what Sewell (2022, forthcoming) called 'racist processing': the reactions that occur in thinking and feeling in an embodied way. For example, a fear response (informed by stereotypes) of a racialised person in an MHA assessment will not relate to one or other of these aspects of processing, but rather a fusion of cognition, feeling and physiological responses. Attending to these feelings will require more than reading and gaining knowledge. Most helpful forms of development of anti-racist approaches will require attention to feelings as well as past racialised traumas remembered by our bodies (Menakem, 2021). Exploration of emotions in relation to racism is supported by work such as DiAngelo (2018) and Saad (2020). Guided body-work can be found in Menakem (2021), drawing on the increasing evidence that trauma is not just a mental or emotional state but exists in the physiology of the body (that is, embodied). The science of the embodied nature of trauma was documented in *The Body Keeps the Score* (Van der Kolk, 2014). Menakem (2021) uses mediations and reflections to bring awareness to the embodied consequences of racial trauma on people who have experienced racism and as well as on people who are part of the oppressor social group (recognising that racism adversely affects everyone and not just those framed as the victims).

The referral

The content of referrals reflects an interaction between the information available and the judgements and biases of the referrer. AMHP practice in general benefits from the critical awareness of what informs the content, timing and nature of the referral. The referrer has power to determine what is amplified and how to frame the presenting problem.

When considering race and ethnicity, it is worth noting that racialised identities are never neutral. Mental health appearance is likely to be the most salient detail that shapes a referral, but the studies of unconscious bias make two pertinent points. First, depending on who is being considered (or interacted with) humans see or hear different things. Second, unconscious bias does not serve as the primary decision-making criteria, but rather nudges a decision in a way that reflects biases or assumptions. The presence of bias may not be detectable as an isolated episode, but becomes more easily apparent when scrutinising patterns in data (Banaji and Greenwald, 2013).

To illustrate the latter point, Kahneman (2011) explored research that identified unconscious bias: that hurricanes with traditionally female sounding names cause a greater loss of life and damage to property. The reason was because of human behaviour; fewer precautions are taken because people (outside of their own awareness) downgraded the perceived risk based on the mental associations they have between the female gender and gentleness. It is likely that each individual had conscious intentionality in their decision making and thus could explain their decision making with plausibility. For example, the conscious reason for a person's decision could have been that they had heard that the eye of the hurricane had passed and they acted without awareness that the gendered name was having an influence on their decision.

When an AMHP receives a referral, as well as paying attention to the explicitly stated concerns there will be merit in remembering that racialised identities will have an influence in the referring process. An AMHP will need to remain alert to stereotypes and associations that may have an influence on what is amplified in a referral and a referrer's hypothesis about diagnosis, treatment and care, which follows any assessment. A belief about how nice or kind a referrer seems is not a reliable guide as to the likelihood of racialised biases affecting the process. (Note that Banaji and Greenwald [2013], experts on unconscious bias, entitled their book *Blind Spot: Hidden Biases in Good People*.) Racist processing of data is a feature of everyone who has been through formal education and socialisation in a country that consistently creates a racialised hierarchy and reinforces it by explicit racism and implicit messaging.

An AMHP does not require certainty of bias to justify an exploration of it. Ambiguity warrants exploration. As an example, if a referral of an 18-year-old young black man included the statement, 'He may pose risks to others, as he is known to have been involved in county lines', there could be a myriad of potential reasons behind this, including the possibility that the risk alert is based on a racist stereotype that links black men to violence rather than verified information about history. A skilled AMHP would find a way of examining that statement in the referral, for example by asking for as much substantiating information as possible. Curious questioning is a helpful way of exploring possible bias and discrimination, as well as referring to the evidence that unconscious bias sometimes affects processes and is, by definition, not intentional, as the term 'unconscious bias' refers to processes outside of a person's awareness. Fear of naming the possibility of bias, unconscious or otherwise, enables its unfettered influence.

Exploration or challenge of bias can feel uncomfortable because it can seem like an accusation. Kendi (2019) stated that this process can be made easier by making it clear that it is the action that is being discussed, rather than the character of the person. This can be a liberating way of approaching a conversation. Less accusatory language can be used, such as: "I wondered what you meant by ...", "What you said to me sounded as if there could be an assumption in this ...", "I wondered what the evidence was for ...". The arrangements leading up to an assessment can be pressured and there is often only time to attend to the absolute essentials. A key decision for the AMHP will be whether the seriousness of racist biases are downgraded for the sake of pragmatism. Such a decision effectively makes the AMHP complicit with racism, which may seem small as isolated events, but that shows up in patterns in mass data.

Toxic interaction theory

Toxic interaction theory (Sewell, 2022, forthcoming) describes the toxic effect of the interaction between racialised people who experience racism and workers in direct mental health practice. Toxic interaction theory suggests that a failure to incorporate an understanding of the various forms of racism in people's lives is a form of non-validation, which arises from a conceptualisation of racism as the visible and offensive harms. An AMHP's practice becomes more anti-racist when they take into account: (a) the visible and tolerated forms of racism, such as long-term racial injustice in data; (b) the visible and considered inconsequential forms of racism, such as epithets and amusing or superficially positive stereotypes (benevolent racism); and (c) the invisible racism in policies and underpinning philosophies for professional disciplines. Failure to attend to these would mean that the majority of racism experienced by the person is not taken into account and is not validated (Sue, 2015).

The model of mental health within which the AMHP function sits is still based on the tradition of psychiatry that individualises problems (Rapley et al, 2011). Bracken and Thomas (2005) outlined the fundamental flaw in a system built on a dualism between mind and body ('Cartesian Dualism', named after Rene Descartes 1596–1650), and additionally a dualism between the internal and external worlds as if the problems that lead to contact with psychiatric services are not related to external conditions invading the person. Any model of mental health that centres on symptoms and individualised perspectives on illness will be detrimental to social groups that face more social disadvantage.

Despite the contested nature of the term 'institutional racism', AMHPs are faced with considering the persistent, pervasive and pernicious racialised experiences from birth that are correlated or causally linked to poor mental health. Banaji and Greenwald (2013) and Kahneman (2011) reported that belonging to a social group does not automatically protect a person from internalising negative stereotypes, as with others who are outside of the group. This means that people from racialised groups live their lives receiving and potentially internalising implicit messages about their status, value and possibilities in terms of aspirations. The constant battle to assert a sense of self-worth and resist internalising racism is manifested as 'racial battle fatigue' (Smith et al, 2020). The greater the appreciation of the multiplicity of ways in which racism affects people's lives, the more equipped an AMHP is to engage in conversations with the person and their family or loved ones about the effects.

One of the challenges faced by many workers in direct practice is that they interpret conversations about race as conversations about the racialised person. This reflects the dominant discourse in society that frames race talk as about the 'other'. Most research or investigations (even on any internet search engine) frames racial issues as those pertaining to people who are not white. An AMHP can address this by recognising that race talk is as much about whiteness as anything else. Whiteness is an ideology that shapes the way the rest of the world's population is viewed. Anti-racist race talk is a conversation about racism, not about race. The decision of an AMHP to include or exclude conversations about race is an act of power, shaped by two key agendas: whether racism is as pervasive and pernicious as it is said to be by people with lived experience of racism (and research); and whether racism is proven to have a causal relationship with poor mental health.

The simplicity of the questions shrouds greater complexity. For many it is evident that the colonial legacy has created conditions that pass on intergenerational disadvantage both materially and, like all traumas, mentally, emotionally and in an embodied way (Menakem, 2021). An AMHP engaging in anti-racist practice must first see racial trauma as real, before being able to take account of it in assessments. It helps if an AMHP understands that diffuse racism, as well and sharp and violent racism, is significant in leading to trauma reactions (Johnstone and Boyle et al, 2018). This understanding will enable an AMHP to help formulate an understanding of problems in a way that includes consideration of the impact of racism.

Risks and the racialised patient

Arguably, mental health services are designed to assess and respond to risk. Barnett et al (2019) concluded that the determinant of admission to psychiatric hospital is not the psychiatric condition itself, but rather the assessed level of risk. The legal and moral imperative on an AMHP is to consider risks, as the MHA created the power to detain a patient 'in the interests of his own health or safety or with a view to the protection of other persons'. Though some AMHPs explicitly examine the risks posed to the person as a consequence of coming into contact with services, these conversations are yet to become routine during and after statutory assessments.

Fernando (2017) and Prins (2010) highlighted that when the content of referrals is controlled for, racialised patients are assessed as posing disproportionately higher levels of risk. Meanwhile, Morgan et al (2017) and Vernon (2020) directed attention to the aversive pathways for Black Caribbean and Black African men, which are disproportionately more likely to be via the criminal justice system. The patterns of disproportionality at the start of contact with services are at best maintained unabated (Morgan et al, 2017) or are worsened (Singh et al, 2007).

The Sainsbury Centre for Mental Health (SCMH) (2002) report highlighted the consequence of what Kahneman (2011) referred to as the 'availability heuristic'. The availability heuristic explains that consistent exposure to partial information creates a truth that may not be consistent with a factual reality, but that becomes a reality to a person or social group. Specifically, the SCMH report described the circularity of the relationship between African Caribbean communities and mental health services, which arose from late contact with services by this community due to fear of adverse treatment based on race and that led to greater acuity on contact. This circularity, in turn, fuelled a belief within services that this demographic (African Caribbean) posed higher levels of risk, which led to hypervigilance and more coercive interventions at an earlier stage, which in turn led to a narrative within that community that services are more punitive towards them, thereby leading to reluctance to contact services and so the cycle deepened.

A number of risks are apparent in relation to black and other racialised populations. It is possible, if not probable, that the availability heuristic will lead to adverse experiences in mental health services based not on the assessment of the individual, but rather a shared bias among mental health professionals. Perceived higher levels of risk will be linked to higher and possibly sustained use of psychopharmacology. As Whitaker (2010, p 112) states, this carries known risks where magnetic resonance imaging (MRI) studies 'show that antipsychotics worsen the very symptoms they are supposed to treat, and this worsening begins during the first three years that patients are on the drug'.

One of the decisions an AMHP takes concerns the extent to which they foreground potential risk to the person. Markham (2018) invoked the concept of 'iatrogenic harm' in considering the experience of detaining a patient under mental health legislation. Iatrogenic harm has its foundations in the inadvertent harm caused to patients in the course of a medical intervention or treatment. An AMHP can apply the interprofessional language of risk by explicitly considering potential harm caused to racialised patients by, for example, the non-validation of the seriousness of their experiences of racism. This process occurs through the application of an individualised illness model.

The conclusions drawn by Morgan et al (2017) are that models of intervention that do not adequately address social inequalities are likely to lead to poorer outcomes for Black African and African Caribbean people. An AMHP has good grounds for highlighting early on that a resource-poor system that is unable to invest adequately in social supports disproportionately affects Black African and African Caribbean people, and is contributing to the entrenched patterns of poorer outcomes that are measured using the UK government's Mental Health Minimum Data Set (NHS Digital, 2022). As discussed above, Sewell (2022, forthcoming) developed toxic interaction theory as a way of understanding that without active consideration of social and historical racism, the relationship between the professional and the person using services contributes to inequality. Interactions occur in a social context where the dominant culture suggests that racism should be downplayed. Without active engagement with the impacts of racism, its detrimental effect is likely to be sidelined. Kendi (2019) cited the notion of the 'white judge', brought to collective consciousness by African American feminist author Toni Morrison and referring to the internalised critical voice of whiteness (derived from exposure to racist narratives) that manifests as self-censorship by African American people. This notion of self-censorship is relevant to all racialised groups in a society that downplays its experiences of racism. Toxicity arises when an AMHP becomes complicit with society's silencing of voices that resist racism (Sewell, 2022, forthcoming). The knowledge that people may not feel entitled to cite racism as an explanation for disadvantage places a responsibility on AMHPs to make clear their commitment to exploring the multiple forms of racisms.

An AMHP's engagement with anti-racist work presupposes that they position themselves as an ally or, better still, someone who forms a coalition. DiAngelo (2018) and Sue (2015) persuasively argued for allyship, which is to stand with the oppressed. In cases of race hate crime, 'standing with' may be in the literal sense. Knowledge is evolving here. Dabiri (2021) suggested that allyship runs the risk of defaulting to the 'white saviour' approach and argued for coalition as a model. The central argument is that allyship locates harm in the other, whereas coalition acknowledges that all parties are harmed by racism, even in the context of whiteness as an 'advantage marker'.

An AMHP can be part of coalitions with individuals and other significant people in their lives by creating space in the assessment process to explore a counter-narrative to the deficit narrative of the lives of black and other racialised people, based on individualised risk-based approaches that diminish the significance of racial injustice. These approaches serve neither the individual, the mental health system nor all other citizens who wish to fully enjoy their freedoms.

Recording

Forms and protocols and custom and practice all inform the way in which an AMHP makes a written record of any assessment. Bracken and Thomas (2005) illustrated the power to create a narrative as being held in the process of recording.

In considering what to record, an AMHP can benefit from being intentional about the legacy that is being left each time they document something that will become part of someone's record. Records become facts. Histories become incorporated into narratives that are associated with a person. They are copied, incorporated and augmented. Each bit of recording lands within a system content. A dominant deficit-based narrative of racialised identities creates an imperative for an anti-racist AMHP to resist this by documenting a counter-narrative. This is not an invitation to distort information, but rather to communicate into the real context rather than an imaginary neutral one. A non-racist way of recording may attempt to be circumspect in not documenting stereotypes or tropes, even in an oblique way. An anti-racist approach would anticipate the potential racist processing of information (most probably unintentionally) and make efforts prospectively to attend to this. For example, an AMHP may meticulously document the precipitating factors for any incident of harm in a person's record, including in this both recent and historical traumas. Trauma-informed AMHP practice not only takes racial trauma into account in terms of causality, but also becomes invested in the service response being trauma informed. A trauma-informed approach is not just about forms of talking therapy, but also embodied work. Menakem (2021, p 7) stated that 'contrary to what many people believe, trauma is not primarily an emotional response'.

AMHPs have a role in contributing to formulations arising from their assessments and specifically in making recommendations to support clinical teams following an admission. AMHPs may benefit from reflecting on their confidence that (a) their recommendations are meaningful in relation to the impact that racism may have had on the lives of the people they access; and (b) the recommendations will be used in informing treatment and care. In a system that is functioning effectively, the insights of all professionals would be harnessed to enable the best possible support for individuals in a crisis.

Trauma-informed recording is therefore not solely the act of taking trauma into account and documenting it, but also proactively using what is recorded to, where possible, inform practice. Van der Kolk (2014), writing about trauma generically, and Menakem (2021), specifically about racial trauma, are unequivocal that a trauma-informed response must include embodied work and attention to the circumstances in the present that retraumatise people. Supporting the mental health system to routinely act on AMHP recommendations and to universally adopt a trauma-informed approach will require collective action.

Conclusion

This chapter sets out the following key decision-making points where an AMHP can use their agency to tackle racial inequalities in mental health:

- personal development to engage critically with race and ethnicity;
- consideration of the referral;

- engagement with racialised people and their networks during an assessment;
- consideration of risks to the racialised patient;
- recording.

The specific lessons for an AMHP in relation to race and ethnicity are rooted in best practice generally: preparation and investing in self-development is key; critical perspectives enable referrals to be evaluated more effectively; and incorporating an understanding of racial justice is central to social perspectives. Taking into account the potential racialised risks within the mental health system is part of critical psychiatry and using recording as a tool for change is a small but essential part of the activist work of critical thinkers in mental health. The decisions of an AMHP around race and ethnicity stand on the extent to which they consider competence in these matters to be critical as an indicator of overall AMHP competence.

To support their practice, AMHPs are asked to think critically about race, drawing on the science of genetics and race as a social construction. This chapter helps clarify that having a critical understanding of race is fundamental to understanding racism, including the specific ways it impacts on people who have contact with mental health services.

While maintaining a perspective on structural racism woven into policy and mental health paradigms, the chapter provides frameworks to support professionals to attend to race and racism in their practice as AMHPs. Studies of unconscious bias and theories for understanding particular manifestations of unconscious bias equip AMHPs to anticipate, detect and mitigate against biases in their own practice and that of others (for example the ways in which racial stereotypes or non-validations might appear in referrals).

The failure of an AMHP to incorporate an understanding of the impact of racism in the lives of people being assessed is effectively a downplaying of its significance, which is a form of non-validation. This non-validation has potential adverse effects, both relationally and in terms of professional judgement. In setting out empirical research evidence on the impact of racism on mental health, the chapter makes a case for why it is important to take account of race and racism. The data in this chapter also indicates how mental health services, rather than being solely beneficial or benign, may inadvertently cause harm by re-enforcing hierarchies in society and non-validating the experiences of people who face racism. As such, AMHPs are invited to consider the potential risks to people as a result of a mental health system that does not appropriately take into account the impact of racism in their lives.

Recording intentionally to address racial inequality is offered to AMHPs as a way of countering normalised ways of seeing and working with people who experience racism. Recording practice is strengthened by ensuring that recommendations made by an insightful anti-racist AMHP are applied in practice. Like most forms of practice, at its best, intentionality is required. Addressing the impacts of racism requires sustained focus and effort.

Note

[1] I have chosen to use lower case for 'black' and 'white' as a resistance to further embedding the notion of race as a reality (as opposed to social construction). It appears preceding Caribbean or African as it relates to ONS categories.

References

Association of Directors of Adult Social Services in England (ADASS) and National Health Service Benchmarking Service (NHSBN) (2018) *AMHPs, Mental Health Act assessments and the mental health social care workforce*. London: ADASS and NHSBN.

Banaji, M. and Greenwald, A. (2013) *Blind spot: hidden biases of good people*. New York: Bantham.

Barnett, P., Mackay, E., Matthews, H., Gate, R., Greenwood, H., Ariyo, K., Bhui, K., Halvorsrud, K., Pilling, S. and Smith, S. (2019) Ethnic variations in compulsory detention under the Mental Health Act: a systematic review and meta-analysis of international data, *The Lancet Psychiatry*, 6(4), 305–17.

Bonilla-Silva, E. (2018) *Racism without racists: colour-blind racism and the persistence of racial inequality in America* (5th edn). Lanham, MD: Rowman & Littlefield.

Bracken, P. and Thomas, P. (2005) *Postpsychiatry: mental health in a postmodern world: international perspectives in philosophy and psychiatry*. Oxford: Oxford University Press.

Commission on Race and Ethnic Disparities (CRED) (2021) *The report of the Commission on Race and Ethnic Disparities*. London: Crown.

Dabiri, E. (2021) *What white people can do next: from allyship to coalition*. Dublin: Penguin.

Department of Health (DoH) (2005) *Delivering race equality in mental health care: an action plan for reform inside and outside services and the government's response to the independent inquiry into the death of David Bennett*. London: DoH.

DiAngelo, R. (2018) *White fragility: why it's so hard for white people to talk about racism*. Boston, MA: Beacon Press.

Eddo-Lodge, R. (2018) *Why I'm no longer talking to white people about race*. London: Bloomsbury.

Fernando, S. (2010) *Mental health, race and culture* (3rd edn). Basingstoke: Palgrave Macmillan.

Fernando, S. (2017) *Institutional racism in psychiatry and clinical psychology*. London: Palgrave Macmillan.

Gajwani, R., Parsons, H., Birchwood, M.J. and Singh, S.P. (2016) Ethnicity and detention: are black and minority ethnic (BME) groups disproportionately detained under the Mental Health Act 2007? *Social Psychiatry and Psychiatric Epidemiology*, 51, 703–11.

Garner, S. (2010) *Racisms: an introduction*. London: Sage.

Grandison, C.P. (2020) *The racial hierarchy: anti-blackness culture and anti-black racism – the causes and consequences*. London: Xenogenesis.

Johnstone, L. and Boyle, M. with Cromby, J., Dillon, J., Harper, D., Kinderman, P. et al (2018). *The power threat meaning framework: towards the identification of patterns in emotional distress, unusual experiences and troubled or troubling behaviour, as an alternative to functional psychiatric diagnosis.* Leicester: British Psychological Society.

Kahneman, D. (2011) *Thinking, fast and slow.* London: Penguin.

Kendi, I.X. (2016) *Stamped from the beginning: the definitive history of racist ideas in America.* London: Bodley Head.

Kendi, I.X. (2019) *How to be an antiracist.* London: Bodley Head.

MacPherson, W. (1999) *The Stephen Lawrence inquiry.* London: HMSO.

Markham, S. (2018) Dealing with iatrogenic harm in mental health. Available at https://blogs.bmj.com/bmj/2018/12/04/sarah-markham-dealing-with-iatrogenic-harm-in-mental-health/.

McManus, S., Bebbington, P., Jenkins, R. and Brugha, T. (eds) (2016) *Mental health and wellbeing in England: adult psychiatric morbidity survey 2014.* Leeds: NHS Digital. Available at https://assets.publishing.service.gov.uk/government/uploads/system/uploads/attachment_data/file/556596/apms-2014-full-rpt.pdf.

Menakem, R. (2021) *My grandmother's hands: racialized trauma and the pathway to mending our hearts and bodies.* Dublin: Penguin.

Morgan, C., Fearon, P., Lappin, J., Heslin, M., Donoghue, K., Lomas, B. et al (2017) Ethnicity and long-term course and outcome of psychotic disorders in a UK sample: the ÆSOP-10 study. *British Journal of Psychiatry,* 211(2), 88–94.

NHS Digital (2022) Mental health minimum dataset. Available at https://digital.nhs.uk/data-and-information/data-collections-and-data-sets/data-sets/mental-health-services-data-set.

Pieterse, J. (1995) *White on black: images of Africa and Blacks in western popular culture* (2nd edn). New Haven, CT: Yale University Press.

Prins, H. (2010) *Offender, deviants or patients: explorations in clinical criminology* (4th edn). London: Routledge.

Rapley, M., Moncrieff, J. and Dillon, J. (2011) *De-medicalizing misery: psychiatry, psychology and the human condition.* Basingstoke: Palgrave Macmillan.

Reid, W. (2021) Ruminations. In W. Reid and S. Maclean (eds), *Outlanders: hidden narratives from social workers of colour* (pp 245–92). Lichfield: Kirwin Maclean Associates.

Rutherford, A. (2020) *How to argue with a racist: history, science, race and reality.* London: Orion.

Saad, L. (2020) *Me and white supremacy: combat racism, change the world, and become a good ancestor.* Naperville, IL: Sourcebooks.

Sarpong, J. (2017) *Diversify.* London: Harper Collins.

Sewell, H. (2019) *Working in mental health with people from black, Asian and minority ethnic groups: a practice guide for social workers and other professionals.* Bradford: HS Consultancy.

Sewell, H. (2022, forthcoming) *Toxic interaction theory: how to have conversations about racism.* Bradford: HS Consultancy.

Shah, S. (2020) *The next great migration: the beauty and terror of life on the move.* London: Bloomsbury.

Singh, S., Greenwood, N., White, S. and Churchill, R. (2007) Ethnicity and the Mental Health Act 1983. *British Journal of Psychiatry,* 191, 99–105.

Smith, W., David, R. and Stanton, G. (2020) Racial battle fatigue: the long-term effects of microaggressions on African American boys and men. In R. Majors, K. Carberry and T. Ransaw (eds), *The international handbook of black community mental health* (pp 83–92). Bingley: Emerald Publishing.

Sue, D.W. (2015) *Race talk and the conspiracy of silence: understanding and facilitating difficult dialogues on race.* London: Wiley.

Ture, K. and Hamilton, C. (1992) *Black power: the politics of liberation.* New York: Vintage.

Van der Kolk, B.A. (2014) *The body keeps the score: brain, mind, and body in the healing of trauma.* New York: Viking.

Vernon, P. (2020) Thirty years of Black History Month and thirty years of overrepresentation in the mental health system. In R. Majors, K. Carberry and T. Ransaw (eds), *The international handbook of black community mental health* (pp 137–48). Bingley: Emerald Publishing.

Walker, S. (2020) Systemic racism: big, black, mad and dangerous in the criminal justice system. In R. Majors, K. Carberry and T. Ransaw (eds), *The international handbook of black community mental health* (pp 41–60). Bingley: Emerald Publishing.

Whitaker, R. (2010) *Anatomy of an epidemic: magic bullets, psychiatric drugs and the astonishing rise of mental illness in America.* New York: Broadway.

4

Gender and forensic services

Rebecca Fish

Introduction

Women are in the minority of those residing in forensic mental health services, yet they are generally perceived to be particularly difficult to manage (Jeffcote and Watson, 2004). Abundant evidence shows how such women are more likely to have histories of victimisation, and experience depression and self-harm (De Vogel et al, 2016) while being confined within a system largely designed around the needs of men. Various policies in the United Kingdom (UK) have acknowledged the differing requirements and experiences of women, calling for gender-appropriate psychiatric care and accommodation, including the Reed Report back in 1992 (DoH and Home Office, 1992), the Corston Report (Corston, 2007) and various Department of Health (DoH) strategies and consultations (see, for example, DoH, 2002; 2010). This chapter will explore some of the reasons behind the need for gender-appropriate placements, using evidence from ethnographic research on three locked wards for women in a forensic hospital referred to as 'Unit C'.

For the Unit C study, the author spent over a year visiting locked wards and spending time with women and the staff who support them, then carried out in-depth interviews with 26 women residents and staff (for a full description of the methodology, see Fish, 2018). The women gave accounts of many things about their day-to-day life, including the restrictions placed on their intimate relationships and contact with family and friends. However, the most striking and memorable theme to come out of the study was the imbalance of power between staff and detained women. This was evidenced through talk about the continuum of coercive and restrictive practices, such as incentives systems, constant observation, physical intervention and seclusion. This chapter uses evidence from this study to explore the discourse and practices of – and about – women on locked wards, and how these work to shape their lives.

Gendered preconceptions

The women who participated in the research experienced high levels of coercive and restrictive interventions, and a key influence for this was that women were considered to be particularly difficult to manage. The assumption was that by the time women had arrived in the secure service, they had experienced a lot of trauma and were very complex, in crisis or extreme distress, displaying behaviours of concern. Consequently, women were sometimes placed in the seclusion room or under staff observation as soon as they arrived.

It seems that even at the point of admission, women are at a disadvantage within the forensic system. Some staff members indicated that the main difficulty of working with women was the way the women were perceived to deal with anger. In general, it was assumed that working with men was more straightforward, because they may be aggressive but this would often blow over quickly (see also Williams et al, 2001), whereas women would tend to keep the issue simmering under the surface for weeks. Therefore, gendered stories created a reputation for the women that preceded them. For example Adele,[1] a staff member, said:

> I think men are a little bit easier to understand in that he gets very angry about this, and he'll hit someone and be aggressive for half an hour, and it's more predictable, whereas I think with women they can keep an incident going for days. It can be verbal aggression, then leading to threats, then leading to hostility, then an actual assault or self-harm, or some act that leads to seclusion and it can carry on. And I think staff get frustrated, desperate, burnt out.

This suggests that anger shown by men is seen to be more predictable, reinforcing the stereotype that women should be more passive. It also does not take into account the way women and girls become shaped from a very young age not to show anger and to be passive (McKeown et al, 2003).

This characterisation of women is reinforced in some of the literature. For example, in their practice-focused chapter 'Thinking About the Needs of Women in Secure Settings', Jeffcote and Travers (2004) acknowledge the particularly detrimental early experiences among these women that can impact on social connectedness. Yet they go on to describe the 'highly charged and behaviourally disturbed' nature of women's wards, as emotionally disabling to staff, and mention that nursing staff prefer to deal with a physically violent male patient than the more 'subtle, complex and covert' forms of aggression presented by women (Jeffcote and Travers, 2004, pp 22–3). Feminist writers acknowledge the antecedents and the contextual nature of women's responses (Sagan, 2020). Williams et al (2004) draw on interviews with staff in a secure mental health unit, concluding that it is inappropriate to consider women's mental health conditions in terms of individual pathology. Rather, they should be considered as 'responses to, and sometimes as creative ways of coping with, damaging experiences that are rooted in their lived experiences of inequality and abuses of power' (Williams et al, 2004, p 32).

Williams et al (2004, p 37) go on to say that 'psychiatric labels supplemented with ward-based jargon are the raw material of women's reputations' and that this information, together with details of their histories, precedes them into all settings. In a different paper, Williams et al (2001) show how the combination of structural inequality, lack of access to resources and processes of hiding injustice such as victim blaming, is particularly significant for women's mental health.

Some of this preconception of women as 'difficult' is related to the diagnosis of emotionally unstable personality disorder (EUPD), also known as borderline personality disorder (BPD). This is a relatively common diagnosis for women who are detained in secure services, and is characterised by impulsive actions, unstable mood and chaotic relationships. Many writers criticise the gendered basis for this diagnosis, as it pathologises women who are detained in these services who are problematised without any recognition of the trauma involved in their pasts (Shaw and Proctor, 2005; Proctor, 2007). Warner and Wilkins (2003) explored the connection between childhood abuse and the BPD diagnosis, concluding that staff perceive relationships and abuse as an internalised difficulty for these women. They point out that 'women are then condemned as essentially problematic' (Warner and Wilkins, 2003, p 34). Past difficulties are therefore constructed as part of the person, rather than as socially situated and relational. Other literature demonstrates how women with past abuse are characterised, proposing a link between abuse and offending in later life (Trauffer and Widom, 2017; Turner et al, 2020), and indeed knowledge of past abuse is claimed to increase risk levels in services (Pollack, 2007).

Aitken (2006, p 727) points out that a sense of 'unsafe uncertainty' is created by this discourse of abuse, constructing women as 'fragile' and 'vulnerable' without recognising the historical contexts that bring this about, and this perpetuates their powerlessness:

> In effect, women are constructed as differently dangerous but more so than men – to services and to themselves. The consequence is that a culture of suppression of rage, anger, frustration, and fear is maintained, as is the communication of women's sense of vulnerability and powerlessness. Women are 'done to' rather than 'being with'.

Women as 'done to' is abundant in the literature. Owen et al (1998) studied residential services for women with long-term mental health needs and found that staff felt that they knew what was best for the women, particularly around the care and treatment offered. Along similar lines, Kristiansen (2004, p 380) discusses the paternalism of services, in terms of an imposed form of 'diminished credibility' where women are not believed or trusted, and everything they do or say becomes interpreted as due to their condition, or 'only to be expected' (see also Young, 2009; McKeown, 2010). It would therefore seem that claims of behavioural disturbance are used as a way to pathologise women and rationalise their placement and retention within forensic services (Travers, 2013; Powell and Taylor, 2015). These behavioural issues are seen to require an environment with greater restrictions in order to modify them, therefore typifying the idea that behavioural stability for women, regardless of milieu or context, determines progression through these services (see also Aiyegbusi, 2002; Alexander et al, 2011; Fish and Morgan, 2019). The appraisal and management of behaviour – and consequently women's progression – is in the control of staff.

Restrictive practices

Erving Goffman's iconic work *Asylums* (1961) describes the lives of people living in psychiatric wards in the mid–20th century. Goffman demonstrated how power disparity becomes embedded in institutional life through various practices that work in continuum, juxtaposing the erasure from outside life with exposure within the unit. He describes various 'violations', which include the recording and collecting of facts only available to staff, and confessionals where details that would ordinarily be concealed are exposed to new audiences. According to Goffman, people detained in hospital have restricted contact with the outside world, whereas staff are socially integrated into it. Information is restricted across boundaries, and hereby people are excluded from decisions regarding their fate. Such exclusion is described by Goffman as giving staff a special basis of distance from (and control over) inmates. The institution comes to be identified as belonging to staff, so the interests of the institution and the interests of staff become interchangeable.

Goffman (1961, p 32) describes events that involve direct exposure, for example a person being placed in a 'constantly lit seclusion room, into whose Judas window any person passing on the ward can peer'. He describes this visibility as the person being rendered *contaminated* by their exposure, never fully alone, always within sight and often earshot of someone. Goffman's use of the word 'contamination' is interesting, connoting enduring pollution or corruption as a way to show the lasting damage of inpatient services. The final aim of these processes of contamination was to cause people to 'self-direct' in a way that fits in with the daily running of the organisation (Goffman, 1961, p 83).

The Unit C study found that restrictive practices can still be seen to work on a continuum, as observed by Goffman over 60 years ago. This begins with the control of information (women were often not told they were staying at the unit until after they arrived, and often felt left out of decisions about their future), through the workings of incentives systems, to restraint and seclusion at the extreme. Some research shows that women are subjected to restraint and seclusion more often than men, with women being restrained or secluded for self-harming (Hui et al, 2013). This disparity is concerning when considering the way restrictive practices are experienced by women who have disproportionately high histories of gender-based or sexual violence and abuse. Being overpowered physically and mentally can retraumatise and revictimise women, creating an environment of insecurity and hostility (Knowles et al, 2015; Evans and Costa, 2020). The women in Unit C experienced restrictive practices as aversive and as punishment or abandonment (Fish and Hatton, 2017). For example, Annie, who had significant experience of sexual violence in the past, reported:

> I have been in one particular restraint by a male and a female where they've ripped my top and I've had no clothes on the top half, where there've been males restraining me.

In her book *Unbroken*, Alexis Quinn (2018, p 54) refers to the experience of being restrained as salient of the power hierarchy: 'This was when the whole compliance thing started. If you don't do exactly what they say, when they say, you're in trouble. They hold all the power and they own you. They can restrain you when they like and fill you with chemicals when they like.' Participants in Unit C understood the continuum of intervention as ending at seclusion. Staff were often told not to engage with secluded women, but this was often the time when women were rendered most vulnerable and in need of engagement and support. In one early visit, a woman called Sarah pointed out the seclusion room:

> Sarah: It's cold in there.
> Rebecca: What does it feel like being inside there?
> Sarah: It's horrible.
> Rebecca: Is somebody watching you?
> Sarah: Yes, staff are watching, in a little room with the window,
>   watching you – observing.

Sarah went on to describe how she feels when in seclusion:

> It makes me more angry, it makes me stressed. I always bang my head,
> when I go in seclusion [pause] – I just smash my head. I had a piece
> of string in my pocket, they looked in my pocket and they didn't get
> everything out and I got the string and cut myself in seclusion.

Many studies over the years have repeatedly indicated that seclusion is a negative experience (Meehan et al, 2000; Hoekstra et al, 2004; Haw et al, 2011), which may be construed as a form of punishment or even torture (Chamberlin, 1985; Holmes et al, 2004; Veltkamp et al, 2008; Cusack et al, 2018). Feelings associated with being placed in seclusion include anger, sadness, abandonment, helplessness and fear.

Quinn (2018, p 74) describes her experiences and perspectives of seclusion clearly and powerfully:

> Seclusion is a constant threat of extreme punishment hanging over
> your head. It's wrong. There's nothing therapeutic about the force
> that comes with the act … It's much quicker and easier to lock
> somebody in a room than to talk things through, identify triggers in
> the environment, and make adjustments.

Experiences of seclusion can have lasting influence. For example, Wadeson and Carpenter's (1976) research asked service users to sketch their experience of a psychiatric unit more than one year after their release. Most of the participants drew the seclusion room experience and reported that they still felt distressed about it; for many that experience symbolised their entire psychiatric illness. Quinn (2018, p 311) also describes the lasting damage of seclusion: 'I know if

I get cold while asleep this can trigger a flashback of my stay in that freezing seclusion room ... The experience of being locked inside a cage has had a severe psychological impact on me.'

It becomes clear that the tools made available to staff for behaviour management are persistently reinforcing the power hierarchy within secure services and 'keeping them in their place', thereby hindering women's progression. This aligns with Becker's (1997, p 140) view that it becomes clear that this focus on behaviour management in services is what shapes the power differential, where 'surely, nothing distances staff so thoroughly from clients as the consideration of their "management"'.

Progression

The requirements for demonstrating progression, such as behavioural stability and signifying passivity, reinforce the marginalisation experiences that women have faced in the community and throughout their engagement with services. For example, in Unit C there was much focus placed on past experiences of abuse, which was being used as a way to render women as 'damaged'. Debate on this topic is divided – some authors consider looking to people's pasts to be problematic, for example in claiming that knowledge of a client's past abuse may adversely inform conceptions of risk and potential for rehabilitation (Pollack, 2007; Adshead, 2011). Conversely, other authors advocate looking to the past in terms of treatment in order to avoid the limitations of the medical model (Rossiter, 2012). It is important that personalised plans take past experiences into account, alongside considerations of women's futures.

In Unit C, the emphasis placed on 'damage' meant that women found it very difficult to demonstrate progress, and that outcomes and goals were designated by the service rather than in collaboration with the women themselves. Sometimes, these designated conceptions of progress worryingly encouraged passivity on behalf of women. For example, Sarah stated:

> Like I got hit last week off [name], I got hit last week off her. And I just sat there and let her do it, I didn't want to hit back and that's why the staff said, "That's good that you didn't hit back." So that's why they're going to move me on.

The service emphasised autonomy and self-sufficiency as a way to progress, in line with policy discourse, thereby disregarding the gendered requirement for relational, collaborative support in combination with professional therapy (see also McKim, 2008; Sagan, 2020).

Power disparity

Powell and Taylor (2015) refer to 'symbolic violence' in secure units as part of the system of domination of women within the hegemonic social order or hierarchy within services. Women's experiences in forensic services mirror those related to social hierarchies encountered throughout their lives – those of gender, class, race and disability. These power dynamics are manifested through practices of behaviour management and imposed parameters of progression. The following intersecting and overlapping aspects underpin and reinforce power disparity on locked wards:

- *Control of information.* Some women mentioned being secluded when they first arrived. This was rationalised by staff as women being moved from higher security, but the women mentioned that they had not been informed about their move by the previous service and this is what caused the crisis. Information about women's conduct throughout life follows them throughout services, and only staff are able to see what information is held. Further, women wanted more information about when restrictive practices would be used and why, as the use was sometimes arbitrary.
- *Restrictive practices.* Both staff and women with experience of being restrained and secluded remarked on the indignity of the experience, including the distress of watching other people being restrained/secluded. This was seen as a display or spectacle of power. Restraint and seclusion were retraumatising, reminding women of previous abuse or trauma and evoking feelings of punishment or abandonment. There was a lack of any sort of debrief or resolution afterwards. Shortages of staff can further add to the use of restrictive practices due to forced changes in routine and restrictions on movement within the service (McKeown et al, 2019).
- *Concepts of progression.* Women were often not involved in planning or decisions about the future. They were not consulted about their own goals or outcomes from rehabilitation, and they were often not aware of how to determine or demonstrate progression.

Eliminating restrictive practices

The women in Unit C had important suggestions for reducing restrictive practices. An important step towards this would be to allow safe and supportive spaces for women to explain their anger. For example, Bonnie suggested:

> If there's another room away from seclusion, you know, like a calm-down room, I reckon that they should talk to us and say, "How do you feel, what can we do to help you?" and that …

Therefore, acknowledgement, rather than repression of anger, needs to take place, and the connection between powerlessness and anger needs to be recognised. Anger is being seen as pathological, yet it is important to acknowledge the frustration that comes from being detained in a locked ward with all its restrictions. Further, opportunities for engaging, learning from and resolving disputes resulting from anger should not be missed.

A good example of this happening in practice is the following quote from an interview with staff participant, Brian. He mentions how the staff managed to stop using restrictive practices with one woman, and she moved back to the community:

> The incidents became far less intense and far shorter in duration, again going from many hours in seclusion, quite wild really for want of a better phrase, to maybe having a half-hour period of being upset and distressed and crying. It's just through being consistent really, through letting people know that they're being supported and it's unconditional support that we offer. Being consistent and having the whole team being consistent and making them feel valued as a person.

Brian shows that by accepting some anger and by remaining beside the person afterwards, the need for restriction can be removed.

The use of restrictive practices is therefore governed by its availability. Staff training programmes often begin with de-escalation, move through breakaway techniques, and then to restraint and seclusion. This is often how escalation proceeds, with conflict only ending when restraint or seclusion is implemented. I would argue that this is because we are not working together with people and taking into account their own needs and recovery requirements enough.

Therefore, power and hierarchies are the key issue here. One of the staff participants, Iona, showed that flattening the hierarchy effectively removed the need for restrictive interventions with a woman called Alison:

> My attitude towards her was very upbeat and very OK. I was never negative towards Alison, if she couldn't do something, I didn't say it in a negative way. And the relationship was very different between some other staff members and her because they'd had all the aggression and I'd never had aggression. We'd have a laugh to be honest, we'd laugh and joke and I think there was an element of – what's the difference?

We can see here, that good therapeutic relationships benefit everyone (Gilburt et al, 2008; McKeown et al, 2014).

Flattening the hierarchy

Taking into account that women are in need of therapy and empowerment rather than containment and security (Powell, 2001), the focus on behaviour management and control within forensic services works to define women by their problematic behaviour and minimise the role of the institution (McKeown, 2010). Quinn (2018, p 312) refers to her 'diminished status' in psychiatric care, where relationships between staff and patients are 'contrived and inauthentic, since the entire system is designed to denigrate. The very essence of you is taken away'. Quinn (2018, p 113) recalls only being helped to recover when she was treated as an equal in the service, stating that the service that provided most help to her was the one that had a 'flattened hierarchy'. This means power is shared between staff and residents, and everyone is working towards the same goals. This is key to a progressive service and in order to achieve a flat hierarchy, it is important to work towards aspirations that change culture and systems.

Rather than focusing on the person and their behaviour, we therefore need to change the systems, as a starting point. The work of Spandler and McKeown (2017, p 90) is useful when thinking about how power relations are established through systems and practices: 'Workers may bear responsibility for quite serious consequences without necessarily having sufficient authority to alter systemic practices or overarching power relations. Most members of the mental health workforce would plausibly deny they entered into this work wishing to abuse, harm or dominate.' Therefore, services need to challenge the system and the tools that are available and then this will help flatten the hierarchy. McKeown et al (2014) advise that services invoke a 'deliberative democracy', wherein all participants are respectful of difference and power imbalances are acknowledged and reduced.

To summarise, there are a number of things that services can implement to reduce power disparity:

- It is important to encourage an awareness of power differentials and actively work to empower women through a 'relational and reciprocal' alliance (McKeown et al, 2014).
- Giving people information is key. People need information about their rights, the situations that warrant the use of interventions, and the requirements for how to progress and move on through the service (and we need to ask the person how they would prefer to receive that information). By having access to information, people can be involved in their treatment and take responsibility for working towards their recovery.
- Women and their families should be involved in planning, while keeping thoughts of progressing back to the community in mind. Consistent and gradual, collaborative, well-managed transitions are fundamental (Cooke and Bailey, 2011).
- Services need to recognise the connection between powerlessness and anger, and to appraise behaviour contextually. It is important to be able to take into account the actions of individuals and how they react in certain situations, but also to look beyond and recognise the often stressful contexts of the ward environment
- The use of trauma-informed care is key: listening to women, believing them and taking them seriously, harnessing the use of trust, privacy and reciprocity to design rehabilitation while encouraging feelings of safety (McKeown et al,

2014; Isobel et al, 2020; Sagan, 2020; Ratcliffe and Stenfert Kroese, 2021). It is also important to look beyond the damage and trauma, to see potential and collaboratively plan for the future

Conclusion

This chapter has demonstrated the link between the practices and the power disparity within forensic mental health units and, in particular, how these relate to the experiences of women, who are already a minority within these services. Rather than focusing on behaviour of staff or the detained women, it is increasingly important that gendered experiences and socialisation are considered when planning services for women. If we acknowledge that women's mental health and their contact with the criminal justice system are linked to oppressive gendered social relations and restricted access to services and material resources in the community, then it becomes clear that trauma-informed care and long-term care planning are key. This shift in approach away from medicalised concepts of 'treatment' would work towards balancing power in services, thereby allowing women to become active in their own recovery (Evans and Costa, 2020).

Note
[1] All names are pseudonyms.

References

Adshead, G. (2011) Same but different: constructions of female violence in forensic mental health. *International Journal of Feminist Approaches to Bioethics*, 4(1), 41–68.

Aitken, G. (2006) Women and secure settings. *Psychologist*, 19(12), 726.

Aiyegbusi, A. (2002) Nursing interventions and future directions with women in secure services. *Forensic Focus*, 19, 136–50.

Alexander, R., Hiremath, A., Chester, V., Green, F., Gunaratna, I. and Hoare, S. (2011) Evaluation of treatment outcomes from a medium secure unit for people with intellectual disability. *Advances in Mental Health and Intellectual Disabilities*, 5(1), 22–32.

Becker, D. (1997) *Through the looking glass: women and borderline personality*. New York: Routledge.

Chamberlin, J. (1985) An ex-patient's response to Soliday. *Journal of Nervous and Mental Disease*, 173(5), 288–9.

Cooke, K. and Bailey, D. (2011) Women's experience of forensic mental health services: implications for practice. *Journal of Mental Health Training, Education and Practice*, 6(4), 186–94.

Corston, J. (2007) *The Corston Report: a report of a review of women with particular vulnerabilities in the criminal justice system*. London: Home Office.

Cusack, P., Cusack, F.P., McAndrew, S., McKeown, M. and Duxbury, J. (2018) An integrative review exploring the physical and psychological harm inherent in using restraint in mental health inpatient settings. *International Journal of Mental Health Nursing*, 27(3), 1162–76.

De Vogel, V., Stam, J., Bouman, Y.H., Ter Horst, P. and Lancel, M. (2016) Violent women: a multicentre study into gender differences in forensic psychiatric patients. *Journal of Forensic Psychiatry and Psychology*, 27(2), 145–68.

Department of Health (DoH) (2002) *Women's mental health: into the mainstream – strategic development of mental health care for women.* London: DoH.

Department of Health (DoH) (2010) *See, think, act: your guide to relational security.* London: DoH.

Department of Health (DoH) and Home Office (1992) *Review of health and social services for people with learning disabilities and others requiring similar services: final summary report (The Reed Report).* London: HMSO.

Evans, J. and Costa, L. (2020) Women's forensic mental health care: the need for gender-based analysis. *Canadian Journal of Disability Studies*, 9(3), 52–77.

Fish, R. (2018) 'Behind this wall': experiences of seclusion on locked wards for women. *Scandinavian Journal of Disability Research*, 20(1), 139–51.

Fish, R. and Hatton, C. (2017) Gendered experiences of physical restraint on locked wards for women. *Disability and Society*, 32(6), 790–809.

Fish, R. and Morgan, H. (2019) 'Moving on' through the locked ward system for women with intellectual disabilities. *Journal of Applied Research in Intellectual Disabilities*, 32(4), 932–41.

Gilburt, H., Rose, D. and Slade, M. (2008) The importance of relationships in mental health care: a qualitative study of service users' experiences of psychiatric hospital admission in the UK. *BMC Health Services Research*, 8(1), 92.

Goffman, E. (1961) *Asylums: essays on the social situation of mental patients and other inmates.* New York: Doubleday & Co.

Haw, C., Stubbs, J., Bickle, A. and Stewart, I. (2011) Coercive treatments in forensic psychiatry: a study of patients' experiences and preferences. *Journal of Forensic Psychiatry and Psychology*, 22(4), 564–85.

Hoekstra, T., Lendemeijer, H. and Jansen, M. (2004) Seclusion: the inside story. *Journal of Psychiatric and Mental Health Nursing*, 11(3), 276–83.

Holmes, D., Kennedy, S.L. and Perron, A. (2004) The mentally ill and social exclusion: a critical examination of the use of seclusion from the patient's perspective. *Issues in Mental Health Nursing*, 25(6), 559–78.

Hui, A., Middleton, H. and Völlm, B. (2013) Coercive measures in forensic settings: findings from the literature. *International Journal of Forensic Mental Health*, 12(1), 53–67.

Isobel, S., Wilson, A., Gill, K. and Howe, D. (2020) 'What would a trauma-informed mental health service look like?' Perspectives of people who access services. *International Journal of Mental Health Nursing*, 30(2), 495–505.

Jeffcote, N. and Travers, R. (2004) *Thinking about the needs of women in secure settings.* London: Jessica Kingsley.

Jeffcote, N. and Watson, T. (2004) *Working therapeutically with women in secure mental health settings*. London: Jessica Kingsley.

Knowles, S.F., Hearne, J. and Smith, I. (2015) Physical restraint and the therapeutic relationship. *Journal of Forensic Psychiatry and Psychology*, 26(4), 461–75.

Kristiansen, K. (2004) Madness, badness and sadness revisited: ontology control in 'mental health land'. In K. Kristiansen and R. Traustadóttir (eds), *Gender and disability research in the Nordic countries*. Lund: Studentlitteratur.

McKeown, A. (2010) Female offenders: assessment of risk in forensic settings. *Aggression and Violent Behavior*, 15(6), 422–9.

McKeown, M., Cresswell, M. and Spandler, H. (2014) Deeply engaged relationships: alliances between mental health workers and psychiatric survivors in the UK. In B. Burstow, B.A. LeFrançois and S. Diamond (eds), *Psychiatry disrupted: theorizing resistance and crafting the (r)evolution* (pp 193–216). Montreal: McGill-Queen's University Press.

McKeown, M., Anderson, J., Bennett, A. and Clayton, P. (2003) Gender politics and secure services for women: reflections on a study of staff understandings of challenging behaviour. *Journal of Psychiatric and Mental Health Nursing*, 10(5), 585–91.

McKeown, M., Thomson, G., Scholes, A., Jones, F., Baker, J., Downe, S. et al (2019) 'Catching your tail and firefighting': the impact of staffing levels on restraint minimization efforts. *Journal of Psychiatric and Mental Health Nursing*, 26(5–6), 131–41.

McKim, A. (2008) 'Getting gut-level': punishment, gender, and therapeutic governance. *Gender and Society*, 22(3), 303–23.

Meehan, T., Vermeer, C. and Windsor, C. (2000) Patients' perceptions of seclusion: a qualitative investigation. *Journal of Advanced Nursing*, 31(2), 370–7.

Owen, S., Repper, J., Perkins, R. and Robinson, J. (1998) An evaluation of services for women with long-term mental health problems. *Journal of Psychiatric and Mental Health Nursing*, 5, 281–90.

Pollack, S. (2007) 'I'm just not good in relationships': victimization discourses and the gendered regulation of criminalized women. *Feminist Criminology*, 2(2), 158–74.

Powell, J. (2001) Women in British special hospitals: a sociological approach. *Journal of Social Sciences and Humanities*, 5, 1–14.

Powell, J. and Taylor, P.J. (2015) Gender, masculinity, contemporary history and the psychiatric secure estate: back to the future? *Journal of World Scientific News*, 22, 145–56.

Proctor, G. (2007) Disordered boundaries? A critique of 'borderline personality disorder'. In H. Spandler and S. Warner (eds), *Beyond fear and control: working with young people who self-harm* (pp 105–20). Ross-on-Wye: PPCS Books.

Quinn, A. (2018) *Unbroken: learning to live beyond diagnosis*. Newark-on-Trent: Trigger Publishing.

Ratcliffe, J.M. and Stenfert Kroese, B. (2021) Female service users' experiences of secure care in the UK: a synthesis of qualitative research. *Journal of Forensic Psychiatry and Psychology*, 32(5), 1–30.

Rossiter, K.R. (2012) *Victimization, trauma, and mental health: women's recovery at the interface of the criminal justice and mental health systems*. PhD dissertation. Simon Fraser University, British Columbia.

Sagan, O. (2020) The lonely legacy: loss and testimonial injustice in the narratives of people diagnosed with personality disorder. *Mental Health and Social Inclusion*, 24(4), 241–55.

Shaw, C. and Proctor, G. (2005) Women at the margins: a critique of the diagnosis of borderline personality disorder. *Feminism and Psychology*, 15(4), 483–90.

Spandler, H. and McKeown, M. (2017) Exploring the case for truth and reconciliation in mental health services. *Mental Health Review Journal*, 22(2), 83–94.

Trauffer, N. and Widom, C. S. (2017) Child abuse and neglect, and psychiatric disorders in nonviolent and violent female offenders. *Violence and Gender*, 4(4), 137–43.

Travers, R. (2013) Treatment of women in forensic settings. In C. Henderson, C. Smith, S. Smith and A. Stevens (eds), *Women and psychiatric treatment: a comprehensive text and practical guide* (pp 68–83). London: Routledge.

Turner, D., Wolf, A.J., Barra, S., Müller, M., Hertz, P.G., Huss, M. et al (2020) The association between adverse childhood experiences and mental health problems in young offenders. *European Child and Adolescent Psychiatry*, 30(8), 1195–207.

Veltkamp, E., Nijman, H., Stolker, J., Frigge, K., Dries, P. and Bowers, L. (2008) Patients' preferences for seclusion or forced medication in acute psychiatric emergency in the Netherlands. *Psychiatric Services*, 59(2), 209–11.

Wadeson, H. and Carpenter, W.T. (1976) Impact of the seclusion room experience. *Journal of Nervous and Mental Disease*, 163(5), 318–28.

Warner, S. and Wilkins, T. (2003) Diagnosing distress and reproducing disorder: Women, child sexual abuse and 'borderline personality disorder'. In P. Reavey and S. Warner (eds), *New Feminist Stories of Child Sexual Abuse* (pp 179–98). Abingdon: Routledge.

Williams, J., Scott, S. and Waterhouse, S. (2001) Mental health services for 'difficult' women: reflections on some recent developments. *Feminist Review*, 68(1), 89–104.

Williams, J., Scott, S. and Bressingham, C. (2004) Dangerous journeys: women's pathways into and through secure mental health services. In N. Jeffcote and T. Watson (eds), *Working therapeutically with women in secure mental health settings* (pp 31–43). London: Jessica Kingsley.

Young, I.M. (2009) Five faces of oppression. In G. Henderson and M. Waterstone (eds), *Geographic thought: a praxis perspective* (pp 55–71). Abingdon: Routledge.

5

Boundaries of risks and rights and personality disorder

Andy Brammer

Introduction

Using the example of Approved Mental Health Professionals (AMHPs) in England and based on findings from a recent research study, this chapter explores aspects of decision making in relation to people who hold suicidal ideas, self-injure or present with other high-risk actions when distressed. This group of people are sometimes referred to as having a personality disorder. The chapter explores the complexities of the decision-making process arising from the interrelationship between the statutory mental health legal framework and the more hidden subjective narratives influencing decisions, including how the dominance of the medical model and associated narratives of risk management, alongside the upholding of a person's rights, can limit independent decision making. Applying theories of alienation, the chapter concludes with an exploration of the impact on the decision maker, as well as practice considerations that can more effectively support AMHPs.

Personality disorder and contested narratives

Arguably, the medical paradigm dominates AMHP practice to such an extent that practitioners experience challenges when trying to apply a perspective that considers matters other than medical – sometimes referred to as the social perspective – within multi-agency frameworks. Medical concepts such as 'mental disorder' are embedded in legislation and everyday practice. For example, AMHPs are regularly exposed to terminology usually associated with medicine, such as (mental) illness, relapse, recovery, episode and concordance/cooperation with treatment. These terms place discussions, ideologically, within a medical model of understanding people's experiences. In theory, AMHPs are aware that the origins of many of these medical beliefs are rooted in psychiatry and pharmacology, but in practice they may struggle to provide practical alternatives or even language that can challenge these dominant narratives (Karban et al, 2021).

The whole area of medical diagnosis of mental health and illness is contested, which is particularly true when it comes to the diagnosis of personality disorder (Pilgrim, 2014; Warrener, 2017). These contested beliefs are reflected in the attitudes of mental health professionals, with some believing personality disorder to be a mental illness and others considering it to be a form of social deviance

(Stalker et al, 2005). There are various personality disorders listed in the *Diagnostic Statistical Manual* (DSM) (APA, 2021) and *International Classification of Diseases* (ICD) (WHO, 2022), the guides that psychiatrists use to diagnose mental illness, and it is not the intention of this chapter to explore this debate. However, the chapter will work from the premise that there are some people that professionals will refer to as having a personality disorder, and these individuals share characteristics (such as impaired emotional management strategies) and are said to behave in a way that is difficult for others to manage or make sense of (including self-injury and high-risk actions such as expressions of suicide) (Nehls, 1999). The author also believes that there is a strong association between many of these expressions of distress and traumatic life experiences, in particular childhood abuse and neglect (Warrener, 2017). Historically, people diagnosed with personality disorders experience exclusion from mainstream mental health services (NIMHE, 2003) and there is said to be very little therapeutic optimism when working with them (Warrener, 2017). The author's own research (Brammer, 2020) found that such perceptions and challenges also influence the considerations of AMHPs when making compulsory decisions, which is the focus of this chapter.

In England, the *National Strategy on Policing and Mental Health* (NPCC, 2020, p 12) estimates that around two thirds of those detained under section 136 of the Mental Health Act 1983 (MHA) (which is the section that gives police power to remove someone who may have a mental disorder to a place of safety for an assessment) are already known to mental health services. For those attended to by street triage services (initiatives that place mental health practitioners alongside police officers in an advisory capacity), it is as high as 88 per cent. The same report also suggests that a relatively small number of individuals make up a disproportionate amount of the whole (NPCC, 2020) and are also those who are most likely to be diagnosed or labelled as having a personality disorder. The figures suggest that only 30 per cent of those who require this type of emergency response have no current involvement with mental health services or other support available to them. The author's own research indicates that AMHPs believe that people with previous diagnosis of personality disorder now account for a large proportion of referrals (Brammer, 2020), and one of the questions this poses is how effective current strategies are if such large numbers are repeatedly seeking help through emergency services.

In response to these challenges, different forms of collaborative care and risk planning have emerged, such as multi-agency agreements on how to respond in situations where the person repeatedly interacts with emergency services (and other agencies) in crisis. These initiatives often focus on people diagnosed with personality disorders and they have not been universally welcomed, especially by some service-user groups. There have been suggestions that such initiatives are a way of denying emergency help, or that they criminalise people as police and other emergency services are involved in mental healthcare planning without the person's expressed agreement. There has also been criticism based on the experience that such initiatives can be externally imposed, rather than being genuinely jointly agreed with the person themselves. It also cannot be assumed that because someone has the offer of support, it is necessarily the right kind, or that the person considers it to be helpful.

Even where jointly agreed plans are in place to guide mental health professionals in their decision making (including possible alternatives to the use of section 136 by police), there are, and will continue to be, situations where the perceived risks are so high that a police officer believes their powers of removal under section 136 to be the only safe option. Even with the availability of the advice of mental health professionals, there can be perceived risk factors that lead decision makers to believe that the person needs to be considered for admission or further detention. It is when this point is reached that the AMHP has certain considerations to make, which the chapter will now go on to discuss.

The practice and the principles

The legal framework of the MHA is multidimensional. Integrated into this apparently objective legal process are two very subjective considerations: first, the medical diagnosis by the doctors, including interpretation of symptoms, perceived risk and the causal link between illness; and, second, the AMHP's own consideration of all the factors of the case before deciding on whether or not to make an application for detention. For the AMHP, this decision making includes social and systemic perspectives to make sense of what is happening, or what could happen dependent on the course of action chosen.

Framing the process of statutory assessment for all the professional participants in England are the guiding principles of the MHA (DoH, 2015). The principle most frequently and explicitly referred to is the least restrictive option, which is intended to promote the consideration of how the best outcome can be achieved with minimum intervention. This principle does not stand alone and should be applied alongside the other principles to ensure the person's involvement and maximising of independence, so that when concluding the process, the action has a clear rationale or purpose. In other words, the action is both proportionate and necessary. The AMHP and the doctors should be considering what their decisions and actions are intending to achieve – for example, either from admission into hospital or, alternatively, input from a community treatment team supporting the person at home.

The AMHP needs to provide a rationale for admission or detention, which may, at its most basic, include the provision of strategies for managing or assessing people who self-harm. The AMHP needs to balance these short-term strategies against the possible longer-term iatrogenic effects of being a psychiatric 'patient', which brings with it a range of negative outcomes for people both socially and medically (Campbell and Davidson, 2017). Being able to take this longer-term view of possible negative impact is challenging for the AMHP. First, because managing self-injurious and suicidal behaviour can be anxiety provoking for several reasons (to be discussed later). Second, the medical narrative holds such a great degree of dominance that people in distress seek help through medical processes, including hospital admissions. The dominance of this narrative is partly generated ideologically and reinforced through access to alternative resources that are currently limited and would otherwise be part of enabling a social or less restrictive alternative.

AMHPs will be familiar with the dilemma of assessing the same people numerous times, sometimes where the person is verbalising suicidal ideas and having already harmed themselves in some way. However, when historical evidence is considered alongside current factors, it suggests that the person's actual intention is not suicide (Brammer, 2020). This does not mean the person is not experiencing mental distress, or that death may not occur intentionally or accidentally through miscalculation. It is in these situations that upholding the right for the person to exercise autonomy and choice is often most challenging for the AMHPs who want to ensure the most therapeutic outcome for the person, and often believe that inpatient admissions are not productive. But what evidence is used to support the decision not to admit or detain? Using a simple actuarial model of probability and an evidence threshold of balance of probability (more likely than not), each additional episode that includes expressions of suicidal thought statistically suggests to the decision maker that it is unlikely that harm through an intentional act of suicide will occur. However, human behaviour and human decision making are more nuanced and complex than such mathematical calculations of probability. It is possible that risk assessments in mental health most often operate on avoiding false negatives of risk, rather than false positives. In other words, more people are detained who are not an actual risk to themselves or others, as opposed to the lay view that we are leaving risky people to cause harm (Szmukler, 2018).

The dilemma, therefore, is the appropriateness of using statutory compulsory powers for people who may be experiencing challenges and are referred to as having a personality disorder. There are various contextual considerations; for instance, someone diagnosed with a personality disorder may be deemed not mentally unwell, even though they have an established diagnosis. This needs to be considered alongside the subjective science of psychiatric diagnosis, or what Pilgrim (2014) calls the 'epistemological fallacy' of turning the observation of symptoms and theoretical constructs into factual claims, without adhering to the standard principles of establishing a valid medical diagnosis. The MHA codifies mental disorder into law and gives doctors the responsibility of applying it.

The primary consideration for use of the MHA and its powers is establishing the presence of a mental disorder. The 2007 amendment to the MHA simplified the definition of mental disorder to 'any disorder or disability of the mind' (s 1). Without the identified presence of a mental disorder by a suitably qualified medical practitioner the MHA has no further role. Personality disorder is identified as a mental disorder within the guidance to the MHA as contained in the Code of Practice (DoH, 2015, para 2.5), making the first step of this consideration relatively straightforward. The Code of Practice (DoH, 2015) also explicitly states that the assessment of a personality disorder should not be considered any differently to other mental disorders for the purposes of the MHA (DoH, 2015, para 2.20). The consideration for compulsory admission also requires the mental disorder to be of a nature and/or degree warranting detention, with at least one of the following grounds being met: health, safety or with a view to the protection of others. Circumstances in which all criteria are potentially met when assessing people with personality disorders are not uncommon, but AMHPs (and doctors) describe a reticence on their part to admit or detain the person, because they believe that a psychiatric admission would not be helpful. AMHPs describe repeated cycles of admission, which they believe reinforce unhelpful coping strategies for the person and reduce the possibility of longer-term positive outcomes (Brammer, 2020).

If we first turn to the criteria of the MHA, the person is seen to have a mental disorder in terms of the law, and a doctor has given them a diagnosis based on symptoms, possibly including self-harm, verbalised suicidal thoughts or emotional dysregulation. Whether or not we accept the logic of medical diagnosis (as opposed to those deemed personality disordered as being a socially oriented construct), we have to acknowledge that the personality disorder diagnosis does sit within the framework for considering admission under the MHA. This does not mean an AMHP has to automatically accept that admission or detention is necessary or helpful for the person. What is required is openness and transparency about the rationale behind decision making and to be able to explain this, particularly to the person being assessed. The AMHP should also be able to articulate their rationale, if reached, for deciding *not* to apply for admission, including possible reasons as to why the person is distressed and what the AMHP really believes is being communicated by this distress.

There is some research evidence (Brammer, 2020) which suggests that decision making about compulsion where a person may have a personality disorder is particularly challenging for AMHPs. The person is experiencing a range of deeper feelings, beliefs and emotions, and AMHPs recognise that they are mentally distressed while simultaneously questioning whether the label of personality disorder constitutes mental disorder. In addition, the person may be assessed as having capacity to make choices and take responsibility for them. How these issues are impacted by other considerations, such as those that need to be considered under the Human Rights Act 1998, especially in relation to risk and rights, are discussed next.

Weighing up rights and risks

Decision making under the MHA should have the person's safety and well-being as the primary focus. Findings from the author's research indicate that, on the one hand, AMHPs expressed the belief that hospital admissions are often unhelpful for the person; but, on the other hand, AMHPs were fearful they would be blamed if the person was harmed or died if admission was not applied for (Brammer,

2020). In addition, AMHPs were seen to be wary of what the coroner, media and public view of their decision would be, as there is often a simplistic narrative of suicide applied to the death of an individual when they have a psychiatric history. AMHPs describe often concurring with the doctor's belief and others that the person is unlikely to intentionally end their life, although a miscalculation while self-injuring may lead to significant harm or even death. This brings with it a perceived risk, either reputationally or to the AMHP's employment or registration. There is a need to factor into the understanding of AMHP decision making the impact of a blame culture in mental health risk management. This discussion also needs to include the AMHP's consideration of the various and sometimes competing human rights involved. The AMHP's statutory role and powers are part of their position as public authorities in relation to the duties defined in human rights legislation. As public authorities, AMHPs have both positive and negative duties, and as independent public authorities there is an additional expectation regarding the personal responsibility for decision making.

As in most situations, there is more than one Article of the Human Rights Act 1998 to be considered, and the implications of each needs to be balanced with the others. In the context of a statutory mental health assessment for someone expressing suicidal ideas, the main ones would be as follows: Article 2 places a positive duty on the state to protect life, therefore risk to the person's life needs to be considered, with the possible use of MHA powers to prevent the person from ending their life, whether intentionally or not; Article 5 protects the person's right to liberty and guards against arbitrary or unnecessary deprivation of liberty; and Article 8 protects the right to private and family life (Allen, 2013). In other words, as decision makers AMHPs have a duty to protect citizens' freedom, autonomy and right to make their own choices, while at the same time protecting their life. Sometimes AMHPs are expected to act to protect the person's life, even when the threat to that person's life comes from the person themself. This begins to illustrate some of the conflicting dilemmas that the legal framework presents. AMHPs' legal and ethical considerations and dilemmas require the balancing of risks to the person, as well as to other people. The positive duties of public authorities to preserve life would appear to be the rational starting point, particularly from the point of view of the non-professional observer, or those investigating decision making after a death has occurred. However, the right to life, although an absolute right, must be balanced with the right to liberty and privacy. It could be argued that, once the person has made their intentions public, their life automatically comes under the protection of public authorities, but, as Gilmore (2017) points out, sometimes the state allows people to die.

In AMHP practice, the dilemma is not whether or if the person has the right to die, most commonly they are trying to determine if the person's expressions of suicide are based on a wish to die or a wish to have their distress acknowledged. This is experienced by the decision maker (in this case the AMHP) as pressure, not least as part of the frameworks within which their decision may be scrutinised if the outcome for the person is significant harm. The duty of public authorities to protect life is enacted if the AMHP believes that someone's life is in immediate danger. The dilemma arises because those assessing are being told that the person has suicidal thoughts, but the background evidence and elements of the person's presentation would suggest that these are thoughts without the intention to act on them. However, as mentioned previously, self-injurious behaviour may be present and miscalculation of the intent of this by the decision maker may lead to serious harm or death. The AMHP must consider the consequences of not putting in place the most restrictive action (detention) and how that perceived lack of intervention will be judged by others. The next section of this chapter will look at the impact of these competing pressures and how it might shape the internal and expressed processing of the dilemmas that AMHPs face.

Pressures on the decision makers

There is a growing body of research into AMHP decision making that has identified the conflictual nature of statutory assessments and the very personal impact this can have on the AMHP. As Dwyer (2012) observes, much of the pressure in AMHP decision making is the practicality and real-time pressures of mobilising the assessment; the AMHP feeling responsible for an entire process including finding doctors, arranging ambulances, negotiating inpatient beds and so on, while at the same time containing the distress felt by the service user and the family. Dwyer (2012) describes the aspiration by the AMHP to exercise good authority in situations of high pressure and concern, which has an inevitable effect on the AMHP's own well-being, with a potential negative effect on the decision-making process.

A similar theme was identified by Gregor (2010) and Hemmington et al (2021), where AMHPs often felt isolated and that their role was misunderstood by others, including their own line manager. Peer support was identified as an important way of addressing these feelings, but was not always available. The multiple pressures of making decisions, which placed pressure on the individual AMHP, were identified as working with limited information and limited time; these were said to be compounded by dealing with complex decisions while holding the responsibility for liaising with others, including police, doctors, the ambulance service and inpatient wards. Vicary et al (2019) describes the behaviour of others, including doctors, as the 'shifting' of responsibility to the AMHP the undesirable elements of the assessment process. For example, Vicary et al (2019) suggest that doctors rarely remain involved in the process once the formal decision to detain has been made, leaving AMHPs to negotiate and coordinate the person's admission often alone. Vicary et al (2019) note how these negative experiences for AMHPs create additional pressures, which also contributes to poor experiences for those being assessed. These poor experiences for the person being assessed can in part be the perceived attitudes of those undertaking the assessment. The question of how we theorise and make sense of some of the negative attitudes and emotions AMHPs may feel when assessing people with personality disorders in repeat crisis situations are considered next, using the concept of alienation.

Experiencing alienation

The Marxist concept of alienation has been applied more generally, for example to social work, where Lavalette and Ferguson (2018) restate the contention that it is the dominant social relations in society that shape people's values and ideas. Because the dominant beliefs of society and the related laws frame our everyday lives and work, self-determination, even for seemingly independent professionals, is curtailed. The focus of this chapter is the impact on decision makers when working with people with personality disorders. In these situations, AMHPs describe themselves as the ones who experience a loss of power, trying to balance what they believe is best for the person with how others may perceive the possible negative outcome of these decisions (Brammer, 2020). This sense of alienation from what AMHPs believe should be their role in helping people in distress – helping them find the right help and support – can turn into its opposite. AMHPs may unwittingly adopt elements of a blame culture that sees the person in distress as the problem.

Watts and Morgan (1994) and Whittle (1997) have used the phrase 'malignant alienation' to describe a process in which relationships between staff and patients progressively deteriorate and staff become unsympathetic, even withdrawing support from the patient as they perceive the patient's behaviour to be unreasonable, provocative or overly dependent. The term 'malignant' derives from the inherent possibility of death arising from the misinterpretation of the patients' behaviour and the negative cycle of deteriorating relationships that develop. Watts and Morgan (1994) argue that malignant alienation arises from the distinct relationships that mental healthcare staff develop with their patients. Unlike medical clinicians, their main therapeutic tool is their relationship, therefore if the person does not recover from their illness represented by their continued challenging behaviours, the practitioner is prone to confuse the professional capacity to heal with their own self-worth.

Watts and Morgan (1994) identify the sometimes intense interpersonal nature of mental health work and how the interaction with others experiencing distress can negatively impact on a practitioner's ability to remain objective. The use of self in therapeutic relationships with people who behave in ways that practitioners find personally challenging may impact on the practitioner's view of their own self. The professional can perceive the person's continued self-harm or self-defeating behaviour as failure on their own part, which can potentially lead to feelings of anger and frustration, resulting in negative cycles of interaction. Another element of this lack of therapeutic optimism on the part of the professional is the over-reliance on medical narratives of illness and recovery. The professional is considered to be offering medical help to aid recovery, but when the person does not 'recover' this is perceived as resistance or even sabotage on the part of the patient. Watts and Morgan (1994) conclude that an essential method for avoiding these negative cycles is for staff to be able to express these thoughts and feelings openly so they can be managed safely, thereby reducing the negative impact on the professional and their subsequent ability to remain objective.

Some suggestions for practice

Trying to support people categorised as personality disordered outside of a crisis situation is essential. However, the AMHP does not always have regular contact with the person in the way that other community and ward staff may do, leading to the possibility that the AMHP becomes part of the narrative of conflict and alienation that has developed in relation to this person. However, the potential for positively influencing those networks also exists. In the author's experience, service users themselves do not wish to remain trapped in cycles of crisis where the interaction with emergency services often feels negative or even punitive. But what often happens is that professionals develop plans for people in crisis situations that don't acknowledge that the person themselves may wish to find other solutions. Support plans tend to be agreed by professionals and externally imposed. Crisis support plans are most effective when they are coproduced or jointly agreed with the person outside of crisis situations and include practical alternatives, such as service-user-led safe spaces/crisis cafes, emergency contacts and clearly stated expectations for the person and services.

This chapter's concluding suggestions are twofold. First, AMHPs need to extricate themselves from a medical narrative when it comes to working with people diagnosed with personality disorders. However, this is possibly easier said than done as the medicalisation of everyday life is a narrative that pervades, including for those people with the medical label of personality disorder. The illness narrative holds out the possibility of cure and places faith in the expert healer. As the theory of malignant alienation suggests, this belief in medicine's power to cure may compound the problem by marginalising the psychosocial roots of a person's distress. As a group of professionals, AMHPs need to become much stronger advocates for a less medical, more engaged and strengths-based approach with the person as their own expert. Second, it is important to engage in a more political form of practice that allies AMHPs with service-user groups and those resisting the reductions in community services, particularly in the voluntary sector.

Conclusion

The decisions an AMHP makes when working with people who may be categorised as personality disordered are framed by structural factors, such as legislation and available resources. Ideological and cultural factors, including medical concepts of illness and the associated narrative around risk also have an influence. This wider context needs to be considered, in particular how these external considerations impact on the AMHP's interpersonal and emotional responses. The concept of alienation has been applied when trying to understand the negative cycles that develop when working within a medical and risk dynamic and it is in this context that this chapter concludes with some suggested implications for practice for AMHPs to consider when making decisions. Understanding these dynamics, as well as the fears and frustrations of the AMHPs, helps to contextualise the sometimes negative feelings that professionals can develop towards those they are assessing. As with all professional practice that involves dealing with the distress of others, safe spaces for discussion and reflection outside crisis situations are essential to consider why we lack optimism and sometimes hold negative attitudes towards the people we are trying to help.

References

Allen, N. (2013) The right to life in a suicidal state. *International Journal of Law and Psychiatry*, 36(5–6), 350–7.

American Psychiatric Association (APA) (2021) *Diagnostic and statistical manual of mental disorders (DSM-5)* (5th edn). Washington, DC: APA.

Brammer, A.D. (2020) *A case study of the factors and processes involved in the use of compulsory powers when carrying out Mental Health Act 1983 (amended 2007) community assessments, from the perspectives of Approved Mental Health Professionals in one local authority in the North of England – A Critical Realist Perspective.* PhD thesis, University of Huddersfield.

Campbell, J. and Davidson, G. (2017) Understanding risk and coercion in the use of community-based mental health laws. In S. Stanford, E. Sharland, N.R. Heller and J. Warner (eds), *Beyond the risk paradigm in mental health policy and practice* (pp 17–27). London: Macmillan International Higher Education.

Department of Health (DoH) (2015) *Mental Health Act 1983: Code of Practice.* London: DoH. Available at https://assets.publishing.service.gov.uk/governm ent/uploads/system/uploads/attachment_data/file/435512/MHA_Code_of_ Practice.PDF.

Dwyer, S. (2012) Walking the tightrope of a Mental Health Act assessment. *Journal of Social Work Practice*, 26(3), 341–53.

Gilmore, S. (2017) The modern judge-power, responsibility and society's expectations by Sir Mark Hedley. *Child and Family Law Quarterly*, 29(2), 187–92.

Gregor, C. (2010) Unconscious aspects of statutory mental health social work: emotional labour and the Approved Mental Health Professional. *Journal of Social Work Practice*, 24(4), 429–43.

Hemmington, J., Graham, M., Marshall, A., Brammer, A., Stone, K. and Vicary, S. (2021) Approved Mental Health Professionals, Best Interests Assessors and people with lived experience: an exploration of professional identities and practice. A report prepared for Social Work England. Available at https://www. socialworkengland.org.uk/media/4046/amhp-bia-research-report.pdf.

Karban, K., Sparkes, T., Benson, S., Kilyon, J. and Lawrence, J. (2021) Accounting for social perspectives: an exploratory study of approved mental health professional practice. *British Journal of Social Work*, 51(1), 187–204.

Lavalette, M. and Ferguson, I. (2018) Marx: alienation, commodity fetishism and the world of contemporary social work. *Critical and Radical Social Work*, 6(2), 197–213.

Nehls, N. (1999) Borderline personality disorder: the voice of patients. *Research in Nursing and Health*, 22(4), 285–93.

NIMHE (2003) Personality disorder: no longer a diagnosis of exclusion. Available at https://www.candi.nhs.uk/sites/default/files/Documents/pd_no_longer_a_diagnosis_of_exclusion.pdf.

NPCC (2020) National strategy on policing and mental health. Available at https://www.npcc.police.uk/Mental%20Health/Nat%20Strat%20Final%20v2%2026%20Feb%202020.pdf

Pilgrim, D. (2014) Some implications of critical realism for mental health research. *Social Theory and Health*, 12(1), 1–21.

Stalker, K., Ferguson, I. and Barclay, A. (2005) 'It is a horrible term for someone': service user and provider perspectives on 'personality disorder'. *Disability and Society*, 20(4), 359–73.

Szmukler, G. (2018) *Men in white coats: treatment under coercion*. Oxford: Oxford University Press.

Vicary, S., Young, A. and Hicks, S. (2019) 'Role over' or roll over? Dirty work, shift and Mental Health Act assessments. *British Journal of Social Work*, 49(8), 2187–206.

Warrener, J. (2017) *Critiquing personality disorder: a social perspective*. St Albans: Critical Publishing.

Watts, D. and Morgan, G. (1994) Malignant alienation: dangers for patients who are hard to like. *British Journal of Psychiatry*, 164(1), 11–15.

Whittle, M. (1997) Malignant alienation. *The Journal of Forensic Psychiatry*, 8(1), 5–10.

World Health Organisation (WHO) (2022) *International classification of diseases (ICD-11)* (11th edn). Geneva: WHO.

6

Reflective supervision, emotional containment and the framing of self and others

Gill Robinson

Introduction

This chapter explores the need to create space at policy and practice level to accommodate the emotional needs of Approved Mental Health Professionals (AMHPs) working with complex cases. This is an overlooked area, despite research signposting the importance of the need for AMHPs to have safe spaces in order to reflect on their work (see Gregor, 2010; Ruch et al, 2014; Hemmington et al, 2021). This chapter argues that a bounded reflective group, underpinned by social psychoanalytic ideas, can bring value to this workforce. I draw on the rich interdisciplinary research undertaken within and across human services on such groups (Balint, 1957; Rustin and Bradley, 2008; Ruch et al, 2014; Lees and Cooper, 2017; O'Sullivan, 2017; Katz, 2020). These authors argue that such reflective spaces can reduce burnout, empower the workforce, build bridges toward deeper understanding and support practitioners to become more emotionally attuned.

This chapter uses material derived from my own research and includes participant psychoanalytic observation that draws on infant observation methods, as well as free association narrative interviews, devised by Hollway and Jefferson (2000). I use two data sets: first, reflective group sessions, including case presentation, discussion and researcher observations; and, second, one-to-one interviews. In addition, the paradigm of 'thinking in cases' (see Forrester, 2017) is applied. By using a case illustration, drawn from a monthly reflective practice group (RPG), the chapter will illuminate the ways in which participants have the opportunity to develop a deeper understanding of their client, their professional selves and also the interpersonal dynamics involved in the work.

Working in statutory mental health settings is seldom routine. It involves working with people in situations that are unique, complex and often uncertain. Mental health services see some of the most disturbed people (Preston-Shoot and Agass,1990), and the capacity to critically reflect upon one's practice, to make connections with previous experience and to apply research to knowledge is a desirable attribute. The political and cultural context of mental health work has been dramatically impacted and shaped by many years of neo-liberal policies, which has resulted in management cultures based primarily on efficiency, effectiveness and economy. As Yelloly and Henkel (1995, p 10) recognise, this culture clashes with the more 'person-centered ethos … creating difficult professional ethical dilemmas'. Nevertheless, mental health professionals often work in challenging environments that require a combination of strong legislative knowledge and technical precision, alongside an ability to cope with the uncertainty and messiness of people's lives (Yelloly and Henkel, 1995). A good holistic reflective practitioner requires learning derived from the analysis of experience or observations, reflections, experimentation and conceptualisation, resulting in a continual process of professional growth and development. Models of reflective practice have arguably become lost in the drive toward throughput and efficiency at the cost to both the professional and the person being assessed. How do we begin to re-envision and enliven the work? How do we balance aspects of care and control as well as the artistry and creativity required in this work? How can we facilitate organisational structures that accommodate and acknowledge the distressing and emotional impact of the work and develop an environment that creates safe and secure spaces for learning (Bion, 1961), space that is somewhat apart, safe, and that allows reflection, thinking and vulnerability to surface?

This chapter discusses the value of leading an RPG with a small group of interested practitioners who were working with complex and challenging cases. Through the application of this blended model, I was interested in exploring whether such a space made a difference to participants' professional selves and their practice. As a psychosocial researcher I have chosen to use a single case illustration (drawn from a presentation at an RPG) to examine the value of the application of an RPG. The RPG model used was a blend of Work Discussion and Balint groups. Both groups originated from the Tavistock Clinic in the 1950s, where Balint chose to further develop the model, specifically with general practitioners (GPs); Work Discussion is used primarily for clinical training undertaken at the Tavistock. Both are underpinned by psychoanalytic theory and are tightly bounded.

There are many reasons why studying such groups is challenging (for a more detailed discussion outlining some of the challenges, see Rustin, 2008; Jones, 2014; Sternleib, 2018). Many variables may change any measure of the impact of the group on the participants, for example: the amount of training and experience of the leaders; the nature of the participation and ongoing commitment of participants; the setting or timing of the group; interpersonal dynamics, including how often the group meets; and, finally, the willingness of the group and participants to embrace a more psychological way of thinking.

For this project, qualitative methods using psychoanalytic participant observation (based on infant observation methods) allows for complexity of meaning to be elicited. As a psychosocial researcher and Balint-trained group leader, my aim was to try and make sense of thoughts and feelings that were all deemed important sources of information and would work within the constraints and limits of the researcher's knowledge, including the knowledge of oneself.

Why is reflective practice of value?

Supervision has been recognised as an important vehicle for facilitating reflective practice. However, increasing concern has been expressed over the managerialist nature of supervision as a way of enabling management oversight (or surveillance) of practice (Ruch et al, 2014; Trevithick, 2014; Cooper, 2018b). Other research findings have reported the quality of supervision to be variable (Manthorpe et al, 2015). With reference to the organisational context, Wilkins et al (2016) suggested that supervision, as it is practised now, all too often results from a system that focuses too much on 'what and when' things happen and not enough on 'how and why'. The emphasis is on procedures rather than the impact of the work on practitioners, and in this climate, compassion and empathy are much more difficult to develop and sustain because the emphasis is on the task, rather than on the person. Others have observed a lack of containment of anxieties and a high level of defensive practice (Hinshelwood and Skogstadt, 2000, p 11).

How is it that such bounded reflective spaces have become the exception rather than the norm – a safe space that any practitioner working with people in need or psychic distress would expect to be part of? Stevenson (cited in Bower, 2005), writing about the importance of reflection and raising awareness of self and others, places the onus of doing so firmly with the agency. She contends that unless the host agency respects the importance and facilitates the development of reflective spaces then there is little chance of them succeeding (Stevenson cited in Bower, 2005). If a culture of curiosity and thinking is to flourish, it must be well supported. The time taken to support this may result in better practice and fewer errors. Nevertheless, leaders also need good supervision and training themselves to lead such groups effectively (Robinson, 2021).

It is as if the procedures have become more important than the quality of the engagement and good outcome with the client. These defensive practices engaged in by many managers – where the agency's requirements take priority, with few opportunities to reflect on fears, contradictions and anxieties of the work – leave them remaining unspoken. In such a climate, the threat is that you will be seen as incompetent if you address them (Goddard and Hunt, 2011). This will be illustrated next, using an example of a group from my own research.

Methodology

My aim was to lead a group, using a blend of Balint Group and Work Discussion models, referred to as an RPG within a local authority setting. This blended model was used following its proven contribution to clinicians working in other caregiving settings (Balint, 1957; Rustin, 2008), both having originated from the Tavistock Clinic in the early to mid-1950s. The first data set was gathered via observing (as leader) the RPG group, including an uncensored account of thoughts and feelings following the observation (Briggs, 2002). The second data set was a based on a one-to-one interview with a group participant, also audio recorded and transcribed. The interview used a free association narrative technique (Hollway and Jefferson, 2000), a method involving forming an open question inviting the participant to speak about their experience of presenting and involvement in the group. It allows the participant to freely associate to the question posed, allowing them to say what comes to mind via emotional and unconscious processes. By eliciting a narrative structured in this way, it is possible to access the participant's preoccupations that would not otherwise be elicited by a more structured style. These observations and transcribed recordings were taken to research and clinical supervision for further discussion and closer analysis. I have used 'practice–near research' (Cooper, 2009) alongside the paradigm of 'thinking in cases' (see Forrester, 2017), together with rigorous data gathering.

Why a case?

In this chapter, the individual narrative of one practitioner has been used to illustrate the findings of the impact that this group had on them. This approach, informed by Forrester (2017), argues that there is great value to 'think in cases'. The case study method was used by Balint and others to demonstrate knowledge in the absence of theory. This approach is critiqued in that it still involves a level of subjectivity, and is isolated from the broader social, political context (Bar Haim, 2020), but it offers a valuable insight into the 'case' and the meaning that emerges from a reflective group of this kind.

The proposal to the local authority was to offer a co–led group, with both leaders Balint-trained and experienced mental health professionals, both white women and non-British nationals. The group was a culturally and ethnically diverse mix of male and female participants, and each group varied in number from three to seven. The participants also varied in their engagement and commitment to the group, with some participants attending only once and others committed to attending on a regular basis.

Firmly managed boundaries encourage free expression

Alongside formal leadership training, the experience of leading and observing this and other RPGs has provided me with a deepening awareness of the emotional work participants undertake. This awareness has been understood through associations with events in my own life, alongside Balint peer supervision and through discussion of the material in a wider research–based group, clinical supervision and my own psychoanalytical psychoanalysis. The case illustration that follows allowed me to understand the possible social defences engaged by participants. It was also an opportunity to see how the RPG provided a safe space for the participants to bring any preoccupations or anxieties they may have about their work. The bounded nature of the group meant that it took place at regular intervals, in the same meeting room, monthly, for an hour, the boundaries of which were tightly held by the joint leaders of the group.

How does the RPG work?

Each participant was encouraged to report freely without written notes about their experience with a service user, allowing all sorts of subjective distortions, omissions, second thoughts, subsequent additions and so on. In an RPG of this kind, the leader asks whether anyone has a case for discussion. The participant offering a case then presents their case to the group. After inviting the group to clarify any factual details, the leader invites the presenter to push their chair back, placing themselves slightly apart from the group while the group discuss the case. There is then an opportunity for the group to excavate the many complex layers that make up this relationship, including some space to think about the client in more depth. There is no right or wrong answer; instead, inductive and associative thoughts are encouraged. This allows the presenter to listen to the group 'work' the case, giving the presenter time to digest and think about what is being said before being invited by the leader to rejoin the group. The focus of the group is not the personality of the presenter; rather, it is on the relationship with the person and/or organisation and a deeper understanding of the blind spots within the relational exchanges (Riordan, 2008). An example of this is outlined in Box 6.1, where Sarah[1] (a mental health professional) presented her 'case' to the group.

Box 6.1: Case summary: Sarah presents the case of Avi

The presenter (Sarah), a white, British 40-year-old, reluctantly stepped forward to present a case. The case involved a 60-year-old Jewish man (Avi). He had inherited the family home (both parents deceased) and was estranged from his only sister. He sold the family home for less than market value, exploited by someone who took advantage of his vulnerability. This still aggrieved and disturbed him, despite it having happened some years earlier.

After repeated efforts to see him, Sarah finally managed to make contact with him. She described him as presenting well, dressing very formally and "were you to see him in public you would have no sense of the state of disorder that he lives in". She further described how his house was completely cluttered, "bursting with stuff, piled high to the ceiling", with no functioning facilities, including electricity, running water or heating. He was well educated, but his life choices, according to Avi, were made as a result of the strong influence of his parents. He had not worked for many years. He attended a local Jewish mental health organisation where Sarah sometimes met with him. Sarah had gone to some lengths to build a rapport with him.

She reported being very anxious about the case and felt strongly that she had not achieved very much. There was an expectation (organisationally) that his property needed to be cleared to mitigate the high fire risk. The fire authorities and other support agencies refused to visit due to the high degree of hoarding. She felt alone with the case and under significant management pressure to make progress and close the case.

Psychosocial researchers' observations of the work of the group

The presenter's feelings of anxiety were intensely reflected through her timidity. She spoke quietly, presenting skeletal detail about the case, leaving many questions of clarity to be asked by the group. The group response was measured and thoughtful, showing their capacity to listen, digest and identify with the material that she had presented. One group member noted how profoundly overwhelming Sarah's anxiety seemed in relation to her work with Avi; her fear of something awful happening while she was involved. Another noted how the presenter felt that she had achieved little, yet in the participant's mind, she had achieved great deal. The group became animated about the presence of shame and grief that they imagined Avi may be carrying, including the loss of his family home, loss of his relationship with his sister, his parents, and how this sense of shame was reflected back to him daily "as he crawled down his corridor jammed with stuff". The group wondered whether this was a reminder and a reflection of his internal world. There was also some discussion about the impact of his intergenerational loss and how this trauma may have impacted him; his frozen mental state, unable to determine what to hold on to and what to let go of. Participants further wondered about his many losses and how these had impacted on his ability to trust anyone. The group gave some thought to the client not keeping his appointments, leaving the presenter to hold him in mind in a way that perhaps his parents had not been able to do when he was younger due to their own internal preoccupations, such as displacement and loss suffered as postwar refugees. The group acknowledged the presenter's ability to tenaciously persevere, attempting many times to meet with him despite the many barriers, slowly building rapport not previously achieved by other workers.

Theorised sense-making

It appeared to me as the leader of the group that the presenter had little time to think and reflect on her own emotions, which were seemingly mixed up in the case. I wondered whether the presenter's anxiety was also about her client's fears projected on to her; fears of abandonment and loss, feelings that he had disowned as his own, feelings that were too unbearable to acknowledge. Casement (1985) defines projective identification as a form of unconscious communication. Without understanding the meaning of the anxiety she was carrying about the case, Sarah may have missed an opportunity to deepen her understanding of the roots of Avi's psychic distress. This is where the projector disowns some aspect of themselves and attributes it to another – in this case Sarah. This primal unwanted feeling is put into another person, for it to be disposed of or made more digestible. If the practitioner can manage these feelings more than the client had been, when a response is found the previously unmanageable feelings become more manageable. This ability to think about the client's internal world, and its relational impact on the worker and their relationship with the client, is an important element of a bounded reflective group.

Later, in her one-to-one interview, Sarah disclosed that the group was the only place where her work with this client had been validated and that it had helped her to think about the client in a meaningful and helpful way:

> [Due] to the hustle and bustle of what we are doing, we don't have time to think or talk about the work. Everyone has too much to do and there is no time to reflect … This kind of work is not the kind of work that can easily be measured. If we were at the point where he could open and close his front door, that would be measurable, but we are still a long way off.

It is evident that Sarah's dependency needs for supervision or containment were not being met organisationally, other than through the space of the reflective group. In such situations, practitioners fear becoming scapegoats, isolated and vilified. Many workers carry the fear of being 'found out', and with mounting anxiety, their capacity to retain thought of any kind about their cases becomes limited (Ferguson, 2016). There was little doubt that Sarah carried a great deal of anxiety about this case. She firmly believed that she had not achieved the stated objective that was to clear the property, thereby making it safe, despite having achieved more than any other previous worker allocated.

In my one-to-one interview with Sarah, it was evident that she was under enormous pressure to demonstrate tangible results to the organisation – in part to lessen the risk to Avi, but mostly out of fear that she would be blamed for his death in the event of fire. In Sarah's eyes, she had not made much in the way of progress, yet through the work of the group she began to see the progress that she had made. This allowed her to begin to recognise her achievements, allowing her to feel professionally validated and valued.

It could be suggested that Sarah was caught in the crossfire between her own anxiety from feeling like she had not done enough, and the secondary anxiety associated with organisational defences. In their work with organisations, Obholzer and Roberts (1994) identified that caregivers need to be sensitised to the emotional atmosphere and to the non-verbal, unconscious communication of feelings in their clients. Hoggett (2015) proposes a different view, stating that the task of the team is 'always problematic, contested and socially constructed', believing that there is no such thing as a 'primary task'. Hoggett (2015, p 51) argues that this essentialises the phenomena and depicts them as somehow 'timeless and context free'. Instead, he advocates for a 'psycho-social' space, one that gives equal weight to the psychological and to the social – 'the space in between, the space of the hyphen' (Hoggett, 2015, p 51). He insists that not all anxieties can be located within the psychological sphere and that some are more located within 'late modernity' which takes the form of collective moral panics. He asserts that these anxieties get into the life of organisations, where they may be contained, embedded, enacted or projected. The presenter located the risk of fire as the root of her anxiety. Hoggett's (2015) notion of both social and psychological seemed to offer a paradigm that helped to make sense of this case. Around the same time there had been a flood of anxiety within the local authority about the risk of fire since the Grenfell Tower disaster. Grenfell Tower was a local authority property, standing 24 floors tall, situated in the same city. A fire destroyed the entire building, resulting in a high number of deaths, creating anxiety for local authorities about the potential of fires in similar buildings. It may also be that this anxiety was one that the presenter could more readily identify, whereas the psychological dimension is perhaps more emotionally taxing, elusive, harder for her to grasp and make sense of, unless supported to do so.

Organisational defences?

Halton (2015) writes about the obsessional-punitive defences within all human services, referring to Menzies Lyth's (1988) work on organisational defences to try and make sense of why this is. He defines a social defence as a shared configuration of emotions that promotes cohesion between multiple groups in an organisation. The conclusions in Menzies Lyth's (1988) study, after a period of observation and inquiry spent on a nursing ward, concluded that high levels of stress, anxiety and fear experienced by the nurses were not caused by the nursing task itself, but rather a systemic downwards projection on to the nurses of imagined aggression towards patients, giving rise to mistrust, followed by obsessive controls and punitive sanctions. Many nurses colluded with this system of care, but many also left. This was understood by Menzies Lyth (1988) to be an aggressive management defence against its own anxieties, phantasies and projections. She concluded that in order to bring compassion back into nursing, it required that the nurse be given time with the patient, as compassion and empathy are based on identification with them. Her proposal was to establish practice based on relationships, feelings and actions instead of control, repression and punishment (Menzies Lyth, 1988).

The obsessional, punitive social defences that Menzies Lyth (1988) alluded to in her research have contemporary relevance. The emphasis placed on Sarah to act, get the job done and close the case negated the complexity of the work, including the skill required to engage the client and build trust to enable him to decide to part with some of his possessions. The 'auditable surface' (Cummins, 2002 cited in Halton, 2015, p 36), and the methods of control and surveillance (such as targets, audits and inspections), may appear to be different, but Halton believes that they are ultimately the same – 'namely, to control the relationship between practitioner and patient' (Halton, 2015, p 36). Menzies Lyth's (1988) study showed that it was this lack of trust by managers and the disempowerment of practitioners that contributed to a lower quality of caregiving and therefore a greater risk for the client. An obsessional and controlling management culture can be more anxiety-provoking for staff than the anxiety arising from the primary task of their work with clients.

Impact on Sarah

Taking the risk of presenting her case to the group was certainly significant for Sarah. Indeed, it was revelatory in the discovery that the work she had done was valued in a manner that had not previously been acknowledged. Presenting the case enabled Sarah to recognise her identificatory overlap with Avi. She explained:

> I'm a bit like him l don't easily let go ... the case is offering all kinds of things ... I'm learning as much from him as he is from me ... my other work does not provide the same professional engagement as this does ... my other work has become mechanistic and does not allow for creative engagement in the way this case allows ... Success now looks very different – recording, funding and getting something at the cheapest rate possible, in the shortest possible time. This is my way of forging professional engagement and holding on to a sense of value and worth.

Though implied rather than explicitly stated, the RPG was a space where her work was valued; a space in which she could explore the complexity of her work with her client in greater depth. Dogged and determined, Sarah wished to continue advocating and supporting her client out of a sense of dynamic engagement, despite management pressure to close the case. This narrative informs us of the richness of her learning through the work of the group. Sarah began to recognise qualities within herself: tenacity, perseverance, creativity, openness to learning and growth. The RPG played a vital part in deepening Sarah's professional self-worth, enlivening her engagement in her work with Avi and also deepening her understanding of her own vulnerabilities. It seemed like a turning point for Sarah professionally: she was at risk of becoming deeply disillusioned and neglected by the manner of her client; instead, it seemed she was emotionally replenished. By giving Sarah an emotional reservoir to draw upon and articulate reasons to remain involved, the group brought about the transformation needed for both her client and her own professional self.

Role of senior managers

The role and support of senior managers is key to the success of reflective spaces. This reflective group had the support of senior managers, but despite this, the culture of the organisation can and often does undermine the work of such groups. In a conversation on such reflective groups, Cooper (2018b) observed that such groups can be subversive by their very nature as they encourage the worker to think for themselves and ask questions, which is perhaps why Menzies Lyth's (1988) research was not embraced and applied in the workplace and as a result of her insights did not have a significant impact (Kraemer, 2015, p 150). All too often, as Kraemer (2015, p 144) identifies, public sector organisations operate on the premise that it's better not to know and to just keep on working – based implicitly on a 'military notion that once trained, you can do the job' and when there are new skills to learn, further training is offered with the 'authority existing with the manager and not in the worker'. Work of this kind can be quite disturbing, so sitting down to reflect and think about what is going on for the worker can be challenging. While most participants are keen to attend such groups because they find them valuable, often practitioners find 'their heads are full of things – urgent or mundane – that need doing, from which it is difficult to drag them away', and entering data on the computer can be a preferred activity, as it offers relief from the disturbance that thinking about the work can sometimes generate (Kraemer, 2015, p 156). However, as Stevens (cited in Bower, 2005) recognised, without the support of a manager it becomes individualised; the practitioner has to resist the pressure being brought to bear on them to close the case.

Working with such complex cases requires a skilled, thoughtful, committed, well-contained professional for real and lasting change to succeed. Yet the message within organisations is split. While the organisation hosting this research seemingly values this reflective space (senior managers gave it their tacit support), inadvertently they also worked to undermine it by placing middle managers under significant pressure to work with larger caseloads, an expectation of volume and throughput, with fewer resources. Managers in turn place pressure on practitioners to close cases and end their work with service users. In the case of Sarah and Avi, the presenter spoke of being subject to constant pressure and challenged to 'act' and to use a more coercive approach such as a 'deep clean' in order to get the work done, regardless of the likely impact on her relationship with her client, which she had taken care and time to establish. Sarah's thoughtful, respectful approach resulted in some success, though progress was slow, and there had been tangible change (she could now see the hallway was clearer).

Conclusion

In conclusion, the case illustrated in this chapter allowed the practitioner to learn through taking the risk of presenting her work to the group. As a result, it seemed that she found a more confident, assured, professional self. Not only does such a group have the potential to help to contain practitioners' anxieties, it also helped this practitioner to become more emotionally attuned to the relational complexity that the work entails. She began to more readily understand and identify some of her client's communications, to tolerate them, be able to think about them and find that these states of mind, in turn, can become more manageable, tolerable and thinkable. The RPG allowed all participants to learn and develop through the experience of the cases presented, as well as develop a sense of dignity and deeper professional engagement with the work. However, achieving a sense of balance is not easy when the participant is faced with possible unmanageable anxiety from the client and seemingly unbearable management pressure, with the practitioner caught in the crossfire, leaving little space for thoughtfulness about the client. Put simply, coming together in the manner of a bounded reflective group offers participants the space to think about the client, thus allowing their professional resources to work more effectively. By taking the opportunity to listen, reflect and sometimes alter the habitual way we go about the work, to bear uncertainty, we can avoid looking for ready-made answers and instead see what there is to be seen. If this happens, our relationship to our professional role may be enriched, thereby benefitting the workforce, as well as those we are there to help.

Note
[1] The names used in this case study are pseudonyms.

References
Balint, M. (1957) *The doctor, his patient and the illness* (2nd edn). Tunbridge Wells: Pitman Medical.

Bar-Haim, S. (2020) Proving nothing and illustrating much: the case of Michael Balint. *History of the Human Sciences*, 33(3–4), 47–65.

Bion, W.R. (1961) *Experience in groups and other papers*. London: Tavistock.

Bower, M. (2005) *Psychoanalytic theory for social work practice: thinking under fire*. London: Routledge.

Briggs, A. (2002) *Surviving space: papers on infant observation* (Tavistock Clinic Series). London: Routledge.

Casement, P. (1985) *On learning from the patient*. London: Routledge.

Cooper, A. (2009) 'Hearing the grass grow': emotional and epistemological challenges of practice-near research. *Journal of Social Work Practice*, 23(4): 429–42.

Cooper, A. (2018a) *Conjunctions: social work, psychoanalysis and society*. London: Karnac.

Cooper, A. (2018b) *In conversation: research group on reflective groups*. London: Tavistock and Portman NHS Trust.

Ferguson, H. (2016) What social workers do in performing child protection work: evidence from research into face-to-face practice. *Child and Family Social Work*, 21(3), 283–94.

Forrester, J. (2017) *Thinking in cases*. Cambridge: Polity Press.

Goddard, C. and Hunt, S. (2011) The complexities of caring for child protection workers: the contexts of practice and supervision. *Journal of Social Work Practice*, 25(4), 413–32.

Gregor, C. (2010) Unconscious aspects of statutory mental health social work: emotional labour and the Approved Mental Health Professional. *Journal of Social Work Practice*, 24(4), 429–43.

Halton, W. (2015) Obsessional-punitive defences in care systems: Menzies Lyth revisited. In D. Armstrong and M. Rustin (eds), *Social defences against anxiety: explorations in a paradigm* (Tavistock Clinic Series) (pp 27–38). London: Routledge.

Hemmington, J., Graham, M., Marshall, A., Brammer, A., Stone, K. and Vicary, S. (2021) *Approved Mental Health Professionals, Best Interests Assessors and people with lived experience: an exploration of professional identities and practice a report prepared for Social Work England*. Sheffield: Social Work England.

Hinshelwood, R.D. and Skogstad, W. (2000) *Observing organisations anxiety: defence and culture in health care*. London: Routledge.

Hoggett, P. (2015) A psycho-social perspective on social defences. In D. Armstrong and M. Rustin (eds), *Social defences against anxiety: explorations in a paradigm* (Tavistock Clinic Series) (pp 50–8). London: Routledge.

Hollway, W. and Jefferson, T. (2000) *Doing qualitative research differently: free association, narrative and the interview method*. London: Sage.

Jones, J. (2014) *A report for the Centre for Social Work Practice on reflective group models in social work*. Available at https://www.brighton-hove.gov.uk/sites/default/files/migrated/article/inline/reflective-practice-report-11.05.15.pdf.

Katz, A. (2020) How to run reflective practice groups. A guide for healthcare professionals. London: Routledge.

Kraemer, S. (2015) Anxiety at the front line. In D. Armstrong and M. Rustin (eds), *Social defences against anxiety: explorations in a paradigm* (Tavistock Clinic Series) (pp 144–60). London: Routledge.

Lees, A. and Cooper, A. (2017) *Evaluation of the Reflective Practice Groups Project: Brighton and Hove Children's Services*. London: Centre for Social Work Practice.

Manthorpe, J., Moriaty, J., Hussein, S. and Stevens, M. (2015) Content and purpose of supervision in social work practice in England: views of newly qualified social workers, managers and directors. *British Journal of Social Work*, 45(1), 52–68.

Menzies Lyth, I. (1988) The functioning of social systems as a defence against anxiety. In I. Menzies Lyth (ed.), *Containing anxiety in institutions: selected essays volume 1* (pp 43–85). London: Free Association Books.

Obholzer, A. and Roberts, Z.R. (1994) *The unconscious at work: Individual and organizational stress in the human services*. London: Routledge.

O'Sullivan, N. (2017) *The dichotomy of 'thinking' and 'doing' in social work practice with neglected infant and toddlers. How do social workers respond to neglect and abuse in infancy, and does this change with the introduction of a sustained case discussion forum?* Professional Doctorate, University of East London.

Preston-Shoot, M. and Agass, D. (1990) *Making sense of social work: psychodynamics, systems and practice*. London: Macmillan Press.

Riordan, D.C. (2008) Being ordinary in extraordinary places: reflective practice of the total situation in a total institution. *Psychoanalytic Psychotherapy*, 22(3), 196–217.

Robinson, G. (2021) *Rolling with defences: a space to think – an exploration of a bounded reflective group for Approved Mental Health Professionals*. PhD dissertation, Essex University.

Ruch, G., Lees, A. and Prichard, J. (2014) Getting beneath the surface: scapegoating and the systems approach in a post-Munro world. *Journal of Social Work Practice*, 28(3), 313–27.

Rustin, M. (2008) Work discussion: implications for research and policy In M. Rustin and M. Bradley (eds), *Work discussion: learning from reflective practice in work with children and families* (pp 267–84). London: Karnac.

Rustin, M. and Bradley, J. (2008) *Work discussion: learning from reflective practice in work with children and families*. London: Karnac.

Sternlieb, J.L. (2018) Demystifying Balint culture and its impact: an autoethnographic analysis. *International Journal of Psychiatry in Medicine*, 53(1–2), 30–46.

Trevithick, P. (2014) Humanising managerialism: reclaiming emotional reasoning, intuition, the relationship, and knowledge and skills in social work. *Journal of Social Work Practice*, 28(3), 287–311.

Wilkins, D., Forrester, D. and Grant, L. (2016). What happens in child and family social work supervision? *Child and Family Social Work*, 22(2), 942–51.

Yelloly, M. and Henkel, M. (1995) *Learning and teaching in social work: towards reflective practice*. London: Jessica Kingsley.

7

Reflective practice, truth-telling and safe spaces

Kevin Stone

Introduction

This chapter will consider the tensions that exist for professionals who make compulsory decisions, in this instance Approved Mental Health Professionals (AMHPs), when they attempt to engage in reflective practice. The chapter identifies some of the barriers, including lack of supervision, personal liability, the complexity of the AMHP role and the impact of the organisational context. It is suggested that a framework that supports AMHPs to engage in reflective practice without anxiety or fear of liability is needed, and that to enable authentic reflective practice, the environmental conditions for that reflection must be carefully considered. AMHPs need safe spaces to reflect and enhance their practice. To ignore the context in which AMHPs work is to ignore the complexity and skill required to undertake statutory mental health work.

Context

AMHP services undertake Mental Health Act (MHA) work 24 hours a day, 365 days a year. With rising numbers of people being detained in England under the MHA (NHS Digital, 2021) and even greater amounts of statutory work going unrecorded, AMHPs can be under pressure to undertake multiple assessments a day, causing pressure and stress (BASW, 2016; Care Quality Commission, 2018; Hemmington et al, 2021), which can affect decision making.

Undertaking AMHP work can come at a personal cost. It is recognised as a complex, exhausting and emotionally demanding activity (Evans et al, 2005; Gregor 2010; Morriss, 2015; Hemmington et al, 2021), involving active and sophisticated use of conflicting emotion or dissonance (Vicary, 2021). The obvious correlation is that, in order for AMHPs to be effective, protective and well-being-enhancing mechanisms need to be in place. One such mechanism is reflective practice, an essential skill that has a prominent and well-established place in professional health and social care education and practice (Sicora, 2017). Reflective practice is overwhelmingly considered to be 'good practice' and cited regularly as such in professional literature (Carpenter et al, 2012) and guidance (DHSC, 2019). Ferguson (2018, p 415) suggests that 'reflective practice is a core concept in social work and probably the most well-known theoretical perspective across the entire applied professions of teaching, health and social care'.

For reflective practice to be effective there needs to be honesty about success and where improvement is needed (Scales et al, 2013), and there can be resistance because of this (Hobbs, 2007). This can mean that a failure to strive for honesty can impact on self-awareness, emotional intelligence and development needs more generally (Bruce, 2013; GMC, 2021; Social Work England, 2021). Honesty, which can be understood as 'truth-telling' to oneself and others, and ultimately reflective practice, focuses on delivering better outcomes to patients and service users (DoH, 2014). The purpose of reflective practice is to increase the well-being of staff, improve patient outcomes and ultimately enhance practice. However, to achieve this the practitioner needs to feel able to be open and transparent to themselves and others about their work, decision making, actions and experiences. This transparency requires trust and confidentiality to enable open reflection that can bring about acceptance, validation, change and learning.

Openness and truth-telling to oneself and others are essential prerequisites for effective reflective practice, alongside the usual critical and analytical thinking (Bassot, 2015). However, feelings of self-preservation can limit that reflective ability generally (Ferguson, 2018, p 421), coupled with the fear (Bassot, 2015) of actual or perceived personal and professional legal liability arising from AMHP decision making (DHSC, 2019).

In England and Wales, AMHPs coordinate MHA assessments where a range of decisions need to be made. Their decisions carry a significant amount of responsibility, some of which may be shared with other professionals, but the AMHP is the only one with the power to make an application to detain a person, or not to make an application when faced with medical recommendations to do so. Removing a person's liberty through making an application for detention is a significant act that carries with it a great deal of accountability and responsibility, both legally and ethically (Buckland, 2016), as does taking positive risks where the end outcome cannot be reliably predicted (Killick and Taylor, 2020). The work can render authentic reflective practice challenging, not least considering the personal and professional liability that comes with undertaking this independent work from the employing local authority, High Court or Coroners Court.

As such, this chapter argues that to enable safe and effective AMHP practice, reflective safe spaces for AMHPs need to be created and facilitated, either for self, one-to-one or group reflection, where openness and honesty can occur without fear. The question posed is what can be done to create these safe spaces for reflection where anxieties and fears can be managed? This chapter also draws on the author's own experiences of using techniques in education and practice to encourage openness and truth-telling, through maintaining anonymity and encouraging participation.

Lack of AMHP supervision

Supervision, in the form of reflective supervision, is commonly one of the cornerstones of support for practitioners and is essential to enable good-quality

AMHP practice to be delivered (DHSC/HEE, 2020, p 29). However, access to supervision, which is one mechanism where reflection can occur, may be unavailable or not appropriate, leading practitioners to seek out their own supervision arrangements from peers and others (Gregor, 2010; Hudson and Webber, 2012). In a recent research study by Hemmington et al (2021), AMHPs continue to report 'absent or poor' supervision arrangements. This is in direct contrast to the national workforce plan for AMHPs in England, which suggests that

> AMHP services should support the independence of AMHP decision-making, while ensuring that they have access to individual, peer and professional support to explore their working practices in a safe manner, including the provision of timely debrief sessions. AMHP supervision should be viewed as the cornerstone of good-quality AMHP practice. (DHSC/HEE, 2020, p 6)

Earle et al (2017, p 3) remind us that, 'reflective supervision offers a safe space for a practitioner to slow down and think, explore possibilities, look for meaning and a way to do their work well'. Therefore, the benefits of supervision for AMHPs as a safe space is recommended, in policy as well as in the literature.

Personal liability

Even where arrangements are in place to support AMHPs' reflection on their practice, it can still be challenging to engage in. This is particularly the case when being open and truthful can be associated with threats arising from being personally legally liable and accountable for decision making, leading to concerns about court involvement or a potential threat to continued employment. Although each professional who is eligible to be an AMHP is committed to reflective practice by means of their regulator and maintenance of good practice (RCOT, 2019; BPS, 2021; NMC, 2021; Social Work England, 2021), the AMHP role remains largely an unregulated activity. At the time of writing there are moves for Social Work England (the social work regulator for England) to bring the AMHP role under their portfolio, but this is currently not the case other than regulating initial AMHP training and there is no indication how this would work for Wales or non-social workers. There are also moves for the Care Quality Commission (CQC) to inspect local authority functions once again through the Health and Care Bill introduced to parliament on 6 July 2021, and AMHP work could be one area of focus within this. However, at the present time the CQC has made it clear that 'although CQC are the regulator for health and social care services and are responsible for monitoring the use of the MHA, AMHP services fall outside our regulatory duties. This is because AMHPs are authorised by local authorities, which are not subject to CQC regulation' (CQC, 2018, np). The implication here is that AMHPs do not currently need to notify the CQC of any notifiable safety incidents in respect of their decision making, since that is not an activity CQC currently regulates (CQC, 2018). This means that AMHP work is currently left to local authority jurisdiction and governance. Although this could change with the aforementioned Bill, it does not reduce the need for AMHPs to feel safe to be able to reflect when undertaking MHA work, which by its nature is a powerful activity.

Although CQC guidance at the time of writing currently excludes AMHPs, the guidance states that health and social care professionals need to uphold a duty of candour and that 'registered persons must act in an open and transparent way with relevant persons in relation to care and treatment provided to service users in carrying on a regulated activity' (CQC, 2014, np). The inference here is that it would be difficult for AMHPs to argue that they shouldn't be held accountable to the same standard. This is despite the 'functions of an AMHP being explicitly detached from being considered relevant social work (a regulated profession) for the purposes of Part 4 of the Care Standards Act 2000' (s 114ZA[3] MHA), and means that there is a clear gap, one that the Health and Care Bill may fill. It is likely therefore that the duty of candour will be as applicable to AMHP work as it is to any other future health and social care profession. There is no argument here that AMHPs should not be open and honest and demonstrate candour, but rather that one barrier to candour – particularly when undertaking powerful work – is a fear of litigation that might arise from reporting or disclosing a failure. There is a difference between incidents of 'safety', where guidance should be followed, and concerns over whether an AMHP has acted in a risk-averse manner and their absolute adherence to legal duties and responsibilities as outlined in the MHA and secondary legislation, where they may be personally liable (s 139 MHA). It is difficult to measure AMHP activity and outcomes, but any anxiety that causes an AMHP reluctance in being open could mean that opportunities for enhancing practice are missed.

Complexity of the AMHP role

The AMHP role is complex, and arguably contains potentially many different hybrid roles (Leah, 2020; Quirk et al, 2000). The work in the main involves making decisions about involuntary admission of others through coordinating MHA assessments that interfere with an individual's private and family life (Article 8, European Convention on Human Rights [ECHR]), and, when necessary, depriving assessed persons of their liberty (Article 5, ECHR), which can involve authorising restraint when conveying a person liable to be detained to hospital (ss 6 and 137 MHA).

Overall, AMHP work can be lengthy, with legal and ethical decision making at every turn. This work can bring aspects of responsibility and accountability to a greater or lesser degree; the most accountable of all is making an application to detain a person in hospital based upon medical recommendations. The complexity of this role and differentiation of functions

Figure 7.1: Articulation of the Approved Social Worker (ASW) role (now AMHP)

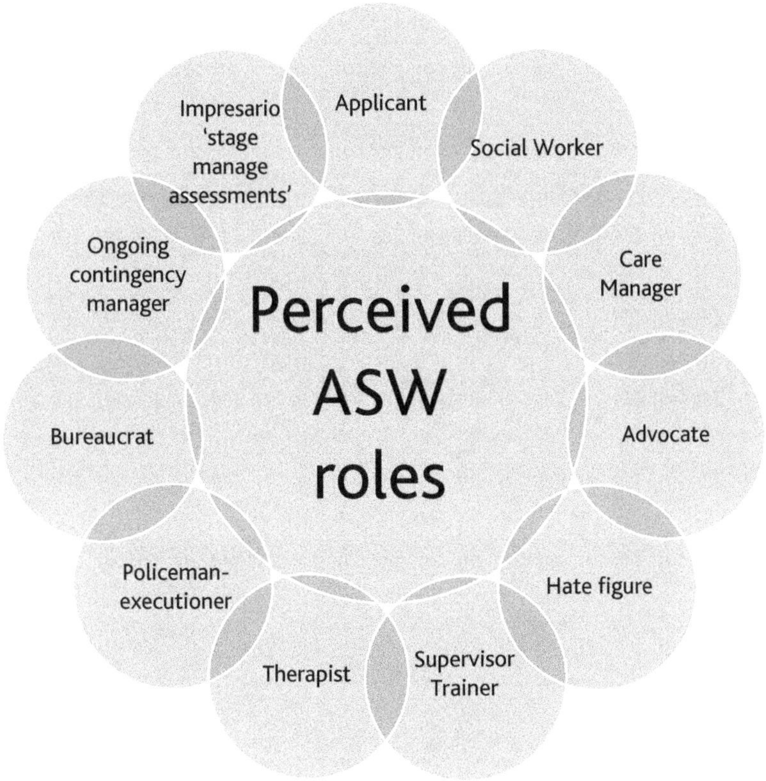

Impresario 'stage manage assessments'

Applicant

Social Worker

Ongoing contingency manager

Care Manager

Perceived ASW roles

Bureaucrat

Advocate

Policeman-executioner

Hate figure

Therapist

Supervisor Trainer

Source: Quirk (2000).

within it is articulated in Figures 7.1 and 7.2, developed by Quirk (2000) and extended by Leah (2020).

There are overlaps within the aspects of the AMHP functions outlined in Figures 7.1 and 7.2, and some may be performed simultaneously. Further, each piece of AMHP work is unique and Figures 7.1 and 7.2 illustrate the variety of the work that AMHPs are involved in, reinforcing the need for reflective practice to make sense of it.

The complexity of AMHP work in England is growing, and hybrid roles and responsibilities may expand further. In May 2020 AMHPs gained a new key role in the Debt Respite Scheme (Breathing Space) Mental Health Crisis Moratorium, under Part 3 of the Debt Respite Scheme (Breathing Space Moratorium and Mental Health Crisis Moratorium) (England and Wales) Regulations 2020. This scheme gave relief to people receiving mental health crisis support with debt from creditors through AMHPs providing written evidence. Furthermore, AMHPs are seen as suitable candidates to undertake the Approved Clinician/Responsible Clinician role.

Figure 7.2: Articulation of the AMHP role

Source: Leah (2020).

Organisational impact

The organisational context in which the AMHP works needs consideration, as this can impact upon their ability to reflect. This impact can be influenced to a greater or lesser degree by how supported an AMHP feels within their organisation. In England, AMHP services have different arrangements: they may be integrated within a health setting (section 75 joint commission arrangement under National Health Service [NHS] Act 2006); co-located (differently commissioned services in the same location); or organised completely separately. Further, the hierarchy within which the workforce sits needs consideration. AMHPs may have a level of seniority within their organisation and could be senior practitioners or managers. What can be seen as peer-to-peer reflective supervision, as both parties are AMHPs, may in effect not be a discussion of such equals within an organisation. This seems to challenge workforce guidance which states that 'local authorities and Mental Health Trusts must ensure that all AMHPs (including those in Mental Health Trusts) have support and supervision in line with the regulations. This must be from senior social workers with AMHP experience' (DHSC/HEE, 2020, p 23).

Accountability in practice

Consideration ought to be given to the accountability arising from undertaking AMHP work. This should not be read as a tale of fear, but of a reality of potential conscious or unconscious thinking when AMHPs are engaging in decision making around compulsion. Although it is rare, those who have been detained may take action under a tort (a civil wrong) for all manner of reasons relating to their detention. Therefore, to protect AMHPs and others from legal action and liability, section 139 of the MHA provides 'protection for acts done in pursuance of this Act'. In essence, section 139 is intended to safeguard AMHPs and others by offering partial immunity for the actions they have taken. Section 139(1) states:

> No person shall be liable, whether on the ground of want of jurisdiction or on any other ground, to any civil or criminal proceedings to which he would have been liable apart from this section in respect of any act purporting to be done in pursuance of this Act or any regulations or rules made under this Act, unless the act was done in bad faith or without reasonable care.

In this legal sense 'bad faith' can be broadly interpreted as actions that could be determined to be untrustworthy, misleading, dishonest or not adhering to legal procedures. Reasonable care will be determined objectively in the ordinary sense of the word as to whether a member of the 'ordinary public' (that is, a hypothetical person on the Clapham omnibus) (*McQuire v Western Morning News*, 1903) might think an AMHP acted reasonably.

Although a distinction could be drawn between an 'act done' and an 'act not done' by an AMHP, Stanley Burton J. in *W, R (on the application of W) v Doncaster Metropolitan Borough Council* (2003) offers some clarity. In passing, Stanley Burton J. indicated that it is unlikely that the provisions of an 'act done' only applies to positive acts. Therefore, although no specific case law authority exists, it is likely that an 'act not done', as long as undertaken in good faith and with reasonable care by the AMHP, would be protected under section 139 MHA similarly.

A further concern for an AMHP can be defending the decision making in civil or criminal court Section 139(2) MHA states:

> No civil proceedings shall be brought against any person in any court in respect of any such act without the leave of the High Court; and no criminal proceedings shall be brought against any person in any court in respect of any such act except by or with the consent of the Director of Public Prosecutions.

Therefore, the provisions of section 139 MHA offer two levels of protection to the AMHP, first:

- leave of the High Court (civil) is needed before proceedings can begin;
- High Court (for civil) Director of Public Prosecutions (for criminal), unless an offence under the Act itself (s 139[3]), such as:
  - forgery, false statements, and so on (s 126);
  - ill-treatment of patients (s 127);
  - assisting patients to absent themselves without leave, and so on (s 128);
  - obstruction (s 129).

Second, it needs to be proven that the 'act done' was in 'bad faith' or 'without reasonable care' (as stated earlier).

However, there still remains potential for other claims to be brought, such as claims made under section 7 of the Human Rights Act 1998, misfeasance in public office, or a writ of habeas corpus as examples (Jones, 2021, pp 661–8). All of which can make an AMHP feel that being open, candid and truthful may bring negative consequences for their employment and in turn make them personally liable. Consequently, this may act, understandably, as a disincentive to being open, reflective and honest where learning needs to occur, creating some significant hurdles at the times when reflectiveness would offer the greatest value to future practice and patient safety.

Under section 13(1) of the MHA, a local social services authority must enable AMHPs to undertake their role if they 'have reason to think that an application for admission to hospital or a guardianship application may need to be made in respect of a patient within their area'. As has been seen, section 139 is required as AMHPs coordinate MHA assessments that can lead to a person being detained in hospital for the purposes of assessing or treating that person's mental disorder when it is in the interests of their own health or safety, or in the interests of others. Therefore, the role of the AMHP carries a great deal of accountability. Alongside this, the function of the role is often articulated as 'independent', for instance through the articulation of 'satisfying himself', as stated in section 13(2):

> Before making an application for the admission of a patient to hospital an approved mental health professional shall interview the patient in a suitable manner and satisfy himself that detention in a hospital is in all the circumstances of the case the most appropriate way of providing the care and medical treatment of which the patient stands in need.

This emphasis on independence of the role is further found in the MHA Code of Practice, in which for the guidance covering England it is clear that 'doctors and AMHPs undertaking assessments need to apply professional judgement and reach decisions independently of each other, but in a framework of cooperation and mutual support' (DoH, 2015, para 14.44). This independence is further galvanised in a statement made by the former College of Social Work (TCSW, 2014), in which they write that each local authority should have a lead AMHP. However, the rhetoric contained within it did nothing to diminish the accountability that AMHPs feel each day in practice:

> The independent nature of AMHP practice means that [local authorities] may struggle to challenge AMHP decision-making and actions, in-depth technical knowledge is required if effective critically reflective supervision is to be achieved, and the [local authority] needs to satisfy itself that AMHPs continue to meet the competencies required of them. (TCSW, 2014, p 7)

The MHA Code of Practice reinforces this independence by also stating:

> Although AMHPs act on behalf of a local authority, they cannot be told by the local authority or anyone else whether or not to make an application. They must exercise their own judgement, based on social and medical evidence, when deciding whether to apply for a patient to be detained under the Act. The role of AMHPs is to provide an independent decision about whether or not there are alternatives to detention under the Act, bringing a social perspective to bear on their decision, and taking account of the least restrictive option and maximising independence guiding principle. (DoH, 2015, para 14.52)

This independence means that AMHPs cannot be instructed by their employer or anyone else to make an application to detain a person. It also means that independence results in individual accountability. However, independence should not translate to mean 'in isolation', although a lack of reflective opportunities can lead to this feeling.

This feeling of personal accountability, isolation and independence is not assisted by suggestions made by Jaconelli and Jaconelli (1998) that section 139 MHA is written in such a way that could enable local authorities employing Approved Social Workers (ASWs; now AMHPs) to avoid their vicarious responsibility as the powers of detention are vested in the AMHP, not the local authority (as is the case with children protection legislation). George (cited in Jaconelli and Jaconelli, 1998, p 163) suggests that this risk of incurring personal liability could influence the calculative nature of decision making.

This fear might also be connected to feelings of being blamed, in turn leading to peer AMHP criticism and employer capability assessments. All of which could contribute to a disincentive on the part of the AMHP to the openness and truth-telling necessary for effective reflective practice, regardless of any potential security they may feel from employers' vicarious liability towards them while engaging in 'risk work' (Davis, 1996) (in the form of AMHP practice), and their needing to have insurance in place (DHSC/HEE 2020, p 29). How, then, are

AMHPs enabled to feel safe to engage in supervision and reflective decision-making mechanisms?

Safe spaces for reflection

It is with this backdrop of accountability and personal liability that the case is made here for a safe space for AMHP reflection; a space where AMHPs can discuss their practice and the dilemmas they have faced, without fear of the negative consequences of being open and truthful, so that their practice can be enhanced. It is pertinent to recognise that a safe space requires consideration of the physical space as well as the psychological (Earle et al, 2017, p 18), to ensure that psychological safety is maximised. This space needs to be able to offer AMHPs an opportunity to discuss their work with confidence in an environment that feels safe for reflection and learning. There are several forms of safe space, which will now be discussed in turn.

Supervision

The MHA regulations for England are clear that AMHPs are legally required to use supervision to enhance their future practice, as the regulations state that they should 'exercise the appropriate use of independence, authority and autonomy and use it to inform their future practice as an AMHP, together with consultation and supervision' (HMSO, 2008, key competence area 5, [f]). However, supervision can come in differing forms, with differing components. One formative stage can be the production of a supervision contract. Although this isn't exhaustive, adopting a thematic approach to supervision will enable the time spent to be focused and structured, as follows:

- practice competence
  - ethical dilemmas
  - value judgements
  - service frustrations
  - legal competence
- trauma and well-being impact

Peer one-one-supervision

A distinction here is being made between peer and management supervision, as the former is undertaken by the practitioner selecting someone to meet for supervision, rather than related to managerial functions of performance. Selecting a person themselves enables the practitioner to identify a person they trust. However, this does place emphasis on AMHPs, rather than the organisation, to facilitate that much-needed competency-based supervision and may therefore serve to undermine the actual goal of supervision.

Peer group supervision

Supervision can be achieved through peer group settings. This brings a different dynamic, as depending on who has organised it, each member may not have the same trust levels as can be achieved in one-to-one methods. Engaging in peer group discussions can work to reduce stress and fearmongering that can occur within teams when managing a great deal of uncertainty. There can also be opportunities for group discussion arising with training sessions and group work.

Group work discussion

Engaging in group discussion could result in differing outcomes. Some AMHPs may find discussion in groups challenging, as discussing decision making and decision outcomes can lead to feelings of exposure and critique.

One technique that can be used to good effect is the use of fictitious vignettes, where the AMHP can reach a decision on their own and then see how others responded, without needing to expose any inaccuracies in their own application of the law, their lack of knowledge or how their decision may be out of line with their peers. Use of technology can encourage AMHPs to feel comfortable giving truthful responses to questions and case studies. For example, online polling enables professionals to offer anonymous responses to case study vignettes or evolving case studies. Used in a group, all participants can see the variety of answers or discuss similarities and differences by engaging with the debates without disclosing their own view. It requires careful chairing and anyone who voluntarily identifies their answers should be encouraged not to, to avoid others feeling pressured to do so.

Recording as an act of reflection

AMHPs have a duty to record their decisions, along with an explanation as to how the grounds for detention were met (DoH, 2015, para 14.93–5), irrespective of whether a person is detained or not. Given the liabilities that exist, AMHPs must be able to offer a defensible account of their actions. The act of writing can simultaneously offer a beneficial form of reflection as it affords an opportunity away from the practicalities and pressures of the assessment.

What needs to occur in reflection

This section considers some key theoretical reflective approaches that can be applied to AMHP practice. Although these theories can be universally applied to all professional practice, the legal, policy and practice context in which AMHPs operate makes utilising these theories effectively more challenging due to their accountability and fear of liability.

One model outlines the stages that a learner progresses through when learning and implementing new skills (Gordon Training International, 1970). This model assists AMHPs to appreciate the differing stages of competence that can be moved through:

- unconscious incompetence
- conscious incompetence
- conscious competence
- unconscious competence

(Gordon Training International, 1970)

One of the key starting points is moving from unconscious to conscious understanding of competence. Unconscious incompetence can initially be felt at the beginning of AMHP training when undertaking an approved programme of study, as the role is very different from the duties associated with the usual primary role of the trainee. However, moving to and maintaining the conscious competence requires objective assessment rather than subjective self-evaluation alone. One of the critiques of this particular model is that it is not linear, as professionals can move from unconscious competence to unconscious incompetence through not maintaining their skills or permitting poor practices to become embedded; or from conscious competence to feelings of unconscious incompetence if an adverse incident occurs.

To gain perspective, AMHPs arguably need to be good at what Schön (1983) describes as 'reflection-in-action' or responding to events as they unfold before them, despite the planning and preparation involved. What reflective safe spaces create is the environment for 'reflection-on-action' (Schön, 1983) to occur after the point where divisive decision making has occurred in the moment. To achieve what O'Sullivan (2011) coined as 'sound decision-making', the AMHP needs to be able to evaluate whether the outcome that was achieved was due to their decision making or just good luck, and whether an unwanted outcome was just bad luck in any event. To achieve this 'soundness' the AMHP needs to be able to process what has occurred in a way that is not challenged perversely by wilful blindness, or conscious or unconscious avoidance brought about by fear of liability, rather than considering whether there was anything that could have been undertaken differently (Ghave, 2008).

In the same way, the AMHP needs to reflect on whether there was any influence from their personal values on their decision making (Thompson, 2016), and whether anti-oppressive practice (Nzira and Williams, 2014) can be implemented in what is an oppressive act of removing a person's liberty. This is important as AMHPs may also not find themselves in competency-based discussions or value and belief conflicts when interpreting statutory provisions or decisions arising from ethical dilemmas and balancing people's human rights.

Conclusion

This chapter argues that the need for a framework that supports front-line AMHPs to engage in reflective practice, without anxiety or fear of liability, is vital. For AMHPs to engage in authentic reflective practice meaningfully, the environmental conditions for that reflection need to be carefully considered. AMHPs need safe spaces to reflect and enhance their practice. To ignore the context in which AMHPs work is to ignore the complexity and skill required to undertake MHA work and the difficulties experienced.

References

Bassot, B. (2015) *The reflective practice guide: an interdisciplinary approach to critical reflection.* London: Routledge.

British Association of Social Work (BASW) (2016) *Report of the Inquiry into Adult Mental Health Services in England.* London: BASW. Available at https://www.basw.co.uk/system/files/resources/basw_53449-9_0.pdf.

British Psychological Society (BPS) (2021) Best practice in CPD. Available at https://www.bps.org.uk/psychologists/professional-development/best-practice-cpd.

Bruce, L. (2013) *Reflective practice for social workers: a handbook for developing professional confidence.* Milton Keynes: Open University Press.

Buckland, R. (2016) The decision by Approved Mental Health Professionals to use compulsory powers under the Mental Health Act 1983: a Foucauldian discourse analysis. *British Journal of Social Work*, 46(1), 46–62.

Care Quality Commission (CQC) (2014) Regulation 20: duty of candour. Available at https://www.cqc.org.uk/guidance-providers/regulations-enforcement/regulation-20-duty-candour.

Care Quality Commission (CQC) (2018) Briefing: Mental Health Act – Approved Mental Health Professional services. Available at https://www.cqc.org.uk/news/stories/wide-variation-uncovered-how-nhs-local-authorities-work-together-when-applying-mental.

Carpenter, J., Webb, C., Bostock, L. and Coomber, C. (2012) SCIE research briefing 43: effective supervision in social work and social care. Available at https://www.researchinpractice.org.uk/media/2568/reflective_supervision_resource_pack_2017.pdf.

Davis, A. (1996) Risk work and mental health. In H. Kemshall and J. Pritchard (eds), *Good practice in risk assessment and risk management 1* (pp 109–20). London: Jessica Kingsley.

Department of Health (DoH) (2014) *Mental health crisis care concordat: improving outcomes for people experiencing mental health crisis.* London: DoH. Available at https://assets.publishing.service.gov.uk/government/uploads/system/uploads/attachment_data/file/281242/36353_Mental_Health_Crisis_accessible.pdf.

Department of Health (DoH) (2015) *Mental Health Act 1983: Code of Practice.* London: DoH.

Department of Health and Social Care (DHSC) (2019) *National workforce plan for Approved Mental Health Professionals (AMHPs).* London: DHSC. Available at https://www.gov.uk/government/publications/national-workforce-plan-for-approved-mental-health-professionals-amhps.

Department of Health and Social Care and Health Education England (DHSC/HEE) (2020) *Approved Mental Health Professional (AMHP) national service standards.* London: DHSC/HEE.

Earle, F., Fox, J., Webb, C. and Bowyer, S. (2017) Reflective supervision: resource pack. Available at https://www.researchinpractice.org.uk/media/2568/reflective_supervision_resource_pack_2017.pdf.

Evans, S., Huxley, P., Webber, M., Katona, C., Gately, C., Mears, A. et al (2005) The impact of 'statutory duties' on mental health social workers in the UK. *Health and Social Care in the Community*, 13(2), 145–54.

Ferguson, H. (2018) How social workers reflect in action and when and why they don't: the possibilities and limits to reflective practice in social work. *Social Work Education*, 37(4), 415–27.

Furminger, E. and Webber, M. (2009) The effect of crisis resolution and home treatment on assessments under the 1983 Mental Health Act: an increased workload for approved social workers? *British Journal of Social Work*, 39(5), 901–17.

General Medical Council (GMC) (2021) The reflective practitioner: guidance for doctors and medical students. Available at https://www.gmc-uk.org/-/media/documents/dc11703-pol-w-the-reflective-practioner-guidance-20210112_pdf-78479611.pdf.

Ghave, T (2008) *Building the reflective healthcare organisation.* Oxford: Blackwell.

Gordon Training International (1970) Learning a new skill is easier said than done. Available at https://www.gordontraining.com/free-workplace-articles/learning-a-new-skill-is-easier-said-than-done/.

Gregor, C. (2010) Unconscious aspects of statutory mental health social work: emotional labour and the approved mental health professional. *Journal of Social Work Practice*, 24(4), 429–43.

Hemmington, J., Graham, M., Marshall, A., Brammer, A., Stone, K. and Vicary, S. (2021) *Approved Mental Health Professionals, Best Interests Assessors and people with lived experience: an exploration of professional identities and practice a report prepared for Social Work England.* Sheffield: Social Work England.

Her Majesty's Stationery Office (HMSO) (2008) *Schedule 2 of the Mental Health (Approved Mental Health Professionals) (Approval) (England) Regulations 2008.* London: HMSO.

Hobbs, V. (2007) Faking it or hating it: can reflective practice be forced? *Reflective Practice*, 8(3), 405–17.

Hudson, J. and Webber, M. (2012) *The National AMHP Survey 2012 final report. Stress and the statutory role: is there a difference between different professional groups.* London: King's College.

Jaconelli, J. and Jaconelli, A. (1998) Tort liability under the Mental Health Act 1983. *Journal of Social Welfare and Family Law*, 20(2), 151–64.

Jones, R. (2021) *Mental Health Act Manual* (24th edn). London: Sweet and Maxwell.

Killick, C. and Taylor, B. (2020) *Assessment, risk and decision making in social work: an introduction.* London: Learning Matters.

Leah, C. (2020) Approved mental health professionals: a jack of all trades? Hybrid professional roles within a mental health occupation. *Qualitative Social Work*, 19(5–6), 987–1006.

McQuire v Western Morning News [1903] 2 K.B. 100 at 109 per Collins MR.

Morriss, L. (2015) AMHP work: dirty or prestigious? Dirty work designations and the Approved Mental Health Professional. *British Journal of Social Work*, 46(3), 703–18.

NHS Digital (2021) Mental Health Act statistics. Available at https://digital.nhs. uk/data-and-information/data-tools-and-services/data-services/mental-hea lth-data-hub/mental-health-act-statistics.

Nursing and Midwifery Council (NMC) (2021) Guidance sheet: reflective practice. Available at https://www.nmc.org.uk/globalassets/sitedocuments/ revalidation/reflective-practice-guidance.pdf.

Nzira, V. and Williams, P. (2014) *Anti-oppressive practice in health and social care*. London: Sage Publications.

O'Sullivan, T. (2011) *Decision making in social work* (2nd edn). Basingstoke: Palgrave Macmillan.

Quirk, A., Lelliott, P., Audini. B. and Buston, K. (2000) *Performing the Act: a qualitative study of the process of Mental Health Act assessment*. London: Department of Health.

Royal College of Occupational Therapists (RCOT) (2019) Principles for continuing professional development and lifelong learning in health and social care. Available at https://www.rcot.co.uk/file/3024/download?token= 1x9mYOVD.

Scales, P., Briddon, K. and Senior, L. (2013) *Teaching in the lifelong learning sector*. Maidenhead: McGraw-Hill Education.

Schön, D. (1983) *The reflective practitioner: how professionals think in action*. London: Maurice Temple Smith.

Sicora, A. (2017) *Reflective practice and learning from mistakes in social work*. Bristol: Policy Press.

Social Work England (2021) Reflection. Available at https://www.socialwork england.org.uk/cpd/what-counts-as-cpd/reflection/.

The College of Social Work (TCSW) (2014) *The business case for the Approved Mental Health Professional (AMHP) lead role: a discussion paper*. London: TCSW.

Thompson, N. (2016) *Anti-discriminatory practice* (5th edn). Basingstoke: Palgrave Macmillan.

Vicary, S. (2021) 'Pull': the active use of dissonance. An IPA pearl to show emotion management in action. *Practice: Social Work in Action*, 33(4), 253–70.

W, R (on the application of W) v Doncaster Metropolitan Borough Council [2003] EWHC 192 (Admin).

8

Practice education: boundaries of knowledge, theory and practice

Che McGarvey-Gill

Introduction

This chapter will focus on the role of practice educators, a role that typically involves an experienced and qualified worker providing support and education for a trainee within a practice setting. Additionally, the practice educator would usually be expected to assess the trainee against capability frameworks (or similar). The themes that will be explored relate to the complexities, challenges and opportunities that practice educators face when supporting trainees to develop and ultimately become skilled practitioners within the field of statutory mental health assessments.

In England and Wales, practitioners working as Approved Mental Health Professionals (AMHPs) are involved in making decisions and applications to hospital where people may be admitted against their will and where treatment can be enforced. Practitioners such as AMHPs are usually non-medical by background, although notably in some locations (such as Australia and New Zealand) the decision to detain may be made by a doctor. Professionals have a vast amount of power over (and responsibility to) those experiencing mental distress. The power to limit another person's human rights to liberty and a private life should never be underestimated or taken lightly. It is therefore imperative that professionals working in this field are conscious of their duties, powers and responsibilities, and uphold the human rights of those they are working with; only taking decisions after they have ensured all other, less restrictive, options have been exhausted.

Non-medical practitioners involved in decision making about compulsion under mental health legislation must be able to manage competing tensions and ensure that professionals who go on to qualify into these roles have a value base that minimises any potential for abuse of the power that is embodied in them. The role of a practice educator can be likened to that of a gatekeeper, who ensures that only those who are assessed as competent can enter and where the duty is to safeguard the interests of those who require assessment, as well as those of their employers (Furness and Gilligan, 2004).

The chapter will consider the role of practice education for AMHPs in greater detail, focusing on the conditions required to support trainees to develop the required knowledge, skills and values. Specific ways of supporting trainees to learn will be explored, including the use of observational (or 'shadowing') opportunities of practice situations, direct observations (where the trainee takes the lead role in a practice situation) and supervision discussions. The chapter will conclude by examining the practice educator's role in the assessment of the trainee and deciding whether they meet the required level of competence to pass the placement. To illustrate this, the national standard of AMHP competences (HMSO, 2008) in England and Wales are used to illustrate and discuss broader concepts of applied knowledge and assessing practice competence. Pedagogy from social work practice education is applied, as the value bases of the two contexts have considerable overlap and share origins.

Preparation of self and context

In England and Wales, a fundamental part of the training to become an AMHP is the successful completion of a practice placement under the supervision of a practice educator who must have relevant knowledge, skills and experience, and who has undertaken appropriate training (Social Care Wales, 2020; Social Work England, 2020). The length, type and form of the placement will differ according to the organisational context. In preparing for a trainee, it is essential that practice educators consider how they will facilitate learning and the development required. Mortiboys (2005) proposes that self-awareness is essential for learning, and it therefore follows that practice educators should reflect on their own experiences in order to think about how they will support the learning journey for the trainee. Parallels can be drawn with the four stages of learning model (Howell, 1982), which shows that learners move through four different stages of awareness, starting with being unconsciously incompetent (or unskilled) and developing towards being consciously competent. It would be impossible for a practice educator to competently support a learner without having first developed self-awareness in relation to their practice. A useful reflective task for practice educators preparing for a trainee is to document their thoughts and feelings about their own learning experiences and expectations:

- What has been helpful?
- What has been unhelpful?
- What does the practice educator want from the trainee?
- How will this be achieved?

Writing reflectively supports the practice educator to develop their own self-awareness and conscious competency.

An essential part of planning for a trainee is considering the practical elements that facilitate learning, for example where they will sit if in an office base, preparing the wider team, frequency of supervision and so on. While this part of the preparation is less intellectually demanding, it is important that the setting and physical environment is seen as a dimension of the learning process.

Supporting trainees remotely

Following the COVID-19 pandemic many employers have actively encouraged employees to work from home and it may be that working practices will continue to change, with more remote working expected. While there are arguably benefits to this, such as greater flexibility, there are also negative impacts such as workers feeling isolated, not being connected to colleagues and lack of collaboration (CIPD, 2021). Research has highlighted the value of peer support for AMHPs (Gregor, 2010; Hudson and Webber, 2012) and many were badly affected by COVID lockdowns since peer support, sharing of knowledge and shared reflection sustained them and acted as a form of supervision protecting them from frustration, stress and burnout (Hemmington et al, 2021). Connection and presence are also particularly relevant for trainees, who need to see good practice modelled by others and who need learning to be facilitated by a practice educator who interacts with them constructively in order to achieve the required outcomes (see Walker et al, 2008; see also section titled 'Modelling good practice' later in the chapter for a discussion of social learning theory). As people work more remotely, practice educators will need to think about how they ensure trainees can be supported.

Although not directly connected to mental health practice, the Law Society of Scotland (2021) has published guidance for remote supervision of trainees, which has been adapted in Box 8.1 for practice educators of statutory mental health trainees.

Box 8.1: Remote supervision

1. Be clear about roles, particularly what to do if the practice educator is on leave, off sick and so on. Consider whether a colleague could offer support to the trainee. Ensure this is communicated.
2. Work out a schedule of communication with the trainee, stick to it but be prepared to change it. There is no one-size-fits-all approach, and some suggestions might include:
   - a daily call at the start of the day to check in that the trainee has the right level of work, knows what they are doing and has an opportunity to ask questions;
   - regular supervision to explore more complex matters;
   - weekly wrap-up feedback sessions: what went well, what didn't and so on, ensuring feedback focuses on their development with reference to competences they need to evidence over the placement.
3. Be approachable. Practice educators will hold a number of other responsibilities and trainees need to feel they can ask for additional support outside of scheduled sessions with their practice educator.

4. Osmosis by design. A lot of observational learning by osmosis can be missed when working remotely (for example overheard telephone calls, observations of body language and so on). Practice educators need to think how to recreate this aspect of the placement. Options here might be having a trainee listen/watch calls via electronic means (for example video calls).

5. Be aware of their situation. Trainees may be reluctant to raise issues relating to their own needs. Practice educators should be proactive, open and show empathy to the trainee.

Learning processes

A significant element when planning for a trainee is considering how to approach adult learning in such a challenging area of practice. Practice educators assessing trainees who are making decisions about compulsion under mental health legislation must ensure that trainees are able to engage in active, deeper levels of reflection. Biggs and Tang (2007, p 24) discuss the difference between surface and deep learning: the former is of low cognitive engagement (such as rote learning); the latter is where a learner understands the underlying meaning of the subject 'appropriately and meaningfully'. Some of the qualities that trainees need to develop when making decisions as AMHPs are much more akin to the definition of deep learning – for example, they must demonstrate the ability to reflect on complex ethical dilemmas and decision-making processes. Surface-level learning has been described as 'superficial', 'memorising' and 'skating the surface' (Walker et al, 2008), and is not always given the same value as deep learning. However, there are benefits to surface learning – for example, knowledge regarding the wording of legislation, relevant knowledge of services that could support people in the local area and so on, which are important areas of knowledge that trainees require but which do not require deeper-level learning. In her analysis of Chinese learning styles, Sit (2013) considers how learning through memorisation can aid understanding and is not necessarily inferior to deep learning.

As a practice educator, it is essential to consider the knowledge and experience trainees bring with them. Practice educators should view the learning process as a democratic and reciprocal form of education, rejecting notions that the trainee is an empty vessel that needs to be filled with enlightenment (Freire, 1972). There should be a co-focusing on the trainee's understanding of the importance of emotional intelligence in the work, given concerns that practitioners experience exhaustion and burnout arising from both the nature of the role (working with people experiencing mental health crises) as well as logistical problems (such as lack of resources) (Samuel, 2019). While research findings identify that the meaning of resilience is broad and varies from one person to another, it is proposed that resilience is a skill that can be learnt and developed (Fox et al, 2014; Grant and Kinman, 2014).

Practice educators should recognise that there may be tensions with supporting trainees who are already experienced in mental health work when they start their post-qualifying statutory mental health training. Some of these tensions are characteristic of adult learning whereby the trainee is goal orientated, driven to build upon pre-existing knowledge, concerned with the relevance of information to their pre-existing perspectives and motivated to seek to place learning in the context of achieving a wider objective (Knowles, 1984). On a broader note, some of these tensions relate to the need for the trainee to make a perceptual shift towards understanding the complex world of practising in a related albeit different role from that which they have been undertaking previously, most likely to a high standard. There is a need for the practice educator to support the trainee to understand the complex ecosystem that is statutory decision making and ensure the trainee does not approach assessments in an atomised and decontextualised manner (Smale et al, 2000). Instead, the trainee should be encouraged to build on and develop relationships with organisations, teams, colleagues and carers to promote best practice and least restrictive outcomes.

A word of caution for practice educators is that it is difficult to make assumptions that all adult learners feel the same way about development opportunities, particularly where organisations direct employees to complete certain training. This is of relevance for practice educators supporting trainees to carry out a role where there are workplace shortages. In England and Wales, it is recognised that there are widespread shortfalls in the number of AMHPs, alongside concerns of staff retention and growing demand (DHSC, 2019). It is possible that AMHP trainees lack internal motivation as the drive instead maybe external, that is from the organisation, with pressure being put on employees to undertake training (Gregor, 2010; Stevens et al, 2018; Bonnet and Moran, 2020).

In order to support trainees to shape the placement to meet their own learning needs, it may be useful to cocreate a learning agreement identifying a trainee's strengths, the learning outcomes they need to achieve, and opportunities required to meet them. Such a tool builds on the process identified by Field et al (2016), which seeks to identify a learner's motivations in order to guide the practice educator's approach. It can also aid openness and transparency in terms of identifying the assessment activities that will form part of the placement.

Modelling good practice

During trainees' learning on placement it is important that they have opportunity to observe (or shadow) experienced colleagues doing the role they will eventually be doing themselves. Through the process of observation, trainees should be active participants who are thinking about how the practitioners they are observing put into place the skills, knowledge and values they are working towards within their placement. Learning through observation is based on the principles of social learning theory (developed by Bandura, 1977), which claims people learn new behaviours themselves through a process of observing how others behave.

After trainees have undertaken observations of experienced colleagues, questions should be asked that seek to promote learning, to ensure the trainee is not a passive observer who will later simply copy what they have seen. Parsloe and Leedham (2009) clarify the importance of enabling the learner to take responsibility for their own development. Supporting the trainee to think *critically* about what they have observed enables them to develop their conscious competence (Howell, 1982). Questions that the practice educator could ask will vary depending on the particular experience that was observed, for example:

- Can you explain what you thought was happening? (Supporting surface-level learning)
- What might you have done in that situation? Or, what would you have wanted to consider? (With both developing deeper-level learning)
- How will you use the observation to support you when you take the lead? (Aiming to bridge the gap between the two roles of observer and leader)

The process of critical reflection aims to facilitate learning but is also important in assessing the trainee's value base. Given the legislative powers that the trainee will hold when qualified (that is, powers to restrict people's human rights and removing people's liberty), it is essential for practice educators to consider the ways in which the trainee's values link to their decision making. For practice educators assessing trainees making decisions about compulsion, it is considered that assessing the value position of the trainee at any given time is a necessary aspect of the overall assessment process. Lynch et al (2019, p 297) state that a relationship between the educator and the trainee in which values can be safely expressed and professional values modelled, cultivates a space in which students report that they 'started to say what we think' and that interactions felt like 'we were all together'.

Direct observation

A vital part of the practice learning experience for trainee AMHPs is their capacity to undertake the role and have observations of their practice by the practice educator, a process known as direct observation. This enables the trainee to carry out the role themselves, but in a safe and supported way. It is also a way in which the practice educator can assess the trainee's skills, knowledge and values.

It is important to highlight that direct observations are extremely anxiety provoking for learners and careful planning is essential (Field et al, 2016). While trainees will hold professional registration already and will be experienced in their field, this does not protect them from experiencing the same anxieties around direct observations as other learners. Practice educators should be alert to the significant number of trainees who may experience 'imposter syndrome', whereby they doubt their abilities despite their success, fearing (mostly without reason) their exposure as frauds (Mullangi and Jagsi, 2019). Prevalence rates of imposter syndrome vary widely (between 9 per cent and 82 per cent), but have been more commonly found in minority ethnic groups (Bravata et al, 2020, p 1271). It is important that practice educators recognise they are not the purveyors of, or arbiters to, absolute truths, and the previous experience trainees bring should be celebrated and promoted to reduce risks of anxiety.

Practitioners involved in decision making about compulsion under mental health legislation will take on complex and competing roles, which can be difficult for trainees to reconcile. Research by Quirk et al (2000, pp 43–5) highlights the multiple roles involved in such compulsory decision making, and there can be tensions where several may be evident in a single assessment. Roles include: 'applicant' (their 'official role' as signatories of the application); 'social worker' (in the context of an existing professional–client relationship causing conflict and feelings of betrayal); 'care manager'; 'supervisor/trainer'; 'advocate'; 'hate figure'; 'therapist' (around informing the client of their right to appeal, thereby attempting to facilitate client control and counter the damaging effects of compulsory admission by exercising a right to be listened to); '(social) policeman-executioner' (locking people up against their will); 'bureaucrat' ('following the rules' and presenting detention as 'nothing personal' to minimise its harmful effects on existing relationships or to counter perceptions of the 'policeman/executioner' role); 'ongoing contingency manager' (a core role due to common unexpected turns of events); and 'impresario' (a key role to successfully 'stage manage' the assessment and make sure it runs smoothly). There may be a quick transition from 'social worker' to 'hate figure' once the person is told they are going to be detained (Quirk et al, 2000). Leah (2020) recently revisited and added to this approach, exploring the concept of professional hybridity (where a professional has two or more roles). Through discussion with AMHPs, different legal roles were identified alongside social justice, advisory and therapeutic roles. The tension between these differing roles is summarised by one of the participants: 'You're the advocate, you're the caring person, you're the judge and I'm going to detain you, but I also care about you!' (Leah, 2020, p 993).

While direct observation of trainees is fundamental, it is important that practice educators recognise one of the greatest tensions that exists within the learning and training relationship is the fact that the trainee may feel inhibited to admit they are being exposed to situations that are far outside their 'comfort zone' (for example, the sense of personal vulnerability in the face of potential harm, identifying that the only hospital bed is over 200 miles away from the person's home, and so on). Field et al (2016, p 119) identify that practice educators need to be skilled in creating safe environments 'in which the student can explore and test their ideas and take responsibility for the intervention'. While that should be the aim of any direct observation, given the nature of the work being described, the ability of the practice educator to minimise the risks so that the trainee feels safe may be limited.

Decision making under mental health legislation

When making decisions under mental health legislation, the ability to work with people experiencing emotional distress is essential. People who access mental health services have often experienced multiple forms of abuse and trauma. Within this context, those responsible for applying for admission are faced with a decision: whether or not to admit a person into hospital, sometimes against their wishes, using legal processes. In England and Wales, the Mental Health Act 1983 (MHA) places specific duties and responsibilities upon AMHPs. They have a responsibility to act in a non-oppressive manner (HMSO, 2008), but a key question is how AMHPs uphold anti-oppressive practice when applying a piece of legislation that is deemed by many to be highly oppressive, and how trainees can be supported to navigate these tensions.

There is little research into the experiences of those being assessed under the MHA in England and Wales, and what research there is has tended to focus on people's experiences once they have been detained. Blakley et al (2021) interviewed ten people who had been assessed under the legislation and their findings explore their subjective experiences. The participants reported that when being assessed under the legislation, the assessment was poorly explained, meaning they weren't aware of who the assessors were or what options were available. Another finding was people felt intimidated by 'the barrage of three' (Blakley et al, 2021, p 3) (in England and Wales the assessment usually involves an AMHP and two doctors), and people experienced this as oppressive and didn't feel involved in the process. This, and other research, highlights some of the difficulties of being assessed under the legislation and the authors recommend that participants are given time to sit and talk to the practitioners (Buckland, 2020; Hemmington et al, 2021). One of the challenges for people who are subject to an assessment under mental health legislation is whether they feel safe to express their feelings freely, when the outcome of doing so may result in compulsory admission to hospital. The practice educator and trainee will need space to reflect upon how best practice is applied in situations where the receiver of that best practice may not perceive it as such.

It is well documented that certain groups are more likely than others to be detained under mental legislation: in England and Wales, Black people are four times more likely than White people to be detained in hospital for mental health treatment (NHS Digital, 2021) and there is evidence of similar findings in the United States (US) and other European countries (Singh et al, 2014). Vinkers et al (2010) identified several reasons why people from Black and Minority Ethnic (BME) backgrounds were more likely to be detained in psychiatric hospitals, which included: higher rates of psychoses; comorbid drug use; delays in help-seeking; and, additionally, mental health professionals were more likely to perceive Black people as 'dangerous'. Given the criteria for detention under mental health legislation are often directly related to the professional's view of 'risk', discussions around how decisions have been made are fundamental between the practice educator and trainee in unearthing bias (whether unconscious or conscious) or oppressive practice.

Linked to anti-oppressive practice must be a focus on emotional intelligence, which is essential for mental health trainees, given the nature of the work. Benefits of emotional intelligence include the ability to relate confidently and empathically with others, improved decision making and the ability to avoid becoming overly involved (Grant and Kinman, 2014). When working with people who are often in heightened or unpredictable emotional states, as is often the case in mental health work, having a high degree of emotional intelligence would seem vital for the role. Koprowska (2010) highlights the dangers that have been found when practitioners lack emotional awareness; for example, people who have experienced abuse are more likely to identify with others who have experienced abuse. Without a high level of emotional intelligence there is a danger that decision making could be based on erroneous decisions regarding risk.

Supervision of trainees

There is little available research in relation to the effectiveness of supervision within statutory mental health settings. However, there is a wide range of literature available on supervision in social work, which, it is argued, is applicable given the considerable overlap between the roles and that currently social workers make up most of the AMHP workforce in the United Kingdom (UK) (DHSC, 2021). There is also considerable overlap in terms of AMHP competences and those of social workers, as these have continued from the Approved Social Worker (ASW) qualification. In his review of social work education, Croisdale-Appleby (2014) identified that social workers must be competent practitioners (who apply skills within their work), professionals (who are aware of their value base) and social scientists (who use and apply knowledge). There are comparisons that can be made with the statutory regulations for AMHPs (HMSO, 2008), and likely other professionals who work as AMHPs. It is proposed that one of the most important skills for practice educators is being able to provide an opportunity for trainees to receive reflective supervision that enables them to develop across these differing but interrelated aspects of the job.

Research relating to supervision within social work (explored in Kadushin and Harkness, 2002) suggests it has three functions: administrative, educational and supportive. The research is relevant for trainees making decisions about compulsion under mental health legislation, given the overlaps identified. The administrative function is found to dominate social work supervision; typically, tasks are associated with 'getting the job done', such as work planning, monitoring and reviewing. For trainee AMHPs, the administrative functions might involve the practice educator supporting the trainee to plan elements of the assessments or exploring how legislation has been applied in work completed. It can be argued that overfocus on administrative tasks does not promote the independence of the trainee/supervisee as the practice educator/supervisor takes responsibility or 'vicarious liability' (Kadushin and Harkness, 2002, p 79).

The educative function of supervision focuses on the development of knowledge, skills and values (Tsui, 2005). During their placement, trainees who are already experienced professionals are required to significantly increase their knowledge in relation to their potential new role. Through supervision the practice educator shares their knowledge and identifies the learning needs of the trainee, supporting them to find solutions and problem solving (Kadushin and Harkness, 2002).

The supportive function of supervision (both psychological and interpersonal) is crucial when working with trainees in such an emotive area of mental health practice. Social work supervision should be an arena where the emotional impact of work situations is acknowledged (Ingram, 2013; Kettle, 2015). In statutory mental health practice this aspect of supervision can be the space created to examine the tensions that arise because of the powers inherent in the legislation. Use of power in mental health can be highly emotive for service users and cause specific tensions for experienced workers and trainees alike.

While it has been identified that supervision is an important arena for exploring emotions, there are barriers that can prevent supervision from being supportive. Trainees may be fearful of being judged or of becoming overwhelmed by emotion. Practice educators may also experience anxieties regarding their ability to respond (Field et al, 2016). Additionally, there is likely to be an added barrier, namely the power dynamic present in the relationship; the practice educator is actively involved in assessing the trainee against competency frameworks. The trainee may therefore choose not to discuss anything they perceive as impacting negatively upon their assessment.

It is important that practice educators and trainees recognise and manage potential barriers to supervision being supportive, such as power dynamics, as it is through supervision that practice educators can support the development of emotional intelligence and resilience, which are essential for the profession. Many workers in the caring professions experience stress and burnout. Research by Evans et al (2005) of social workers undertaking statutory mental health assessments (then ASWs) and social workers not practising as ASWs found that both groups reported high levels of stress, but that working as an ASW increased the risk of becoming 'burnt out'. In more recent research with over 1,000 social workers in the UK, Ravalier (2019) found that a large number reported stress, intention to leave, low job satisfaction and absenteeism. Kettle (2015) identifies that supervision can reduce the risk of burnout and increase personal accomplishment.

Grant and Kinman (2014) highlight that the social work curriculum places little emphasis on the development of strategies to support practitioners with stress management and self-care. One of the reasons that could account for this is the value society places on certain types of knowledge over others; studies around intelligence focused only on cognitive ability until the 1920s, when Thorndike proposed the concept of 'social intelligence' to explain the ability to 'act wisely in human relations' (cited in Held, 2009, p 107). Feminist researchers identify that research fields have been dominated by patriarchal views that equate knowledge with reason, logic and objectivity by devaluing subjectivity and failing to attribute value to emotion (Evans and Hardy, 2010). One of a number of ways that emotional intelligence can be supported is to use cognitive behavioural techniques in practice (Grant and Kinman, 2014). The benefits of the cognitive model in facilitating learning, resilience and capacity for practice are that experiences can be clearly examined and the interrelationship between thought, action and emotion made visible. This can be a positive way in which challenging ethical issues can be explored and used to develop emotional resilience.

Placement outcomes: pass or fail?

As highlighted, practice educators will usually be expected to make a recommendation regarding whether trainees have met the competences required and will decide whether they have passed or failed the placement (specific arrangements will depend on the requirements of the jurisdiction). As mentioned earlier, practice educators are 'gatekeepers' for the entry into the profession and they must have the confidence to fail the trainee if required (Clarke, 2017). Given the complexity of the AMHP role and the risks to service users and organisations of having professionals practising who are not competent, the practice educator must overcome any personal fears of failing a trainee.

It is important that practice educators and trainees are clear about the requirements of the placement and how assessment will take place. For trainee AMHPs in England and Wales, guidance is provided by Social Work England (2020) and Social Care Wales (2020) in relation to the criteria that trainees are assessed against; they go on to be approved in line with statutory regulations (HMSO, 2008). In Scotland, the equivalent role of the Mental Health Officer (MHO) has standards and practice competencies that are regulated by the Scottish Social Care Council (2021); for Northern Ireland, the role is that of an ASW (DHSS, 1992). It is essential that the practice educator and trainee are aware of the assessment standards set by the regulatory body.

Factors that impact practice educators' decisions

Research with practice educators of social work trainees by Furness and Gilligan (2004) identified that there were significant differences among practice educators regarding what constitutes 'good enough' practice. Some practice educators were concerned that while trainees appeared to demonstrate that they meet the competences required, they nevertheless had reservations about the trainee's fitness for practice. While the research considered student social workers on placement (that is, social work trainees who are not yet qualified), there could be parallels with AMHPs.

Walker et al (2008) consider the processes involved in assessing social workers (relevant to the assessment of AMHPs given the parallels previously identified), highlighting that making judgements is complex and assessment against competence standards implies that practice educators can be 'neutral and objective', while the reality is that social and cultural contexts in which decisions are made impact the outcome. Furness and Gilligan (2004) also suggest that trainees can be reluctant to share their own needs related to disability with practice educators for fear of being judged in advance. Trainees with ongoing mental health needs were more likely to share this with practice educators if they felt safe, valued and that they could trust the practice educator. Learners who identified as gay or lesbian were unsure whether to share this with practice educators. If trainees do not feel able to share relevant information around their own individuality or needs, they are unlikely to receive the support they need or do as well in their placements as other learners.

As highlighted earlier, professionals from BME backgrounds are more likely to experience 'imposter syndrome' compared to professionals who identify as White (Bravata et al, 2020), but there are additional factors that must also be considered by practice educators. Fairtlough et al (2014) consider the experiences of BME student social workers. They identify that while there are more BME student social workers compared to many other university degree courses in the UK, BME students are more likely to fail the course compared to other students. There are multiple factors identified in the study that explain why this might be, ranging from language difficulties, economic hardships and the increased caring responsibilities found among BME students. Students also reported feeling that they were stereotyped, that their practice educators put them under more scrutiny and that expectations were higher. Practice educators must be alert to these issues to ensure that trainees are supported and assessed fairly. There also needs to be an awareness of the recognition that groups of AMHPs are often less ethnically diverse than social workers overall (Skills for Care, 2021), and that this has the potential to compound the problem.

It is important that practice educators reflect on their relationships with trainees with this knowledge in mind, in order to safeguard trainees against unfair treatment or assessment while they are on placement. It is also important that when decisions are made in relation to passing or failing a trainee there is sufficient evidence to justify the decision. Parallels can be drawn between the practice educator's dual role as a practitioner, as they must approach assessments of people in mental health crisis with an awareness of their power and how they take steps to promote anti-oppressive practice. A hospital admission and detention under legislation should only ever be made if there is evidence to justify the decision and this must include reflection on behalf of the professional that they have not acted upon unconscious biases.

Conclusion

This chapter has explored the role of practice educators who provide support and education for trainees within a practice setting. This is an essential part of the learning experience for professionals undertaking the requisite additional training to become qualified AMHPs.

The chapter provides practice educators and trainees with a useful resource that supports and guides the placement and relationship in the context of compulsory decision making under mental health legislation. Although this has been grounded in the author's own experience of practice within England, arguably these themes are applicable to other jurisdictions where (mostly) non-medical practitioners are making decisions about compulsory admission and treatment for people who are experiencing mental health crises.

Given the overlap between social work and AMHP work, a significant amount of literature and research has been applied from the discipline of the former to the latter. However, given the differences between the roles, such as meeting the competences required, it would be incorrect to assume that social work knowledge could be used without careful consideration.

The themes explore the placement setting chronologically, beginning prior to the practice educators meeting the trainee they will be working with. In this phase the practice educator must prepare by considering practical aspects of the placement, which include how the trainee will be supported and how adult learning takes place. Once trainees are assigned a placement, it is considered that learning agreements or contracts are helpful in setting out expectations and aims of the placement; additionally, these can be used to highlight the strengths the trainee has already, so they can more readily draw on their existing experiences in order to adapt and apply them to AMHP practice.

Trainees must be made aware that the placement has two functions, which are arguably contradictory: they are both assessed and supported by the practice educator through different learning experiences. These can include learning through observing practice being modelled by the practice educator, as well as observations of the trainee's own practice by the practice educator and through reflective supervision discussions. These elements of practice placements allow for different skills, knowledge and values to be explored and examined by the practice educator and trainee. Given that the nature of the work involves assessing people in mental distress, there are significant impacts on people's rights to liberty, and decisions may, at times, go against the person's own wishes; it is therefore necessary for both practice educators and trainees to consider how emotional intelligence can be fostered within the placement.

Finally, it is argued that the evidence from other disciplines suggests that the diversity and needs of trainees undertaking practice placements are not always recognised. Practice educators must not only recognise that trainees come with different needs, but that they may also be reluctant to acknowledge or share due to fears of doing so impacting negatively on the assessment of their performance. Overall, this chapter aims to give people working in this area a useful framework with which to approach the practice placements of trainees seeking to work in statutory mental health fields.

Acknowledgements

This chapter has been created over a period of some years with information kindly shared by colleagues at both Cumbria County Council and the University of Central Lancashire. Many thanks to Jonathan Ashworth, Lesley Faragher, Matt Graham, Steve Nellist, Becky Squires and Alla Stoica.

References

Bandura, A. (1977) *Social learning theory*. Englewood Cliffs, NJ: Prentice-Hall.

Biggs, J. and Tang, C. (2007) *Teaching for quality learning at university: what the student does*. Maidenhead: Open University Press.

Blakley, L., Asher, C., Etherington, A., Maher, J., Wadey, E., Walsh, V. et al (2021) 'Waiting for the verdict': the experience of being assessed under the Mental Health Act. *Journal of Mental Health*, 31(2), 1–8.

Bonnet, M. and Moran, N. (2020) Why do approved mental health professionals think detentions under the Mental Health Act are rising and what do they think should be done about it?. *The British Journal of Social Work*, 50(2), 616–33.

Bravata, D., Watts, S., Keefer, A., Madhusudhan, D., Taylor, K., Clark, D. et al (2020) Prevalence, predictors, and treatment of impostor syndrome: a systematic review. *Journal of General Internal Medicine*, 35(4), 1252–75.

Buckland, R. (2020) Power as perceived in MHA assessment contexts: a scoping review of the literature. *Practice*. 32(4), 253–67.

Chartered Institute of Personnel and Development (CIPD) (2021) Coronavirus (COVID-19): flexible working during the pandemic and beyond. Available at https://www.cipd.co.uk/knowledge/fundamentals/relations/flexible-working/during-COVID-19-and-beyond#gref.

Clarke, L. (2017) How we're supporting struggling practice educators. Available at https://www.communitycare.co.uk/2017/11/02/supporting-struggling-practice-educators/.

Croisdale-Appleby, D. (2014) Re-visioning social work education, an independent review. Available at https://assets.publishing.service.gov.uk/government/uploads/system/uploads/attachment_data/file/285788/DCA_Accessible.pdf.

Department of Health and Social Care (DHSC) (2019) *National workforce plan for Approved Mental Health Professionals (AMHPs)*. London: DHSC. Available at https://assets.publishing.service.gov.uk/government/uploads/system/uploads/attachment_data/file/843539/AMHP_Workforce_Plan_Oct19__3_.pdf.

Department of Health and Social Care (DHSC) (2021) *The Approved Mental Health Professional workforce in the adult social care sector*. London: DHSC. Available at https://www.skillsforcare.org.uk/adult-social-care-workforce-data/Workforce-intelligence/documents/AMHPs-Briefing.pdf.

Department of Health and Social Services (Northern Ireland) (DHSS) (1992) Mental Health (Northern Ireland): Order 1986 Code of Practice. Available at https://www.rqia.org.uk/RQIA/files/84/84f400a2-a3a7-44f1-b096-6afa54a8f8e5.pdf.

Evans, S., Huxley, P., Webber, M., Katona, C., Gately, C., Mears, A. et al (2005) The impact of 'statutory duties' on mental health social workers in the UK. *Health and Social Care in the Community*, 13(2), 145–54.

Evans, T. and Hardy, M. (2010) *Evidence and knowledge for practice*. Cambridge: Polity Press.

Fairtlough, A., Bernard, C., Fletcher, J. and Ahmet A. (2014) Black social work students' experiences of practice learning: Understanding differential progression rates. *Journal of Social Work*, 14(6), 605–24.

Field, P., Jasper, C. and Littler, L. (2016) *Practice education in social work: achieving professional standards*. St Albans: Critical Publishing.

Fox, J., Leech, J. and Roberts, E. (2014) Supporting emotional resilience within social workers: practice tool. Available at https://www.rip.org.uk/resources/publications/practice-tools-and-guides/supporting-emotional-resilience-within-social-workers-practice-tool-2014-.

Freire, P. (1972) *Pedagogy of the oppressed*. Harmondsworth: Penguin.

Furness, S. and Gilligan, P. (2004) Fit for purpose: issues for practice placements, practice teaching and the assessment of students' practice. *Social Work Education*, 23(4), 465–79.

Grant, L. and Kinman, G. (2014) The importance of emotional resilience for staff and students in the 'helping' professions: developing an emotional curriculum. Available at https://www.advance-he.ac.uk/knowledge-hub/importance-emotional-resilience-staff-and-students-helping-professions-developing.

Gregor, C. (2010) Unconscious aspects of statutory mental health work: emotional labour and the Approved Mental Health Professional. *Journal of Social Work Practice*. 24 (4): 429–23.

Held, S. (2009) Emotional intelligence and collaborative leadership. In J. McKimm and K. Phillips (eds), *Leadership and management in integrated services* (pp 106–21). Exeter: Learning Matters.

Hemmington, J., Graham, M., Marshall, A., Brammer, A., Stone, K. and Vicary, S. (2021) *Approved Mental Health Professionals, Best Interests Assessors and people with lived experience: an exploration of professional identities and practice – a report prepared for Social Work England*. Available at https://www.socialworkengland.org.uk/about/publications/amhp-bia-and-people-with-lived-experience-research.

Her Majesty's Stationery Office (HMSO) (2008) *Mental Health Act (Approved Mental Health Professionals) (Approval) Regulations 2008, Schedule 1*. London: HMSO. Available at https://www.legislation.gov.uk/uksi/2008/1206/pdfs/uksi_2008 1206_en.pdf.

Howell, W. (1982) *The empathic communicator*. Belmont, CA: Wadsworth Publishing.

Hudson, J. and Webber, M. (2012). *The National AMHP Survey 2012*. London: King's College London.

Ingram, R. (2013) Locating emotional intelligence at the heart of social work practice. *British Journal of Social Work*, 43, 987–1004.

Kadushin, A. and Harkness, D. (2002) *Supervision in social work*. New York: Columbia University Press.

Kettle, M. (2015) Achieving effective supervision. Available at https://researchonl ine.gcu.ac.uk/ws/files/40380381/iriss_insights_30_23_06_2015.pdf.

Khalifeh, H., Moran, P., Borschmann, R., Dean, K., Hart, C., Hogg, J. et al (2015) Domestic and sexual violence against patients with severe mental illness. *Psychological Medicine*, 45, 875–86.

Knowles, M. (1984) *The adult learner: a neglected species*. London: Gulf Publishers.

Koprowska, J. (2010) *Communication and interpersonal skills in social work*. Exeter: Learning Matters.

Law Society of Scotland (2021) Remote supervision of trainees. Available at https://www.lawscot.org.uk/qualifying-and-education/qualifying-as-a-scott ish-solicitor/the-traineeship/information-for-trainees-and-practice-unit/supp ort-for-traineeship-providers/remote-supervision-of-trainees/.

Leah, C. (2020) Approved mental health professionals: a jack of all trades? Hybrid professional roles within a mental health occupation. *Qualitative Social Work*, 19(5–6), 987–1006.

Lynch, M., Bengtsson, A. and Holleets, K. (2019) Applying a 'signature pedagogy' in the teaching of critical social work theory and practice. *Social Work Education*, 38(3), 289–301.

Matthews, S. (2014) Underpinning themes, theories and research. In S. Matthews, P. O'Hare and J. Hemmington (eds), *Approved mental health practice: essential themes for students and practitioners* (pp 7–22). London: Palgrave Macmillan.

Mortiboys, A. (2005) *Teaching with emotional intelligence*. London: Routledge.

Mullangi, S. and Jagsi, R. (2019) Imposter syndrome: treat the cause, not the symptom. *Journal of the American Medical Association*, 322(5), 403–4.

NHS Digital (2021) Mental Health Act statistics, annual figures 2019–20. Available at https://digital.nhs.uk/data-and-information/publications/statistical/mental-health-act-statistics-annual-figures/2019-20-annual-figures.

Parsloe, E. and Leedham, M. (2009) *Coaching and mentoring*. London: Kogan Page.

Quirk, A., Lelliott, P., Audini, B. and Buston, K. (2000) *Performing the Act: a qualitative study of the process of Mental Health Act assessments*. London: Royal College of Psychiatrists Research Unit.

Ravalier, J. (2019) Psycho-social working conditions and stress in UK social workers. *British Journal of Social Work*, 49(2), 371–90.

Samuel, M. (2019) Councils urged to tackle AMHP salary disparities and stress in national workforce plan. Available at https://www.communitycare.co.uk/2019/11/11/councils-urged-tackle-amhp-salary-disparities-stress-national-workforce-plan/.

Scottish Social Care Council (2021) Introduction to the standards and practice competences to achieve Mental Health Officer award: Scottish Social Services Council. Available at https://www.sssc.uk.com/knowledgebase/article/KA-01818/en-us.

Singh, S., Burns, T., Tyrer, P., Islam, Z., Parsons, H. and Crawford M. (2014) Ethnicity as a predictor of detention under the Mental Health Act. *Psychological Medicine*, 44(5), 997–1004.

Sit, H. (2013) Characteristics of Chinese students' learning styles. *International Proceedings of Economics Development and Research*, 62, 36–9.

Skills for Care (2021) *The Approved Mental Health Professional Workforce in the adult care sector*. Leeds: Skills for Care.

Smale, G., Tuson, G. and Statham, D. (2000) *Social work and social problems*. London: Palgrave Macmillan

Social Care Wales (2020) Specified named course requirements for the Approved Mental Health Professional award. Available at https://socialcare.wales/cms_ass ets/file-uploads/Specified-named-course-requirements-for-the-Approved-Men tal-Health-Professional-Award.pdf.

Social Work England (2020) Approved Mental Health Professionals (AMHP) course guidance. Available at https://www.socialworkengland.org.uk/educat ion-training/amhp-course-guidance/#mapping%20AMHP%20criteria%20 to%20the%20education%20and%20training%20standards.

Stevens, M.J., Martineau, S.J., Manthorpe, J., Steils, N. and Norrie, C.M. (2018) *Who wants to be an Approved Mental Health Professional?* London: Social Care Workforce Research Unit, King's College London.

Tsui, M. (2005) *Social work supervision: context and concepts*. London: Sage

Vinkers, D., De Vries, S., Van Baars, A. and Mulders, C. (2010) Ethnicity and dangerousness criteria for court ordered admission to a psychiatric hospital. *Social Psychiatry and Psychiatric Epidemiology*, 45, 221–4.

Walker, J., Crawford, K. and Parker, J. (2008) *Practice education in social work: a handbook for practice teachers, assessors and educators*. Exeter: Learning Matters.

9

Compulsory mental health work and multi-professional frames: occupational therapy in AMHP work

Rachel Bloodworth-Strong

Introduction

In England, if someone needs to be admitted to a psychiatric hospital under a compulsory legal framework, specifically the Mental Health Act 1983 (MHA), the decision maker has traditionally been a social worker. Since 2007, occupational therapists, along with mental health nurses and psychologists, have been permitted to train as an Approved Mental Health Professional (AMHP) – a role conceived as a counterbalance to the possibility of medical authority enforcing treatment and deprivation of liberty. As an occupational therapist AMHP, the author is still in a minority, with most AMHP colleagues being social workers.

The need to consider alternatives to detention is becoming ever more critical. According to the Care Quality Commission (2018, p 4) during 1998–2008 the number of psychiatric beds in England reduced by more than 50 per cent, but the rate of compulsory detention increased by the same percentage, leading to a 'vicious cycle where pressure on beds leads to clinical practices that increase the likelihood of patients being detained, which itself increases the pressure on beds'. This pressure has led to a government commissioned review of mental health legislation in England and Wales, concluding that 'compulsory treatment must be a last resort' (DHSC, 2018, p 34). Skills for Care (2019) forecasts an increased need in the adult social care workforce of 36 per cent to meet the demands of an ageing population, leading to greater workforce pressures across all sectors including on community services that could act as viable alternatives to hospital admission. Recruiting more AMHPs, including allied health professionals, has become ever more pertinent. Despite this, a government-commissioned data survey found that 95 per cent of professionals working as AMHPs remain social workers, 4 per cent were nurses, but only 1 per cent were occupational therapists (Skills for Care, 2021). The aim of this chapter is to explore the relationship between occupational therapy and statutory mental health work and to make a case for recruiting more AMHPs from this profession. It also considers the significance of professional background and explores the ways in which occupational therapy can inform decision making on compulsion.

The extent to which occupational therapy brings something unique as a profession has not been considered in any depth in studies in literature relating to statutory mental health work and decisions about compulsion. Experience by the author as an occupational therapist carrying out a dual role in mental health work and compulsion has led to reflection on whether this core profession brings any distinct value in the arena, as well as considering what barriers there are to occupational therapy colleagues following the same path. Gaining more understanding about the uniqueness of occupational therapy skills could offer potential solutions in terms of the recruitment of occupational therapists as AMHPs.

The MHA Code of Practice (DoH, 2015, para 14.52) lays out the purpose of the AMHP role, which is to 'provide an independent decision about whether or not there are alternatives to detention under the Act, bringing a social perspective to bear on their decision and taking into account the least restrictive option and maximising independence principle'. A key question is whether occupational therapy lends itself to the AMHP role, in light of this description.

At the heart of the discussion in this chapter is one aspect of the AMHP role – namely, how bringing a 'social perspective' is understood and interpreted in practice. Historically, the development of a social model of mental disorder led to the creation of the AMHP equivalent role – the Approved Social Worker (ASW) – previously only open to social workers because they are considered to bring a distinctive social and rights-based perspective to their work (Allen, 2014). In a study by Karban et al (2020), 12 AMHPs were interviewed regarding how they understand the social perspective in compulsory decision making. Findings referenced the 'cornerstones' model proposed by Tew (2005), namely: a holistic lens; a recognition of trauma; highlighting strengths, both social and individual; a collaborative approach to recovery; and a recognition of the impact of power imbalance in the MHA assessment process. They comment that 'some of those participating in this study explicitly linked their understanding of social perspectives to their professional identity as social workers' (Karban et al 2020, p 14), but recognise that only social workers participated in the study and call for more research involving other how professions interpret the 'social perspective' (while also acknowledging that the individual accounts in the study are nuanced and diverse in their understanding of the concept of bringing the social perspective). As one commentator suggests, an occupational therapist may well be suited to considering the person in a mental health crisis from a strongly social perspective (Tew, 2011), an assertion that will be explored next.

The value of occupational therapy

At the heart of occupational therapy is the belief that the ability to participate in meaningful occupation is fundamental to health and well-being, and that occupation has intrinsic therapeutic value. The core skills of an occupational therapist focus on the assessment of occupational needs and 'facilitating participation in day-to-day activities chosen by the client' (Hemmington et al, 2021, p 84). However, the Royal College of Occupational Therapists (RCOT), the professional body for occupational therapists, recognises 'the increasing diversity and breadth of occupational therapy practice' (RCOT, 2021, p 1), which might encompass decision making about compulsion. Research has for some time debated the value of occupational therapists practising their specific occupation-centred practice in community mental health teams versus generic care coordination (Culverhouse and Bibby, 2008; Lama et al, 2021). In a study by Lama et al (2021, p 583) occupational therapists were found to support clients in their recovery to 'find their best occupational self', working intentionally on client-centred goals such as establishing routines and therapeutic groups on exercise and budgeting. Culverhouse and Bibby (2008) propose that occupational therapists are best utilised in community mental health teams promoting rehabilitation through skills training or introducing clients to new roles. It might therefore be argued that occupational therapists are ideal candidates for compulsory mental health work, with their ability to notice detail about a person's environment and behavioural patterns – crucial skills for gauging if someone is safe to stay or return home. Indeed, the Health and Care Professions Council (HCPC) Standards of Proficiency for Occupational Therapists (HCPC, 2013, p 10) highlight the need to 'recognise the socio-cultural environmental context within which people live', and this may apply in generic as well as occupational therapy specific roles.

Health enablers

A fundamental value of the occupational therapy profession centres on a holistic, whole-person and client-centred approach (RCOT, 2021). Kielhofner's (2008) model of human occupation (MOHO) views the person within their environment, placing emphasis on their occupational performance in terms of their roles and routines (habituation), and their values, interests and motivations (volition). The person, environment, occupation model (Law et al, 1996) reflects the ideas and concepts of the social perspective discussed earlier.

Respondents in a study by Stevens et al (2018) consider that occupational therapists are suited to compulsory mental health work because their training covers both medical and social perspectives. This conclusion resonates with the wording in the MHA Code of Practice, stating that the AMHP 'must exercise their own judgement based on social and medical evidence' (DoH, 2015, para 14.52). Such suitability is also reinforced by the professional body, which states that 'occupational therapists are unique in being trained to work across health and social care settings and within mental health, physical health or learning disability teams', and they may 'migrate between specialisms across their career, giving them a broad perspective … working across boundaries' (RCOT, 2016a, p 4).

While the qualifying degree of occupational therapists is science based, unlike social work, the training also differs from that for mental health nurses in that it does not specialise in physical or mental healthcare. Occupational therapists also work across the age span. The training undertaken by occupational therapists gives them an understanding of how conditions affect a person's occupational performance; but essentially, rather than seeking to solve medical problems, they are health enablers (RCOT, 2016b). It is the value of such health enablement that is the focus of this chapter.

Occupational therapists view themselves as experts in promoting independence (RCOT, 2021), not only in their core values but also through their creative and practical skills in keeping people out of hospital. Occupational therapists offer rehabilitation, specialist equipment, environmental adaptation and education as alternatives to structures of care or treatments that lead to institutionalisation or dependency. They are trained to assess a person's cognitive, physical and functional abilities and can expedite safe discharges from hospital. This knowledge enables them to 'navigate care and support systems efficiently, liaise appropriately, and work effectively in multidisciplinary settings; they are the key workforce when it comes to reducing hospital-related pressures' (RCOT, 2016b, p 4). While occupational therapists are seen as key enablers in physical health settings, the same skills would lend themselves to the AMHP duty to 'make necessary arrangements for treatment or care' when a person is discharged from a place of safety under MHA section 136(2). This is in line with the AMHP competence 4(e), which is to 'consider the feasibility of and contribute effectively to planning and implementing options for care as alternatives to compulsory admission, discharge and aftercare' (HMSO, 2008a).

Occupational therapists have a professional duty to embrace positive risk taking (Boardman and Roberts, 2014) and reduce the possibility of iatrogenic harm from a long hospital stay (Karban et al, 2020). They have expertise in assessing and minimising risk. These values are enshrined in RCOT's *Professional Standards for Occupational Therapy Practice, Conduct and Ethics* (RCOT, 2021), which are very much in keeping with the MHA guiding principles, including: 'least restrictive option and maximising independence', 'empowerment and involvement' and 'respect and dignity'. This duty also reflects the AMHP competence 4(f): 'recognising, assessing and managing risk effectively' (HMSO, 2008a). The RCOT (2018a) guidance *Embracing Risk; Enabling Choice* cites an example of a person kept in hospital because their cluttered home was perceived as a risk, which was outweighed by the negative outcome of becoming institutionalised. With appropriate adaptation and support in place, this situation might have been prevented. Du Feu (2012) observes how a trainee occupational therapist AMHP could notice the effects of antipsychotic medication on a person's balance and gait. A personal example encountered through AMHP practice is being able to recommend plans for an older person's discharge home with intensive support and reablement, as opposed to discharge to a long-term care home. This was based on professional experience in assessment of daily living skills and occupational performance. In the context of an MHA assessment for someone who was an amputee and wheelchair user to see if the criteria were met for a longer hospital detention, occupational therapy knowledge was used to advocate for them to be discharged home, as opposed to a care home placement. It had been assumed that the person could not go home based on the fact that they were relying on the care of nurses on the psychiatric hospital ward, when actually their home environment was, or could have been made, more suitable for their physical needs, along with community support for their mental health.

Alternatives to hospital

The RCOT (2010) report *Recovering Ordinary Lives* asserts that 'occupational therapists will be seen as professionals who have the knowledge and experience to deliver creative solutions to complex problems'. Creek (2005) describes occupational therapy as a 'complex intervention' involving 'non-linearity and unpredictability' and 'shifts of perspectives'. In a survey of occupational therapists by Craik et al (1998), when asked what factors attracted them to work in mental health they cited uncertainty and challenge of the work, along with the need for flexibility and opportunities for creativity autonomy – the very skills that lend themselves to 'considering the person's case' (s 13[1] MHA) and the 'alternatives to detention' (DoH, 2015, para 14.52).

Embracing alternatives to detention (DoH, 2015) is very much in keeping with the fourth and fifth guiding principles in the MHA Code of Practice (DoH, 2015) – namely, 'purpose and effectiveness' and 'efficiency and equity'. For example, three separate reports highlight where these alternatives are. First, RCOT's (2016b) *Improving Lives Saving Money* campaign cites improved quality of life for people experiencing mental and physical health conditions in a variety of areas where occupational therapists are strategically placed, which include general practitioner (GP) practices and working with paramedics or in Accident and Emergency (A&E). Second, the report *Getting my Life Back* (RCOT, 2018b) cites evidence of occupational therapists improving physical health outcomes for people with mental illness by, for example, promoting involvement in active, healthy meaningful occupation. Where occupational therapists work in education or workplaces, their practical problem–solving approach in recommending reasonable adjustment enables people to stay in employment or education, reducing the likelihood of referral to primary or secondary mental health services. While seeming to be removed from compulsory mental health work, this points to the heart of the occupational therapy profession to steer people away from purely medical solutions. Third, an 'Adult Mental Health Fact Sheet' from RCOT (2017, p 1) asserts, with reference to several studies, that 'timely occupational therapy interventions can: prevent unnecessary hospital admissions; improve wellbeing and patient experience; facilitate early discharge; enable recovery and social inclusion'.

Independence

AMHPs are expected to make the decision about detention and 'exercise their own judgement, without being told by the local authority or anyone else whether or not to make an application' (DoH, 2015, para 14.53). A key area of AMHP competency (Area 5) is the 'ability to make and communicate informed decisions' (HMSO, 2008a). Du Feu (2012, p 15) highlights how an occupational therapist AMHP trainee had a unique 'flair for decision making', with an ability to quickly 'identify workable alternatives to hospital', distinguishing between those cases where a patient would need detention on safety grounds, and those that could be supported in the community. A key standard for occupational therapy is to 'practise as an autonomous professional exercising their own professional judgement' (HCPC, 2013, p 8). Occupational therapists are accustomed to being the key decision makers in how public resources are distributed in an equitable manner when someone applies for a disabled facilities grant, in accordance with legislation following the Housing Grants, Construction and Regeneration Act 1996 and the Equality Act 2010.

Occupational therapy skills

The clinical reasoning undertaken by occupational therapists may also be particularly suited to AMHP practice. Neistadt (1996, p 677) describes occupational therapists using a combination of 'narrative reasoning, interactive reasoning, procedural reasoning [and] pragmatic reasoning': narrative reasoning deals with the client's story; interactive reasoning deals with the client's illness experience and the therapeutic relationship; and procedural reasoning involves systematic gathering and interpreting of client data, akin to scientific or diagnostic reasoning. This thought process focuses on the client's disease or disability (Mattingly and Fleming, 1994). Mattingly (1991, p 979) argues that occupational therapy and medical decision making overlap here, but may diverge in that occupational therapy can offer a 'deeply phenomenological mode of thinking ... more than a simple application of theory ... as understood in the natural science'. It may involve improvising 'an approach that addresses the unique meaning of disability as it relates to a particular patient'. Pragmatic reasoning considers the environment and what is practically possible. This strongly resonates with the complexity of compulsory decision making, whereby AMHPs must be 'satisfied the statutory criteria for detention are met' (DoH, 2015, para 14.49), while considering 'all the circumstances of the case' (s 3 MHA).

  In the process of considering the case for compulsory detention, a key AMHP duty is to 'interview the patient in a suitable manner' (s 13.2 MHA). There is no reason why occupational therapists should outperform other professional groups in terms of skill and proficiency in this area. Nevertheless, the HCPC (2013, p 11) standards of proficiency for occupational therapists stress the need to listen and 'communicate effectively' and 'select, move between and use appropriate forms of verbal and non-verbal communication'. Occupational therapists are likely to have encountered a huge range of differing types of communication impairments among the people they work with (from stroke-related aphasia or head injury through to autism or dementia). These experiences would equip them with the ability to efficiently plan an assessment, supply 'appropriate equipment' (DoH, 2015, para 14.42), arrange for an interpreter or simply be sensitive communicators.

A unique core skill of an occupational therapist involves activity analysis (Brown and Hollis, 2013) – breaking the task down into steps or components – and this is normally discussed in the context of observing someone perform an occupation for an assessment or manipulating it as a therapeutic medium to effect an improvement in function by graded steps. However, it is possible that these skills lend themselves well to the practical planning involved in an MHA assessment around compulsory detention. Bringing together doctors, police, paramedics, interpreters, involving relatives, considering the needs of children and keeping the person at the centre is the overall responsibility of the AMHP (DoH, 2015, para 14.41). It may also involve considerations about pets and property under the Care Act 2014. These are key areas of AMHP competence 4(i), namely the ability to 'plan, negotiate and manage compulsory admission to hospital'; and (4j) coordinating the legal and practical processes (HMSO, 2008a). Occupational therapists develop expertise in thinking through the detailed steps about how something is going to work, for example a hospital discharge involving people and equipment arriving in one place at one time, a new group being set up, or how a warrant might be executed. Getting this right will likely achieve the best outcome for the person.

Occupation therapy and AMHPs: the research

Little evidence has so far emerged about the relationship between occupational therapy and AMHP practice (Knott and Bannigan, 2013). Academic enquiry in this area tends to view the problem in terms of workforce capacity or barriers to recruitment. There has also been interest in similarities and differences between professional roles and identities in compulsory decision making (Karban et al, 2020). The literature originates from other disciplines and study participants tend to be social workers, who make up the majority of AMHPs, along with a small number of nurses.

Stevens et al (2018) investigated barriers to health professionals adopting the AMHP role; samples were small and therefore not necessarily generalisable, with only 12 occupational therapists, although this is the most so far in any study. This research cited organisational or structural barriers between health services and local government, whereby in some areas occupational therapists are not funded to train or do not feel supported, a finding echoed elsewhere (Du Feu, 2012; DHSC, 2019). The lack of awareness that this role is open to non-social workers is widely acknowledged.

Differences in culture and thinking underlying professional roles have emerged as barriers to health professionals in compulsory mental health work (Stevens et al, 2018). There is a perception that has emerged from some studies that the AMHP role could conflict with therapeutic relationships that health professionals hold with patients, or clash with client-centred values. Leason (2004) cautions that for nurses adopting the AMHP role, detaining people may threaten the independence of that role, but also questions whether nurses would actually want to potentially damage therapeutic relationships. Coffey and Hannigan (2013) highlight the challenge for nurses combining traditional biomedical with social approaches. On the other hand, Watson (2016, p 4) found that both nurses and social workers were motivated to train 'in compulsory mental health roles because the ability to stand up for an individual's rights, when their liberty is at stake, was seen as rewarding and congruent with their personal values'. Vicary et al (2019) note the example of a nurse standing up to a doctor in the context of statutory decision making, challenging the notion that this role is best executed by social workers. Vicary et al (2019) also suggest that AMHPs from a nurse background may challenge the way in which AMHP work is undertaken. It may be assumed that occupational therapists, as with nurses and nurse AMHPs, might tend to ally themselves with doctors (Stevens et al, 2018; Stone, 2019; Hemmington et al, 2021); however, these perceptions have been challenged.

There is evidence that people with lived experience of MHA assessments are unaware of professional role differences. A study by Hemmington et al (2021, p 53), based on interviews with professionals as well as those with lived experience of MHA assessments, found that in a mental health crisis, professional roles might not matter (although it should be noted that only a very small number of occupational therapists took part in the study). One participant reported: 'I think I would have loved to have been assessed by an occupational therapist AMHP 'cause I've met some fantastic occupational therapists in the past ... they are non-judgemental, and "normal" although, like nurses, are kind of adding to the medical model'.

Stone (2016; 2019) used vignettes to explore the decision making of ten social work and ten nurse AMHP trainees to consider how professional roles determine risk-taking and detention rates. Variation was found between individuals but not between the two professions, thereby challenging traditional assumptions about role difference. Indeed, Leah (2018) proposes the notion of those working in this compulsory mental health arena as 'hybrid' professionals, whose roles span beyond their own boundaries. Similarly, Pilgrim (2020, p 158) describes the 'overlap of roles and approaches across the mental health workforce', so that the identity of the practitioner is defined by their own individual orientation, to the extent that they may lose 'a sense of belonging to their own original occupational group'. This is further reflected in the National Workforce Plan for AMHPs (DHSC, 2019, p 6), which states that 'the role still has human rights and a social approach at its heart – regardless of the profession undertaking the role', and is supported by research identifying that considerations about human rights are dominant within AMHP decision making (Buckland, 2014; Laing et al, 2018; Dixon et al, 2019).

A literature review by Knott and Bannigan (2013) specifically explores occupational therapy and the AMHP role. The span is wide-ranging and extracts four key themes: values, social perspective, independence of the AMHP role and impact on therapeutic relationships. Knott and Bannigan (2013, p 118) argue for 'coherence' between social work and occupational therapy values in terms of 'empowerment, autonomy and working in collaboration with service users'. They find little basis for the AMHP role damaging relationships with the client, and concur with Carr (2007) that the occupational therapy approach might be valued by service users, although this is not explored further and they acknowledge their own potential bias as occupational therapists. Furthermore, Du Feu (2012, p 14) describes the experience of supervising an occupational therapist in AMHP training and notes 'initial hesitancy … for some workers … in the transition from the medical model to one of rights and safety-based work with a focus on the Human Rights Act', but that they can flourish 'once they have grasped the concept of rights and liberty, in the development of the least restrictive practice'.

A reading of the professional code of ethics for occupational therapy and social work highlights the congruence in values between these professions, which is highly relevant in compulsory mental health work, with repeated references in both to human rights, holistic practice and collaboration. The AMHP regulations outline key AMHP competencies that are closely aligned with core social work and occupational therapy values. These include: 1(a) challenge discrimination; 1(b) respect for diverse backgrounds; 1(c) promote the rights, dignity and self-determination of patients; and 1(d) sensitivity to personal choice. The fourth area of key AMHP competencies is working in partnership (HMSO, 2008a).

Occupational therapists, like social workers, are trained to apply legislation in their work, including the Human Rights Act 1998 and Mental Capacity Act 2005, which form a key part of compulsory decision making. This echoes the second area of key AMHP competency, focusing on knowledge and ability to apply law and policy in practice (HMSO, 2008a). Occupational therapists routinely consider a person's ability to make an informed decision in all aspects of their work, from equipment provision to mental health care and treatment planning. Occupational therapists also train as Best Interests Assessors (BIAs), although, as with AMHP practice, they are in the minority compared to social workers. A report by Hemmington et al (2021, p 84) – albeit with limited responses from and about occupational therapists BIAs – found evidence that 'the Mental Capacity Act 2005 is embedded in every aspect and area of occupational therapy practice'; that the core philosophy of occupational therapy is about maximising independence and using specialist knowledge of equipment and aids that can help reduce restrictions allowed people more freedom, and, further, that occupational therapists were thought to be good at writing well-structured reports and used a solid analytical approach.

AMHPs may be recruited from occupational therapists working alongside social workers in local government, rather than from those who work in health services alongside psychiatric nurses, although there is no formal data collection by profession (ADASS, 2018) and a national register of AMHPs has been called for (CQC, 2018). RCOT's (2016a) *Care Act 2014: Guidance for Occupational*

Therapists – Prevention recognises 'a close correlation between the philosophy, skills and practice of occupational therapists' and the principles of the Care Act 2014, including prevention, well-being and a focus on a person's strengths, thereby minimising restrictions. Statutory guidance recognises occupational therapists, along with registered social workers, as two of the key professions in adult care and support (DoH, 2015, para 6.82), pointing to the correlation of values between both professions and therefore parity in terms of suitability for the AMHP role.

The case for occupational therapy

Curious as to why so few occupational therapists become AMHPs, the author undertook a service improvement project to enquire further. Data was gathered using semi-structured interviews with five occupational therapists who had not trained as AMHPs. This was a small-scale qualitative enquiry, focused on occupational therapy attitudes to AMHP training, their knowledge of the role, barriers to them becoming AMHPs and how they relate the AMHP role to their professional values. Using thematic analysis (Braun and Clarke, 2006; Davies, 2007; Bryman, 2012), a mirroring of themes emerged between barriers and solutions.

Respondents highlighted the following as potential barriers to occupational therapists becoming AMHPS: a lack of awareness about the AMHP role; the fact that occupational therapists traditionally are not AMHPs; the AMHP role may conflict with establishing a therapeutic relationship with clients or they may be perceived or perceive themselves as less suitable than social workers, even lacking confidence; the AMHP role could be perceived as stressful; there may be lack of time to train effectively and their own team may not allow it since occupational therapists are in demand in other areas.

In terms of the value of occupational therapy to the AMHP role, respondents talked in eloquent and positive ways about how they felt very suited to be AMHPs in terms of core skills, closely aligned with their focus on social perspective that the AMHP is supposed to bring. The recurrent themes were that occupational therapists are creative and practical people, able to problem-solve and seek out alternatives; they are holistic in their approach and trained in both mental and physical health work; and as a profession they are skilled at understanding the broad social and environmental influences on a person (Law et al, 1996; Kielhofner, 2008). Appreciating the scope of their role and how it could be valuable to AMHP practice, respondents were positive about promoting their role to other professionals, enhancing their own development and benefiting them, their team and the service and service users. The constraint of team pressures could therefore be turned into a benefit for everyone and stressful situations in AMHP practice could be a learning platform to gain confidence in making decisions. From this emerged an intervention plan consisting of a virtual educational event to promote the AMHP role directly to occupational therapists, and interest in the role was enhanced as a consequence of this project.

At a national level, the government has commissioned a national workforce plan for AMHPs recommending a 'specific pathway supported by the regulatory and professional organisations … to support the development of the AMHP role in the other professional groups, according to their regulatory and professional frameworks, and a nationally agreed data collection process for the AMHP role' (DHSC, 2019, p 21). The absence of formal data collection by profession is acknowledged (ADASS, 2018). A 2019 report by the All-Party Parliamentary Group on Social Work (APPG) and British Association of Social Work (BASW) highlighted a need to recruit more AMHPs overall, including from among health professionals (APPG, 2019; see also Carson, 2018; Stevens et al, 2018; DHSC, 2019). The APPG (2019) notes that a small minority (around 5 per cent) of AMHPs are from professions other than social work and would welcome 'requirements on local authorities to provide AMHPs with more diverse experience'.

Conclusion

Occupational therapists can be highly suited to compulsory mental health work. Their work as health enablers, expertise in considering alternatives to hospital, promotion of independence through their clinical reasoning, decision making and communication skills potentially adds to the scope and skills of the workforce. Raising awareness about occupational therapy values and skills and how these relate to human rights work in the mental health context could be a vehicle to promote the occupational therapy profession, inspire therapists to train in these roles and improve AMHP recruitment. There is a need to promote awareness about the role among health professionals through involvement of their professional bodies, as well as a call for further research (Knott and Bannigan, 2013; Stone, 2016; ADASS, 2018; Stevens et al, 2018; DHSC, 2019; Stone, 2019).

References

Allen, R. (2014) The role of the social worker in adult mental health services. Available at https://www.basw.co.uk/system/files/resources/basw_112306-10_0.pdf.

All-Party Parliamentary Group on Social Work (APPG) (2019) *Inquiry report: social work, social workers and a new Mental Health Act.* London: BASW. Available at https://www.basw.co.uk/resources/inquiry-report-all-party-parliamentary-group-appg-social-work-social-workers-and-new.

Association of Directors of Adult Social Services (ADASS) (2018) *National findings: AMHPs – Mental Health Act assessments and the mental health social care workforce.* London: ADASS.

Boardman, J. and Roberts, G. (2014) Risk, safety and recovery: IMROC briefing. Available at https://www.centreformentalhealth.org.uk/publications/risk-safety-and-recovery.

Braun, V. and Clarke, V. (2006) Using thematic analysis in psychology. *Qualitative Research in Psychology*, 3(2), 77–101.

Brown, H. and Hollis, V. (2013) The meaning of occupation, occupational need, and occupational therapy in a military context. *Physical Therapy*, 93, 1244–53.

Bryman, A. (2012) *Social research methods* (4th edn). Oxford: Oxford University Press.

Buckland, R. (2016) The decision by Approved Mental Health Professionals to use compulsory powers under the Mental Health Act 1983: a Foucauldian discourse analysis. *British Journal of Social Work*, 46(1), 46–62.

Care Quality Commission (CQC) (2018) *Mental Health Act: Approved Mental Health Professional services*. London: Care Quality Commission. Available at http://www.cqc.org.uk/publications/themedwork/briefing-mental-health-act-approved-mental-health-professional-services.

Carr, J. (2007) The introduction of new roles under the Mental Health Act 2007. *Mental Health Occupational Therapy*, 12(3), 99–100.

Carson, G. (2018) Approved Mental Health Professional numbers continue to decline, Community Care finds. Available at http://www.communitycare. Co.uk/2018/02/14/approved-mental-health-professional-numbers-continue-decline-community-care-finds/.

Coffey, M. and Hannigan, B. (2013) New roles for nurses as Approved Mental Health Professionals in England and Wales. *International Journal of Nursing Studies*, 50(10), 1423–30.

Craik, C., Chacksfield, D. and Richards, G. (1998) A survey of occupational therapy practitioners in mental health. *British Journal of Occupational Therapy*, 61(5), 227–34.

Creek, J. (2005) Valuing occupational therapy as a complex intervention. *British Journal of Occupational Therapy*, 68(6), 281–4.

Culverhouse, J. and Bibby, P.F. (2008) Occupational therapy and care coordination: the challenges faced by occupational therapists in community mental health settings. *British Journal of Occupational Therapy*, 71(11), 496–8.

Davies, M.B. (2007) *Doing a successful research project: using qualitative or quantitative methods*. Basingstoke: Palgrave Macmillan.

Department of Health (DoH) (2015) *Mental Health Act 1983: Code of Practice*. London: DoH. Available at https://www.gov.uk/government/publications/code-of-practice-mental-health-act-1983.

Department for Health and Social Care (DHSC) (2018) *Modernising the Mental Health Act: increasing choice, reducing compulsion – final report of the Independent Review of the Mental Health Act 1983*. London: DHSC. Available at https://assets.publishing.service.gov.uk/government/uploads/system/uploads/attachment_data/file/763547/Modernising_the_Mental_Health_Act___increasing_choice__reducing_compulsion___summary_version.pdf.

Department of Health and Social Care (DHSC) (2019) *National workforce plan for Approved Mental Health Professionals (AMHPs)*. London: DHSC. Available at https://www.gov.uk/government/publications/national-workforce-plan-for-approved-mental-health-professionals-amhps.

Dixon, J., Wilkinson-Tough, M., Stone, K. and Laing, J. (2019) Treading a tightrope: professional perspectives on balancing the rights of patients and relatives under the Mental Health Act in England. *Health and Social Care in the Community*, 28(1), 300–8.

Du Feu, M. (2012) What did the OT say to the AMHP? *Professional Social Work*. Available at https://www.basw.co.uk/system/files/resources/basw_21951-10_0.pdf.

Health and Care Professions Council (HCPC) (2013) Standards of proficiency for occupational therapists. Available at https://www.hcpc-uk.org/resources/standards/standards-of-proficiency-occupational-therapists/.

Hemmington, J., Graham, M., Marshall, A., Brammer, A., Stone, K. and Vicary, S. (2021) *Approved Mental Health Professionals, Best Interests Assessors and people with lived experience: an exploration of professional identities and practice – a report prepared for Social Work England*. Sheffield: Social Work England. Available at https://www.socialworkengland.org.uk/media/4046/amhp-bia-research-report.pdf.

Her Majesty's Stationery Office (HMSO) (2008a) *Mental Health Act (Approved Mental Health Professionals) (Approval) Regulations 2008*. London: HMSO. Available at https://www.legislation.gov.uk/uksi/2008/1206/contents/made.

Her Majesty's Stationary Office (HMSO) (2008b) *The mental health (hospital, guardianship and treatment) (England) regulations 2008*. London: HMSO. Available at https://www.legislation.gov.uk/uksi/2008/1184/contents/made.

Karban, K., Sparkes, T., Benson, S., Kilyon, J. and Lawrence, J. (2020) Accounting for social perspectives: an exploratory study of Approved Mental Health Professional practice. *British Journal of Social Work*, 51(1), 1–18.

Kielhofner, G. (2008) *Model of human occupation: theory and application* (4th edn). Philadelphia, PA: Lippincott, Williams & Wilkins.

Knott, G. and Bannigan, K. (2013) A critical review of the Approved Mental Health Professional and occupational therapy. *British Journal of Occupational Therapy*, 76(3), 118–26.

Laing, J., Dixon, J., Stone, K. and Wilkinson-Tough, M. (2018) The nearest relative in the Mental Health Act 2007: still an illusionary and inconsistent safeguard? *Journal of Social Welfare and Family Law*, 40(1), 37–56.

Lama, T.C., Fu, Y. and Davis, J.A. (2021) Exploring the ideal practice for occupational therapists on assertive community treatment teams. *British Journal of Occupational Therapy*, 84(9), 582–90.

Law, M., Cooper, B., Strong, S., Stewart, D., Rigby, P. and Letts, L. (1996) The person-environment-occupation model: a transactive approach to occupational performance. *Canadian Journal of Occupational Therapy*, 63, 9–23.

Leah, C. (2018) *Approved Mental Health Professionals: negotiating dialogic identities as hybrid professionals.* PhD thesis. University of Manchester. Available at https://ethos.bl.uk/OrderDetails.do?uin=uk.bl.ethos.779587.

Leason, K. (2004) Independence under fire. Available at http://www.communitycare.co.uk/Articles/2004/10/07/46549/Independenceunder-fire.htm.

Mattingly, C. (1991) What is clinical reasoning? *American Journal of Occupational Therapy*, 45(11), 979–86.

Mattingly, C. and Fleming, M.H. (1994) *Clinical reasoning: forms of inquiry in a therapeutic practice.* Philadelphia, PA: F.A. Davis.

Neistadt, M.E. (1996) Teaching strategies for the development of clinical reasoning. *American Journal of Occupational Therapy*, 50(8), 676–84.

Pilgrim, D. (2020) *Key concepts in mental health* (5th edn). London: Sage.

Royal College of Occupational Therapists (RCOT) (2010) *Recovering ordinary lives: the strategy for occupational therapy in mental health services 2007–2017 – a vision for the next ten years.* London: RCOT. Available at https://www.rcot.co.uk/sites/default/files/ROL-results-update.pdf.

Royal College of Occupational Therapists (RCOT) (2016a) *Care Act 2014: guidance for occupational therapists – prevention.* London: RCOT.

Royal College of Occupational Therapists (RCOT) (2016b) The College of Occupational Therapists' Improving Lives Saving Money campaign. Available at https://www.rcot.co.uk/promoting-occupational-therapy/occupational-therapy-improving-lives-saving-money.

Royal College of Occupational Therapists (RCOT) (2017) Adult mental health fact sheet. Available at https://www.rcot.co.uk/files/adult-mental-healthpdf.

Royal College of Occupational Therapists (RCOT) (2018a) *Embracing risk; enabling choice: guidance for occupational therapists* (3rd edn). London: RCOT.

Royal College of Occupational Therapists (RCOT) (2018b) *Getting my life back: occupational therapy, promoting mental health and wellbeing in England.* London: RCOT. Available at https://www.rcot.co.uk/sites/default/files/Getting-my-life-back_England.pdf.

Royal College of Occupational Therapists (RCOT) (2021) *Professional standards for occupational therapy practice, conduct and ethics.* Available at https://www.rcot.co.uk/publications/professional-standards-occupational-therapy-practice-conduct-and-ethics.

Skills for Care (2019) *The state of the adult social care sector and workforce in England.* Available at www.skillsforcare.org.uk/stateof.

Skills for Care (2021) *The Approved Mental Health Professional workforce in the adult social care sector.* Available at https://www.skillsforcare.org.uk/Adult-Social-Care-Workforce-Data/Workforce-intelligence/documents/AMHPs-Briefing.pdf.

Stevens, M.J., Martineau, S.J., Manthorpe, J., Steils, N. and Norrie, C.M. (2018) *Who wants to be an Approved Mental Health Professional?* London: Social Care Workforce Research Unit, King's College London.

Stone, K. (2016) *Decisions on risk and mental health hospital admission by Approved Mental Health Professionals.* Thesis. University of Bristol.

Stone, K. (2019) Approved Mental Health Professionals and detention: an exploration of professional differences and similarities. *Practice*, 31(2), 83–96.

Tew, J. (ed.) (2005) *Social perspectives in mental health: developing social models to understand and work with mental distress*. London: Jessica Kingsley.

Tew, J. (2011) *Social approaches to mental distress*. Basingstoke: Palgrave Macmillan.

Vicary, S., Young, A. and Hicks, S. (2019) 'Role over' or Roll over? Dirty work, shift and Mental Health Act assessments. *British Journal of Social Work*, 49, 2187–206.

Watson, D. (2016) Becoming an approved mental health professional: an analysis of the factors that influence individuals to become Approved Mental Health Professionals. *Journal of Mental Health*, 25(4), 310–14.

10

Nurses as AMHPs: from 'unclean' to 'honorary social worker'

Sarah Vicary

Introduction

Since 2000, government policy in relation to mental health professionals in England and Wales has been underpinned by a growing trend towards integration, a development based on the belief that most roles can be fulfilled by any profession, irrespective of professional background, profession-specific education and professional identity. Two broad policies encapsulate this development: New Ways of Working in Mental Health (DoH, 2007; NIMH, 2008), an England-wide programme whose rationale is the extension of professional roles and promotion of the sharing of knowledge, skills and competences. In parallel, driven by the belief that the number of eligible professionals were decreasing at the same time as the work was increasing (Huxley, Evans, Gately et al, 2005; Huxley, Evans, Webber et al, 2005), reform of mental health legislation in England and Wales has resulted in the reconfiguration of certain statutory mental health roles by opening them up to other non-medical professions.

One such statutory role, the Approved Mental Health Professional (AMHP), is now extended to mental health nurses. Under the pre-reformed legislation, social workers fulfilled the equivalent role exclusively. In addition to nurses, the role is also now open to occupational therapists and psychologists. An AMHP is responsible for making a decision about, and being the applicant for, the formal detention in hospital of a person with a mental disorder. The assessment of mental disorder is part of a medical decision carried out by the eligible doctor(s) who recommend hospital admission based on this opinion, and in accordance with the Mental Health Act 1983 (MHA) (DoH, 2015). The role involves the coordination of the assessment process, while considering and dealing with the person's social and domestic circumstances, and is underpinned by an independent, non-medical perspective (Manktelow et al, 2002; HMSO, 2008).

Background

The change in legislation has had a mixed response; it is seen by some as providing an opportunity for nurses to develop professionally (Hurley and Linsley, 2007). However, the impact on independence of decision making has been queried, with others contending that nurses might be more likely to defer to, rather than challenge doctors (Haynes, 1990; Quirk et al, 2000; Walton, 2000), a contention that also suggests that social workers maintain independence of medical influence (Davidson and Campbell, 2010). It is argued that being trained in the social sciences, social workers are best placed to understand the social dimensions of a person's circumstances, such as the impact of poverty on mental well-being (Hatfield, 2008). Nurses themselves report fears that AMHP work would impact negatively on their therapeutic relationship with patients (Hurley and Linsley, 2007). The opening up of the AMHP role has therefore given rise to the concern expressed at the time of its inception that it would not be fulfilled as envisaged (Rapaport, 2006; Gregor, 2010).

Hughes (1971) contends that every profession, including mental health, is underpinned by status – that is, is the notion that some professions are more desirable than others and fulfilled by those who are accepted, by peers, into them. There are competing views about the status of AMHPs and their predecessors: one is about it being an elite role; the other is that it is not a desired role, but 'dirty' (Morriss, 2015). Using binary constructs of difference, where dirt is 'matter out of place' and clean is 'ordered arrangement' (Douglas, 1966, p 36), a long-standing sociological theory, dirty work, has been applied to professional identity and its nature. This concept also concerns exploring the frontier between the roles of doctor and nurse, and how such boundaries change or are 're-sorted' (Hughes, 1971, p 314; Vicary et al, 2019).

This chapter seeks to address the question of whether professional identity has any impact on compulsory decision making in light of extending a statutory role to mental health nurses.

Methods

The data upon which this chapter is based heralds from a larger study examining the AMHP role from the viewpoint of those fulfilling it in order to explore whether professional identity has any impact on role fulfilment (Vicary, 2016). The study was underpinned by the methodological approach of interpretative phenomenological analysis (IPA) (after Smith, 1996), a methodology committed to the examination of how people make sense of major life experiences (Smith et al, 2009, p 1). IPA seeks to understand the person's own experience, the meaning they make of it and, crucially, the interpretation the researcher makes of the person's meaning. This process is regarded as central to knowledge making and is referred to as the 'double hermeneutic' (Smith and Osborn, 2003). Two further reasons support the use of IPA for this study: that identity is one of the main constructs to have emerged (Smith, 2011) and that it 'fits' exploration of the comprehensive experience (Smith et al, 2009, p 205). The focus of this chapter is the comprehensive experience of nurse AMHPs.

What follows are the findings that emerged: a four-stage process illustrated with verbatim quotes from participants. As befits the double hermeneutic, this framework is an interpretation by the researcher making meaning of what participants were saying and not a conscious self-presentation by the participants.

Findings

Stage one: convergence – 'there's no difference'

At the outset of the analysis, nurse participants perceive their non–AMHP role as like that of social workers. One nurse participant has no doubt that these two professions converge:

> There's no, I mean to be honest I am a nurse by training, but I'm not particularly bothered what I am. I'm not. (Nurse 03)

He repeats this assertion:

> I'm not really bothered what my role is. I've got a nursing ticket, but I wouldn't say I was particularly proud to be anything, I just come to work and get on with it. (Nurse 03)

According to him, the one difference between a nurse and a social worker is the ability to administer medication:

> My argument is why be so fiercely loyal to your role and your profession? Why, what is it? Because, essentially, we are all in it, we are all doing the same thing, it's just I can go to the med … there's a couple of social workers in our team and the only difference between mine and their job is that I can go to the medicine cabinet and get some tablets out, it's no different other than that. (Nurse 03)

This, seemingly inconsequential, difference is also echoed by a second nurse participant who is surprised to recall that a colleague is not the same profession:

> I often forget [name] is a social worker because she's the only social worker here, but her role isn't really much different from any of our roles. I mean, the only way I see difference between that is medication. (Nurse 05)

Again, apart from dealing with medication, she sees no difference between nurses and social workers. She even goes on to exuberantly welcome such changes as she calls for it to be 'brought on':

> Much like social workers you know. There again looking at the social aspects with the family stuff like that, but they don't deal

with medication but as regard[s] the knowledge on clients that are mentally ill, how to manage them, the plan of care and stuff, bring it on. (Nurse 05)

During this initial transition stage, the sense made by mental health nurse AMHPs about the relationship between a mental health nurse not in the AMHP role and social work is shown as a convergence.

However, through further analysis and interpretation these same nurses begin to make sense of fulfilling the AMHP role as mental health nurses, and go on to acknowledge the need to overcome divergence. They make sense of this shift, in the words of one participant, by moving from unclean to honorary, or clean.

Stage two: overcoming divergence: from 'unclean' to 'honorary social worker'

One nurse participant suggests that, even though he is a qualified nurse, the AMHP role is attractive to him because he is not a typical nurse. In other words, in order to fulfil the AMHP role, he has to adopt attributes different to a typical nurse:

> I really enjoyed it really enjoyed it because it's, although I'm a nurse – don't know if we are coming to this later – but although I'm a nurse, I'm not your typical nurse. (Nurse 03)

He is attracted to the AMHP role because it aligns closely with the social model of care, adding that because of this he enjoys doing it:

> I mean, I enjoy it. It's something I'd looked at doing erm 'cause the reason I worked in assertive outreach teams. It was a very social model of care anyway. (Nurse 03)

Similarly, a different nurse participant at first perceives what she does as an AMHP as 'just an assessment' and thereby an equivalent or extension of their usual role:

> Assessments are assessments. I think they are our bread and butter, we've done them for years and the assessment is what it is. The assessment isn't a hard part of my life. An assessment, or an AMHP assessment, to me isn't a huge problem because it's what I do day in and day out and I'm comfortable with doing assessments. (Nurse 05)

For this nurse participant, when undertaking her AMHP training she reports her surprise at having been advised that, in order to fulfil it, she would have to 'change hats'. The implication being that there would be a difference in the way in which she fulfilled the AMHP role:

> When I first was doing my AMHP training I used to go out with these
> AMHPs, one of them in particular, we used to do these assessments
> and she'd be saying to me, "Right, put your AMHP hat on now
> when you do this assessment", and I'd go in and I'd be sitting there
> thinking me AMHP hat, me AMHP hat. Does that mean I have to
> do my assessment any differently? (Nurse 05)

The hat analogy is used again by the same participant, but this time she *contradicts*
her earlier claim. On this occasion she feels that, when she is being an AMHP,
she must put on a different hat:

> Yeah, the AMHP hat on – yes to me it isn't a different hat. (Nurse 05)

During this stage of the transition as a nurse AMHP, this participant is changed.
She is not the same nurse fulfilling a different role, but she is assuming a
different professional identity. For her, the difference is based on value-driven
considerations. Even though she was aware of matters such as human rights
previously as a nurse, these considerations had not, for her, been to the forefront.
This is a divergence; her former professional identity as a nurse must be overcome
in order to fulfil the role of the AMHP:

> I say you had a better awareness of, because nurses really you know
> about the Human Rights Act and it's always there in the background,
> but you don't really work with it on a day-to-day basis as in it's not
> there. It's in the background and you are aware of it, social workers
> are aware of it and work with it more, but we don't when I did my
> AMHP training. That, it's at the front instead of at the back after
> that. (Nurse 05)

A different nurse participant describes the difficulty she first experienced in what
for her was the need, psychologically and cognitively, to separate out nursing in
order to fulfil the AMHP role:

> At first, I did have difficulty separating in my own head the two roles
> I did think going with my AMHP head on today. (Nurse 04)

She also describes social workers in a similar position:

> And I know of social workers who think the same thing: I am going
> in with my AMHP head on, not social worker. (Nurse 04)

For her, the difference between the social worker as an AMHP is much
less than that of the nurse as an AMHP; the need to forefront principle-
driven considerations:

But the difference is more advanced between the nurse role and the AMHP role, because the principles between the AMHP role and the social work role are quite similar, whereas it's quite poles apart really from nursing assessment. (Nurse 04)

One other nurse participant recounts their initial experience of AMHP training. Here, she reports on the apparent coincidence that had occurred when she and other, unknown nurse colleagues had unwittingly sat next to each other:

When I did my AMHP training there was me and three other nurses and I trained at [place name] where there was only a small group, 12 of us; 8 social workers and the rest nurses and, interestingly, on the very first day when we walked in nobody knew anybody and all the nurses sat together. (Nurse 02)

She at first makes light of this, musing as to whether nurses can sense each other, or 'give off vibes', and similarly wonders whether social workers are certain types:

Whether it was because we were all giving off the same sort of vibes or whether social workers are a certain type of people, but we don't know, but yeah, they did say it was quite funny. (Nurse 02)

However, she also recalls the initial attitude of the trainers and her belief that she and nursing colleagues were almost treated as outsiders, or 'unclean':

Tutors would come into the room and say, "I believe we have some nurses present", and it was almost as if we were unclean, unclean and we had to identify ourselves. (Nurse 02)

Nonetheless, this initial reception of the nurses changed once they had 'proved' themselves and were thereafter referred to as 'honorary social workers', as if they had been accepted into a special grouping:

Although certain nurses have proved themselves and they call us honorary social workers. (Nurse 02)

The sense this nurse participant is making of being initially considered as an outsider is also recalled when she reports some social workers as being 'quite confrontational' and 'unhappy' when first aware that the AMHP role was to be extended to mental health nurses:

I know a lot of social workers do actually say to me, and quite openly say to me, that they weren't happy when they first found out [that nurses were eligible to train as AMHPs]. (Nurse 02)

Entering favoured company is also described by a different nurse participant. Here, fulfilling the AMHP role is not nursing in its traditional sense, rather it is undertaking social work and being afforded such parity, or being allowed entrance into a special group alliance:

> It's not nursey nursing, we are honorary social workers. (Nurse 02)

Overcoming divergence is central to the sense mental health nurses make of their AMHP experience. In order to fulfil the role of the AMHP they feel that they must be accepted as 'honorary' social workers and assume aspects of a professional role not usually expected of nurses. This transition is made sense of by one nurse participant as moving from 'unclean' to 'honorary social workers'. This ascription of the role as honorary, or special, launders what is perceived as dirty into that which is clean and in turn demonstrates the impact that role fulfilment has on the professional identity of the nurse.

However, to extend the analogy further, once clean these same nurses use the AMHP role to challenge the traditional nurse–doctor relationship and ultimately the AMHP role itself. Such praxis is a new understanding of the impact of role fulfilment.

Stage three: change to medical processes – nurses as AMHPs

The traditional, and arguably deferential, relationship between nurses and doctors might suggest that the former will not be 'properly' able to fulfil the AHMP role. This is illustrated when participants discuss the specific relationship with doctors and is reported by one nurse participant when she recalls her initial failure to be supported to train:

> I, initially, was unsuccessful in my interview to do the AMHP training first time around. I applied and it was a different lead AMHP and she was less accommodating of nurse AMHPs nurses doing their AMHP training and she did actually say to me, she didn't ask me, she did say to me in the interview, "You know, as a nurse you would find it extremely difficult to disagree with a consultant", which I thought was a bit presumptuous really. (Nurse 02)

The participant goes on to point out what for her is the irony of this misguided opinion. She makes sense of her role as an AMHP when she challenges previous practice or, in other words, the praxis influences her professional identity. She feels that now as an AMHP, she challenges doctors, more so than some of her social work AMHP colleagues – albeit she puts this ability to confront down to individual personalities, rather than a particular professional identity:

And, ironically, I feel I do challenge doctors now a lot more than certain social workers, but I don't think that's anything to do with them being social workers, I think that's to do with people's personalities. (Nurse 02)

According to her, other professionals almost expect that she as a nurse will go along with what the doctor says and, moreover, that this acquiescence would be unquestioned:

[During] assessments on inpatient units I think there's kind of, because there's an expectation [that because] I am from a nursing background that there is going to an automatic, that I will go along with. (Nurse 02)

Another nurse participant repeats her sense that nurses based in inpatient settings believe that she will fulfil her AMHP role in a different way to social workers because of her nurse identity. The perception is that she will have a perspective that aligns with the doctor:

From all, I think perhaps more with the nursing staff from the environment where I have previously worked, although there has been a number of years so I have not really worked with any of the staff on the inpatient units, but I think it is the background where they are from – that there is more expectation that you will view it quite different from a nursing background than a social worker. (Nurse 04)

The same participant reflects on the nursing role and believes that it remains influenced by the medical model. Fulfilling the AMHP role requires the need to overcome this influence:

I think it's very much more medicalised, the nursing role. As much as we say we are going to move away from that, and there has been, but doing this makes me realise we are not as moved away as you think and there is still quite a focus on medication, particularly in terms of treatment and admission to hospital. (Nurse 04)

For her, nurses when fulfilling the AMHP role challenge medical processes. She provides two instances. First, the conduct of assessment interviews. In her experience as a nurse, it had been a doctor who has led this process, but as an AMHP this role is reversed:

In terms of the interview itself, because previously from a nurse background it's kind of been the doctor that's led the assessment, because obviously [for] the Mental Health Act assessment it's the

AMHP that introduces the situation and speaks first and explains the proceedings. (Nurse 04)

Second, her professional identity when fulfilling the AMHP role is based on the different perspective between herself and the doctor:

So again, that was quite a shift from what I was previously used to. And then the questions are obviously different, which, to be fair, I did expect because the information that's required to do, with the perspective you are doing the assessment from. (Nurse 04)

This participant also believes she has moved away from the traditional nurse identity and is willing instead to consider other value-driven options, a shift for her:

I am now much more aware in doing assessment[s] as alternatives to that and least restrictive and trying [the] least restrictive option first. (Nurse 04)

Albeit subtly, the transition stage has now gone beyond being honorary, or clean. In effect, the praxis of role fulfilment influences professional identity and shows the use of this to challenge or re-sort traditional role boundaries.

Stage four: changes to the AMHP role: nurses as AMHPs

In stage four a nurse participant makes sense of differences she perceives between nursing and being a nurse AMHP. The latter, she feels, is more aligned to social work:

Things happen when you work with a nurse professional and when you've got them coming in a particular role, [which] previously was a social work role, they still kind of think to a certain extent it is very much the AMHP role that they have to do, not the nursing role, I think. (Nurse 04)

But this is not to suggest that this nurse always believes that when social workers fulfil the AMHP role they do so correctly. She recalls a first observed MHA assessment as a trainee AMHP, and in particular her sense of shock at the different working practices she experienced, on this occasion relating to safety:

First thing was when we did an assessment on an inpatient ward. Whereas previously from a nurse background the first thing you think about is where you are positioned in the room and you always make sure that you are the person nearest the door, but then when

> we went in the practice assessor I was with just walked into the room and walked down to the bottom of the room and sat down, which took me aback a bit because, as I say, we make sure that our chairs were positioned nearest the door, so I found that different. (Nurse 04)

She attempts to explain this sense of shock by viewing the positioning as perhaps more relaxed for the person being assessed, but nonetheless, given that this was in a psychiatric intensive care unit (PICU), she remained surprised. For her, safety should dictate such practices. She therefore begins to question this instance of the AMHP role as fulfilled by a social worker:

> I mean I could see it from both views. It was more relaxing for the person in that somebody goes in and it's more comfortable and walks down and sits rather than looking where they are positioning themselves, but then it was on a PICU so there's, I was also thinking obviously there are reasons why this person is on a PICU, there's that side. (Nurse 04)

This example is therefore illustrative of how the praxis of role fulfilment for this nurse is beginning to challenge how the AMHP role itself is fulfilled.

Discussion

To begin, nurse participants discuss convergence – that is, a belief there is a generic mental health professional role undertaken in the same way, irrespective of professional background. As such, this would suggest that integration, as encapsulated in the policy drive New Ways of Working (NIMH, 2008), is substantiated and strengthens the proposed opening up of the AMHP role (Huxley and Kerfoot, 1994; DoH, 1999). However, in the interpretation of participants making sense of their experiences as AMHPs, the need to overcome difference emerges, not least the adoption of a professional perspective more akin to social work. This second stage of transition therefore involves overcoming divergence. By putting a name on value-driven considerations, attributes are described that, while present in nursing, are not at the forefront. Such understanding would need to be acknowledged in the training and development of nurse AMHPs and assuage the doubt that non-social work AMHPs could fulfil the social perspective (Rapaport, 2006; Hatfield, 2008). In addition, the interpretation shows that participants change key aspects of orientation in their original professional identity; nurse AMHP role fulfilment involves value-driven considerations, attributes now foregrounded. The praxis of role fulfilment is shown to influence professional identity.

Participants experience the AMHP role as moving from being typical to atypical nurses; or, in the words of one participant, from 'unclean' to 'honorary social workers'. This ascription of the role as honorary, or special, launders matter out of place into that which is accepted or clean, indicating acceptance by peers and providing further evidence of the competing notions of status in AMHP work as understood through the concept of dirty work (Morriss, 2015). As such, the binary concepts of dirty and clean (Douglas, 1966) underpin the praxis of role fulfilment by nurse AMHPs and provide valuable insights into how the fulfilment of the role impacts on professional identity.

Participants also go beyond this acceptance, as emerges in the third stage. This finding is of note since it suggests that the AMHP role has influence on professional identity, rather than the reverse, as was originally hypothesised. 'Re-sorting' (Hughes, 1971) of role boundaries is shown in the characteristics and behaviours of nurses as AMHPs. This finding is ironic; when the AMHP role was extended, one fear expressed was that nurses in particular would automatically defer to a medical lead (Haynes, 1990; Quirk et al, 2000; Walton, 2000). Participants are shown to experience a significant change from how they usually relate to doctors, and this is engendered by fulfilling the role. Their questioning of AMHP practice in this third stage is a fundamental illustration of nurses fulfilling the AMHP role. This new relationship boundary is a behaviour that is a change to the expected nurse–doctor deference and represents a new way of working – albeit maybe not as originally envisaged in the New Ways of Working initiative (NIMH, 2008).

Finally, interpretation shows that nurses are beginning to challenge the way in which the AMHP role is accomplished, thereby potentially creating a different way of working for all AMHPs. This finding challenges the notion that AMHP work is exclusive to social work and thereby starts to introduce new ways of working, regardless of professional background; however, this finding requires further enquiry due to the relative newness of nurse AMHPs. More insights will be gained once they have fulfilled this role over a longer period. A progression of the study upon which this chapter is based, therefore, would be to revisit longer-term nurse AMHPs and to examine other mental health roles that have been subject to similar legislative reconfiguration, such as the Approved Clinician.

Conclusion

In this chapter a four-stage process of the impact of role fulfilment on professional identity is provided, beginning with the notion that professions converge. However, in making sense of the fulfilment of the AMHP role participants describe a shift from 'unclean' to 'honorary social worker'. Overcoming divergence in this way is required for acceptance of nurses into the AMHP role by their social work peers. To extend the analogy, once clean, nurse AMHPs begin to 're-sort' the traditional nurse–doctor relationship and the beginnings of a challenge to the AMHP role, as it is ordinarily perceived, emerges. The transition from 'unclean' to 'honorary social worker', and beyond, demonstrates a change in professional identity and also its reverse – the impact professional identity has on role fulfilment. As such, this is a new understanding of the influence of professional identity on decision making. The relevance for practice is that the education and development of mental health nurses should forefront the social perspective, thereby assuaging any doubt that such value-driven considerations can be fulfilled by this professional group; that mental health nurses when undertaking statutory roles can be accepted by social work peers as being able to do so; and that when undertaking statutory roles, mental health nurses change the traditional medical–nurse relationship and boundary, and may even undertake such roles in a way that challenges the original perception of them.

References

Davidson, G. and Campbell, J. (2010) An audit of assessment and reporting by Approved Social Workers (ASWs). *British Journal of Social Work*, 40, 1609–72.

Department of Health (DoH) (1999) *Review of the Mental Health Act 1983: report of the expert committee*. London: DoH.

Department of Health (DoH) (2007) *New ways of working for everyone: a best practice implementation guide*. London: DoH.

Department of Health (DoH) (2015) *Mental Health Act 1983: Code of Practice*. London: DoH.

Douglas, M. (1966) *Purity and danger: an analysis of concepts of purity and taboo*. London: Routledge and Kegan Paul.

Gregor, C. (2010) Unconscious aspects of statutory mental health work: emotional labour and the Approved Mental Health Professional. *Journal of Social Work Practice*, 24, 429–3.

Hatfield, B. (2008) Powers to detain under mental health legislation in England and the role of the Approved Social Worker: an analysis of patterns and trends under the 1983 Mental Health Act in six local authorities. *British Journal of Social Work*, 38, 1553–71.

Haynes, R. (1990) After 1983: Approved Social Workers' perceptions of their changing role in emergency psychiatric assessments. *Practice: Social Work in Action*, 4(3), 184–98.

Her Majesty's Stationery Office (HMSO) (2008) *The Mental Health (Approved Mental Health Professionals) (Approval) (England) Regulations*. London: HMSO. Available at https://www.legislation.gov.uk/uksi/2008/1206/contents/made.

Hughes, E. (1971) *The sociological eye: selected papers*. Chicago, IL: Aldine Atherton.

Hurley, J. and Linsley, P. (2007) Expanding roles within mental health legislation: an opportunity for professional growth or a missed opportunity? *Journal of Psychiatric and Mental Health Nursing*, 14, 535–41.

Huxley, P. and Kerfoot, M. (1994) A survey of Approved Social Work in England and Wales. *British Journal of Social Work*, 24, 311–24.

Huxley, P., Evans, S., Webber, M. and Gately, C. (2005) Staff shortages in the mental health workforce: the case of the disappearing Approved Social Worker. *Health and Social Care in the Community*, 13(6), 504–13.

Huxley, P., Evans, S., Gately, C., Webber, M., Mears, A., Pajak, S. et al (2005) Stress and pressures in mental health social work: the worker speaks. *British Journal of Social Work*, 35, 1063–79.

Manktelow, R., Hughes, P., Britton, F., Campbell, J., Hamilton, B. and Wilson, J. (2002) The experience and practice of Approved Social Workers in Northern Ireland. *British Journal of Social Work*, 32, 443–61.

Morriss, L. (2015) AMHP work: dirty or prestigious? Dirty work designations and the Approved Mental Health Professional. *British Journal of Social Work*, 46(3), 703–18.

National Institute for Mental Health in England (NIMH) (2008) *Mental Health Act 2007: new roles*. London: NIMH.

Quirk, A., Lelliott, P., Audini, B. and Buston, K. (2000) *Performing the Act: a qualitative study of the process of Mental Health Act assessment*. London: Department of Health.

Rapaport, J. (2006) New roles in mental health: the creation of the Approved Mental Health Practitioner. *Journal of Integrated Care*, 14(5), 37–46.

Smith, J.A. (1996) Beyond the divide between cognition and discourse: using interpretative phenomenological analysis in health psychology. *Psychology & Health*, 11(2), 261–71.

Smith, J.A. (2011) Evaluating the contribution of interpretative phenomenological analysis. *Health Psychology Review*, 5, 9–27.

Smith, J.A. and Osborn, M. (2003) Interpretative phenomenological analysis. In J.A. Smith (ed.), *Qualitative psychology: a practical guide to methods* (pp 53–81). London: Sage.

Smith, J.A., Flowers, P. and Larkin, M. (2009) *Interpretative phenomenological analysis: theory, method and research*. London: Sage.

Vicary, S. (2016) *An interpretative phenomenological analysis of the impact of professional background on role fulfilment: a study of approved mental health practice*. Manchester: University of Manchester.

Vicary, S., Young, A. and Hicks, S (2019) 'Role over' or roll over? Dirty work, shift, and Mental Health Act assessments. *British Journal of Social Work*, 9(8), 2178–206.

Walton, P. (2000) Reforming the Mental Health Act 1983: an Approved Social Worker perspective. *Journal of Social Welfare and Family Law*, 22(4), 401–14.

11

Who do you think you are? Hybrid professionals, boundaries and the context of AMHP practice

Caroline Leah

Introduction

This chapter will examine Approved Mental Health Professionals' (AMHPs') practice through the lens of hybrid professionalism (Noordegraaf, 2015). It will consider the role of the AMHP and address how hybridity intersects dynamically with boundary working. AMHPs are hybrid professionals in a number of interrelated ways. First, they cross-cut professional boundaries via the broad knowledge areas they draw upon when they make an independent decision about whether or not to detain an individual under the Mental Health Act 1983 (MHA). This is apparent via AMHPs' application of a biopsychosocial model of mental health, a model that arguably pivots distinctive (yet often contradictory) legal, social, psychological and medical perspectives. Second, hybridity refers to professionals who are of a 'mixed origin' (Gittell et al, 2010). This idea applies to AMHPs as they are drawn from social work, nursing and occupational therapy professional backgrounds. Finally, it applies to professionals who straddle multiple roles, for example a social worker who is an AMHP and a care coordinator. Interprofessional collaboration during MHA assessment further involves AMHPs working in liminal spaces and physical places that other professional groups, such as psychiatrists, traditionally occupy. The main argument that will be progressed throughout the chapter is that AMHPs are a profession of interstitiality; a profession whose job it is to mediate between all others (Leah, 2018).

The context of AMHP practice

The current MHA White Paper (DHSC, 2021) is the UK government's response to the review of the MHA published in 2018 (DHSC, 2018). It advocates for a systematic and radical reform to the way individuals are supported during an acute relapse of their mental health condition. Although the White Paper offers a welcomed opportunity to enhance the autonomy of individuals subject to the MHA, providing more rights and aiming to minimise detention, it fails to recognise the limitations of professionals working in resource-constrained environments, underpinned by years of economic austerity (Karban et al, 2021). Additionally, the review has been criticised for failing to acknowledge the broad-scale reconfigurations in the English and Welsh health and social care system, which are themselves situated in larger international sociopolitical arenas that influence how professional work is operationalised by those individuals undertaking multiple professional roles (Noordegraaf, 2015). Growing political and public concerns about mental health services have fuelled debates about the pressures and tensions involved in public sector delivery for AMHPs, and the burdens they experience through the perceived interference in the role during multidisciplinary working. This includes the prolonged impact on service users from a lack of resources (for example the reduction in psychiatric inpatient beds) and on the ability of AMHPs to undertake the AMHP role effectively due to the limited financial investment from government in resourcing the numbers of AMHPs (Leah, 2018; Stevens et al, 2018; Bonnet and Moran, 2020).

It is commonplace for AMHPs to routinely undertake several generic roles, including acting as care coordinators under the Care Programme Approach (DoH, 2008), having the opportunity to become an Approved Clinician (s 135, MHA), or a Best Interests Assessor, or undertaking leadership roles as senior mental health practitioners or managers. Both the complexity of specific social care roles and the broadening out of professionals occupying multiple roles are modern features of health and social care organisations, which are enforced and enacted at institutional, group and individual levels in contemporary society (Noordegraaf, 2015; Leah, 2020) and illustrate hybrid professionalism.

The erosion and marginalisation of mental health social work and that of the AMHP has received much attention from scholars who argue that it is a core concern, even going so far as to suggest it has become an identity crisis, particularly when AMHPs are situated in healthcare trusts with larger numbers of health professionals within mixed professional teams (Rapaport and Manthorpe, 2008; Nathan and Webber, 2010; Allen, 2014; Morriss, 2016). Despite the promotion of multi-professional teamwork there is still a degree of hesitancy by colleagues valuing other team members from different professions, particularly as health professionals are viewed as protagonists of the medical model (Nathan and Webber, 2010). These features of professional marginalisation are symbolic of the marginalisation of the social perspective within mental health organisations, and the dominance of National Health Service (NHS) agendas and medical professionals within integrated social and health structures (Nathan and Webber, 2010). These issues have influenced how the roles of the Approved Social Worker (ASW) and latterly the AMHP have been understood, and provide an important context for understanding the ways in which AMHPs enact hybrid professionalism as hybrid professionals and as boundary workers (Noordegraaf, 2015; Leah, 2018). Such issues include a consideration of how AMHPs' commitment to a value base of social justice and human rights can be reconciled with the types of mental health practice dominated by health and managerialist concerns.

Hybridity definitions

Hybridity is a complex concept and subject to numerous interpretations. Hybrid professionals are perceived as occupying both hybrid roles and complex professional identities (Croft et al, 2015; Spyridonidis et al, 2015), with hybridity further signifying the liminal space between two or more original approaches (Croft et al, 2015). Although scholars' definitions of hybridity and their empirical conceptualisations offer different positions on its manifestation, one key area of agreement is that hybrid professionals merge different and potentially contradictory sets of values and ideological positions (Croft et al, 2015; Noordegraaf, 2015).

One consequence of the reforms to the MHA introduced in 2007 was the professionalisation of AMHPs. The term 'professional' entered the AMHP title from the previous ASW title. AMHPs therefore became a new form of public professional. When professional associations are successful in (re)making a new professional, as witnessed by the change from the ASW to AMHP role, the enactment of change can provoke changes in jurisdictional boundaries and how a role is practised (Noordegraaf and Van der Meulen, 2008). Noordegraaf (2007) presents a useful analytical framework for summarising reconfigurations in the professionals he identified from differing and broad professional areas, including social workers, one of the primary professional backgrounds from which AMHPs are predominantly drawn. Noordegraaf (2007) categorised professionals into a typology comprising 'pure' ('pure, pressured, purified'), 'situated' and 'hybrid' ('hybridised' and 'mixed-up').

The concept of concern here is that of the 'hybrid professional', defined by a focus on professionals who are reflective practitioners (for example Schön's [1983] managers) and broadened out to include a less restricted use of the term that values 'artistic, intuitive processes which some practitioners do bring to situations of uncertainty, instability, uniqueness and values conflict' (Schön, 1983, p 49). The 'hybrid professional' is a relational concept, which requires 'interdisciplinary knowledge and interactive skills' (Noordegraaf, 2007, p 775).

Hybrid professionals are arguably adept at operating within ambiguous public domains. They have hybridised knowledge that enables them to cross traditional role boundaries when working for hybrid organisations (for example health and social care trusts in the UK). Additionally, their work is malleable, in that it shows a nuanced response to contextual factors. Significantly, 'their links with outside worlds are part of their professionalism' (Noordegraaf, 2007, p 771).

Hybridised professionalism is a means of bridging 'expertise-induced gaps between professional control and managerial control' (Noordegraaf, 2007, p 776). AMHPs, for example, are required to operate under market-orientated conditions, so that notions of professionalism enacted through daily practice encompass performance measurement – a form of managerial control to preserve the ongoing professional socialisation of roles (Evetts, 2006, p 137). Hybrid professionalism incorporates a way of controlling complexity, ambiguity and the contested professional domains where role boundaries can be blurred – for example, AMHPs persuading bed managers for access to local psychiatric beds, a duty formally given to psychiatrists but found to be requested by AMHPs (Leah, 2018). This is when professional practice becomes positioned within resource-constrained environments that are managed, restraining the opportunities for professionals to exercise autonomy.

The often uneasy elements of the contested nature of organisational control require professional hybrids to balance decisions that include a consideration of the imposition of efficiency, financial and resource agendas on their practice (Flynn, 2004). Work that involves dealing with 'trade-offs' is a common feature, arising from coping with service users' needs in the face of financial constraints and reduced capacities, and as a response to the uncertainties experienced in contemporary life, in risk societies (Evetts, 2006; 2013). It comprises professionals' ability to manage risk-based decisions (Noordegraaf, 2007).

Hybrid professionals also have influence within the complex organisations they work for and have been found to be 'lords of the dance' because they are able to influence changes in institutional arrangements (Scott, 2008). This is partly due to hybrid professionals' areas of expertise; such expertise involves practice knowledge that cross-cuts traditional boundaries (Noordegraaf, 2007; McGivern et al, 2015; Spyridonidis et al, 2015). Due to these changes in how professionals and their professionalism can be conceptualised, links can be made to AMHPs occupying multiple roles that are nested within the legally defined role (Leah, 2020).

Blomgren and Waks' (2015, p 79) definition of hybrid professionals as 'professionals who operate within broad knowledge areas, who have developed competence outside of their main area of expertise … in situations characterised by institutional complexity', where work cross-cuts multiple organisations and intersects with several disciplines, for example psychiatry and law, was applied as the main definition in the author's AMHP research study, which will be subsequently discussed within the chapter, using illustrative verbatim excerpts to demonstrate AMHPs as hybrid professionals.

Hybridity is therefore a concept that can illuminate professional roles in the ways it speaks to formations of new professional identities, the mixing of multiple identities and how professional roles could be hybridised through boundary working. In summary, notions of hybrid professionals are 'highly relevant in mixed occupations' (Noordegraaf, 2015) such as AMHPs, where meaningful connections are required between service users' public and private domains, where issues are 'soft' and there are multifaceted interactions that require linking 'street-level work' with organisational and professional worlds (Lipsky, 1980).

Professional role(s) and boundaries of practice

Professional roles are best understood in context, and this includes the policy context in which a profession delivers its key functions and duties (DHSC, 2018). There are key events illuminated in policy, legislation and commentaries that impact on AMHP practice. Legislative changes, policies, research and commentaries highlight the pressures placed on AMHPs through increases in workloads, the dismantling of community resources and a reducing workforce (McNicholl, 2015; ADASS, 2018). They highlight a profession that straddles boundaries due to various intentions for generic practices.

Although AMHPs have a fixed role and coherent jurisdiction in terms of making applications for detention into a psychiatric hospital, they cross-cut several jurisdictional boundaries, specified as legal, bureaucratic, social and administrative in nature (Rapaport, 2006). These boundaries are spaces of interprofessional action and tensions. The spaces show how the AMHP role is more than a legally defined professional role within which AMHPs employ narratives that are both congruent and incongruent. AMHPs indeed occupy multifarious roles (Quirk et al, 2000; Rapaport, 2006; Gregor, 2010; Morriss, 2014; 2015; 2016; Leah, 2020).

Research by Morriss (2017) extended the concept of the multifarious roles AMHPs inhabit by considering the ways social work AMHPs work in liminal, and often invisible spaces, occupying the gaps left by other professions. One of her participants, Eva,[1] is quoted as saying:

> It's a job about so many hats, isn't it? It is quite difficult to say what we do and err perhaps you get the feeling that what we do is paper up the gaps in all the other professionals, the bits that are complicated or tricky that's the bits that, "Oh we'll get the social worker to do that", and that's what we do [laughs]. (Morriss, 2017, p 1349)

This is similar to the author's study (Leah, 2018), where Diana described the AMHP role as 'sweeping up the odds and ends' to signify the unfinished business that is not part of the legal role that AMHPs routinely undertake. Diana's statement signified the pragmatic parts of the role, such as arranging for pets to be cared for, packing clothes for a person's hospital stay, or securing an individual's property following MHA detention. The multifarious roles AMHPs enacted were researched via semi-structured interviews with AMHPs from social work, nursing and occupational therapy primary professional backgrounds (Leah, 2020). AMHPs were found to occupy multiple roles (for example 'quasi-judge', 'custodian of social justice', 'advocate') (Leah, 2020), and this was important for examining conceptualisations of AMHPs as hybrid professionals and the ways AMHPs could benefit from hybridisation in their professional practice.

AMHPs have been granted 'jurisdictional autonomy' (Abbott, 1988) by law and this is used for standardising knowledge, skills, values for selecting and training members and by enforcing codes of professional conduct. These are examples of the *structuring* features of professional roles. Thus, to be professional, to enact a professional role, is to feel part of a certain professional field; it is not only functional but also normative, relational and institutionalised, influenced by power and control in the professional arena.

Places in which AMHPs undertake their work are not static locations, because their work takes place in organisations and places controlled by other professionals belonging to other establishments, such as in residential homes, hospitals, police stations, prisons, accident and emergency (A&E) departments and within the private domain of individuals' homes. AMHPs are part of broad networks comprising individuals, teams, services and organisations. They interface with users of these services and in the complex environment around them. AMHPs do have autonomous decision-making duties enshrined in law, which Evetts (2013, p 786) suggests is 'part of the appeal (or ideology) of professionalism'. Such contextual factors 'call for an ambivalent understanding of present-day professionalism' (Noordegraaf, 2007, p 771). Professionalism can be perceived to be both pluralistic and individualistic, comprising the attitudes and behaviour an individual possesses towards their own profession, with performance indicators via management structures that monitor accountability, a key component of professionalism in contemporary knowledge-based societies (Evetts, 2013). Thus, for professionalism to be meaningful it must illuminate the everyday practice realties of the professional enacting a professional role.

Boundary working

While hybrid professionals operate within broad knowledge areas and have competence perceived by others as being outside of their primary area of expertise, boundary spanners are professionals operating at the boundaries of their organisation, mediating between it and wider societal structures. Boundary spanners work together with other professionals, to assess and manage risk (Nissen, 2010; Beech, 2011; Oliver, 2013). A key component of the boundary spanner is their ability to integrate different perspectives into their practice through interprofessional dialogue that involves negotiating shared goals and meanings (Williams, 2002; Nissen, 2010; Beech, 2011; Oliver, 2013).

AMHPs boundary-work both between organisations and other professionals attending to the whole system, while dealing with its comprised parts (Nissen, 2010). AMHPs act as societies' safety net when they detain persons against their will in the interests of their own health and safety, or with a view to protecting other persons. They reconcile the conflicting and divergent professional views and coordinate the collective professional group, providing a means of connection and transition with general practitioners (GPs), psychiatrists, ambulance crew and bed managers in the best interests of the service user. Similar to Nissen (2010), Leah (2018) defines boundary spanners, as professionals whose role it is to work between health and social care systems, and whose care and treatment goals – though superficially complementary – may carry inherent conflicts requiring mediation, negotiation and strategy. AMHPs are well placed to be conceptualised as boundary spanners because their role spans the kind of organisational boundaries envisaged by Steadman (1992). Boundary spanning is salient for AMHPs because they tend to conceptualise systems broadly. The individual, family, community, organisations and society all constitute systems.

While relationship-building is a core skill in many professions, boundary spanners must, by definition, build relationships with people who are different from themselves (Williams, 2002; Nissen, 2010; Oliver, 2013). For this they need to be able 'to acknowledge and value difference in terms of culture, mind-set, [and] professional role' (Williams, 2002, p 110), to competently work in different contexts with a variety of workers with different professional roles and identities. In interprofessional work, 'living with difference' (Frost et al, 2005, p 190) is a key competence, and includes accepting the limits of what, for each profession or discipline, contributes to shared practice. It necessitates an honest interrogation of the different perspectives that professionals enact and espouse.

Boundary spanners need to know how to illuminate difference and how to manage the conflict that often results (Klein, 1990; Nissen, 2010). This is familiar terrain in AMHP practice, particularly as the commitment to diversity, social justice and the intrinsic worth of all people is written into the profession's ethical code (HMSO, 2008; DoH, 2015), but may jar with the medical perspectives of psychiatrists.

Boundary spanners are adept in exercising the kind of non-hierarchical, facilitative leadership for which highly developed communication and interpersonal skills are required (Steadman, 1992; Williams, 2002; Nissen, 2010). It is particularly important that these skills can be applied to a whole group or network (Klein, 1990) through 'persuasion and friendly influence' (Weick et al, 1989, p 350; Quirk et al, 2000) to effect change. Boundary spanners' primary means in securing allies and resources that cross-cut traditional boundaries is through negotiation skills and collaborative relationships, applied both to individuals and the networks in which they operate (Oliver, 2013). As such, boundary spanners are 'agents of change'; a boundary spanner addresses and reconstruct tensions within and across systems (Nissen, 2010). This necessitates some critique of MHA processes and a willingness to experiment with alternatives. In seeking alternatives to traditional ways of practising, boundary spanners need to take calculated risks (Klein, 1990; Williams, 2002). They must be prepared to cross boundaries to be effective, to operate on the edge of what is comfortable and known. The ideal boundary spanner is 'an open-minded person with the ability to take risks without being strident or careless; to have vision but stay practical; to be courageous while attending to the politics; and to systematically create and nurture infrastructure for support and guidance' (Nissen, 2010, p 381).

The boundary-spanning approach provides conceptual support for engaging with multiple roles and working across fields of practice (Kerson, 2004). The gains made through conceptualising AMHPs as boundary-spanning hybrid professionals and framing this as a core element of the AMHP role is clear. AMHPs navigate real-world problems that are extremely complex, enmeshed and dialogically enacted. As Roy (1977 cited in Klein, 1990, p 35) argues, 'the real problems in society do not come in discipline-shaped blocks'. Complex problems cross professional, disciplinary and organisational boundaries, and require complex responses that do the same (Williams, 2002; Hood, 2012). These ideas have resonance in the fields of health and social care. They have led to a growing, albeit contested public policy commitment in health and social care to 'joined-up working' and integration across roles, teams and organisational structures (Frost et al, 2005; Denis et al, 2015). This in turn has renewed interest in boundary spanning (Masterson, 2002; Williams, 2002; Oliver, 2013). The following section will illustrate AMHPs as boundary spanners through drawing on excerpts of interview data from the Hybrid Identities Project (Leah, 2018).

Hybrid Identities Project: a case study of the AMHP role

A research study, undertaken by the author, of AMHPs' boundary-spanning activities mapped out the tensions involved in enacting roles and identities to reveal how the jostling between other professionals during MHA assessments could be understood (Leah, 2018). AMHPs' espoused identities featured claims for knowledge and what was unique as a means for exercising their legitimate control over work areas. These work areas were considered legitimate by AMHPs because they possessed knowledge of the relevant legal framework. Boundary spanning was interpreted through AMHP practice with other professionals involved in MHA assessments when working across boundaries, with participants (AMHPs who were social workers, nurses and occupational therapists) filling the liminal spaces where other professionals refused to go. This negotiation was typified by the comment from one AMHP of "sweeping up the odds and ends". The research found that participants were often stuck in liminal spaces where interagency partnerships had differing and often competing priorities.

Boundary spanning across different organisations was typified by participants' professional practice during MHA assessments, where their professional work was connected to multiple organisations, where AMHPs took the lead, particularly when enforcing adherence with duties under the MHA mediating between their own organisation and wider social structures. For example, one AMHP (Bernie) advised magistrates of their duties to provide her with a warrant. This involved a negotiation to correct their misunderstanding of the law so that a warrant to enter a person's property could be authorised and Bernie "had to tell them what the rules of section 135 were". In doing so she crosses into the legal jurisdiction of the magistrate, and she finds this is "quite often what an AMHP does". Bernie articulated her knowledge in the courtroom dialogically, as her knowledge was not taken for granted and involved negotiating her status as a knowledgeable and legally bound professional. Rather than retreat and seek the safety of a closed professional role and function, AMHPs highlighted the way they routinely rose to the challenges of complex organisational encounters and used their significant, highly hybridised knowledge to dialogically achieve the outcome they desired. This was achieved in the spirit of collaborative working.

In Elizabeth's story, of the 'hottest day of year', she uses her legal knowledge and skills of persuasion to communicate a different approach for sensitively supporting a distressed service user who was at risk of being handcuffed by police officers. This was an exercise where Elizabeth enacted her knowledge of safe conveyancing in a clear manner, and in doing so she entered the practice territory of the police officers, correcting what they believed was the appropriate way of dealing with the situation. This example illustrates how AMHPs 'encroached' on other professionals' 'distinctive space(s)' (Bourdieu, 1986). They appeared at the court room, in A&E departments, in outpatient clinics, but the spaces belonged to magistrates, lawyers, doctors and nurses.

Elizabeth's experience demonstrated that boundary spanning was both difficult and real, and was enacted in spaces of interprofessional tensions and conflicts. It involved reconciling conflicting and divergent professional views, coordinating a collective professional group, and providing a means of connection through discussion with other professionals, to achieve what AMHPs believed to be in the best interest of the service user. Boundary spanning therefore became a way of articulating AMHP professional roles and identities at the intersection of these systems dialogically with other people.

In the study, adaptability was a key component of boundary spanning among AMHPs; sophisticated relational skills were required to establish relationships that were close enough to enable an understanding of the often implicit concepts and meanings with which different professions and disciplines may approach a shared task, but distinct enough to maintain a systems perspective (Bartel, 2001; Oliver, 2013). As boundary spanners, AMHPs were adept at breaking down boundaries between themselves and others to build trust and appropriate care and treatment plans, within the context of managing risks. AMHPs responded on the boundaries of practice to other professionals who brought uncertainty with increased buffering to strengthen their professional boundaries and jurisdictions of practice. To operate effectively when power was dispersed across systems, AMHPs needed 'relational agency' (Edwards, 2011). This response was present in AMHPs' ability to elicit and utilise individuals' motivations and strengths to create plans that were responsive to, and made best use of, the wide range of perspectives and resources available. AMHPs delimited others' professional agency in these encounters through pre-empting or correcting any action transgressing the favoured assessment outcome, often acting as an 'agent of change' (Nissen, 2010); but in doing so, they experienced emotional labour, in the sense of remaining calm and collected when negotiating with 'challenging others' (Gregor, 2010, p 432):

> So, it's about working with all, trying to work with their team but it takes an awful lot of energy trying to pull (it) back together. (Elizabeth, Interview 1)

In this example, Elizabeth cross-cuts team boundaries, using dialogue to resolve some of the tensions involved in working across different organisational priorities and professional remits.

The skill of mediation was key, as illustrated by another participant, Annette:

> I think the role for me is one of mediator ... I think across the different organisations ... sometimes you soften the responses between organisations to make the bridges work better ... gets a better outcomes for the service users. (Interview 3)

Navigating the differences in how other professionals view the individual's mental health presentation involves balancing the views of others, while ensuring the legal duties are not transgressed. Such navigation can be difficult to manage, but the law and the accountability of the AMHP provided protection for Annette:

> My default place for everything is "What does the law say?" ... Sometimes you've got to do that because boundaries have slipped, you've got to reinforce those doors ... to protect the service users and protect your role. (Interview 3)

Reinforcing 'those doors' reveals professional jostling and tensions in exercising MHA duties, so although AMHPs ultimately have the authority to arrange transport to take the person to a hospital, this does not extend to AMHPs being able to enforce a specific time of travel and therefore the arrangement may be subject to 'false start and delays' (Quirk et al, 2000).

However, AMHPs' boundary working can sometimes be so liminal it was felt to be invisible by them:

> Doctors section people according to the media and the world and the people on the street, and nobody knows what the nuts and bolts of it is, and the nuts and bolts of it is us. (Bernie, Interview 2)

Boundary working was intimately connected to moral values and political focus on social justice; on being able 'to make the wheels turn' so the service user did not get a 'bum deal', navigating pathways to make them more just and least damaging for service users.

AMHPs navigated multiple organisations and cross-cut these boundaries within a day's work. Inevitably, when organisations changed policies and procedures, AMHPs got caught up in the crossfire. As different organisations had different priorities, AMHPs were pressurised into adapting to meet other organisations' priorities in order to safely and humanely detain individuals in hospital. Improvisation was key to how they navigated these conflicting priorities; it involved dealing with a high degree of both professional and personal risk:

> Now they're saying they want someone in the back of the [police] van
> with them, so that was another layer and it was just one night of horror.
> I'd gone home and it had gone on and on and I'm on the phone to
> the AMHP – its 10 pm at night and in the end bed managers said,
> "Go and get a taxi and leave your car in X" (a dangerous place). You
> get in the back of the van, go all the way to the hospital in the dark
> and then go back in a taxi to your car. I thought this is just madness.
> She said, "No, she's on her own, no!" (Tina, Interview 1)

Coordinating the assessments, as illustrated in Tina's example, shows how high-
risk situations were fraught with tensions, with multiple professionals having
a view on how the MHA assessment should be managed, despite it being the
AMHPs role to coordinate it. Following discussion, it was agreed that a paramedic
travelled in the back of the police van.

Boundary working involved cross-cutting service areas with different
professional groups – notably, psychiatrists, police officers and paramedics:

> Thinking about it from a Mental Health Act assessment point of view
> may be easier: first of all, you are liaising with different agencies in
> mental health services or different professions in mental health services
> to start with. I suppose you would be talking to care coordinators,
> which could be nurse, or occupational therapist generally and then
> you go from there. You would speak with the GP and a different
> psychiatrist who is on call, maybe a section 12 doctor. Then, setting
> up the actual assessment, you'd be looking at, maybe looking at support
> from paramedics or from the ambulance service or from the police as
> well. That tends to be the main focus really. (Matthew, Interview 3)

The dominant practice focus was on navigating various organisational and
professional groups, as responses often differed within the same professional
groups; nothing was taken for granted. An example was given of a police officer's
response to a section 136 (police power to remove to a place of safety):

> I've found that it's not just the same response that you get from the
> police each time that you do [section] 136, it can be varied depending
> on their pressures and their sergeant may be asking them to leave,
> do you need X to be there when questioning the case, which is fair
> enough, there has to be a rationale there. So it would be very much
> that you'd be weighing up the situation and you be saying either, "Yep
> you're fine to go", or "This person is presenting this way, would you
> mind staying and helping us out." I guess it is ultimately up to them if
> they wish to go … we can only request that something that happens or
> doesn't. I think we have more of a discussion, put suggestions forward,
> but we see what they say really. (William, Interview 3)

The example involved a discussion with William about his professional remit, where he tried to get some understanding of the situation from the police's perspective. In the excerpt, he traversed between an authoritative directive stance and a caring ethos. In doing so, he invoked different skills to highlight the differences in professionals' remits and to manage the conflicts that resulted.

In exploring boundary spanning, this study illustrated the dynamic enactment of the positioning and repositioning of participants' work across professional and organisational boundaries (Leah, 2018). AMHPs worked across both integrated and dispersed systems, which involved the negotiation of both emotional and social processes inherent in interprofessional working (Cooper, 2017). Within working arrangements, participants were found to attach meaning to their professional jurisdiction, through speaking across, alongside and with a range of stakeholders.

AMHPs interacted with individuals, families, communities, other professionals and a variety of organisations as boundary-spanning professionals. They routinely cross-cut systems, providing a means of connection for people in mental health crisis, and filled the liminal spaces left by other professionals. In doing so they engaged in dialogic exchanges with others – namely, psychiatrists, police officers and ambulance crews – doing whatever was necessary to secure the most dignified and humane intervention for people experiencing mental distress.

The enactment of boundary spanning was found to be a mostly positive aspect of AMHPs' professional role(s) as hybrid professionals in the study. AMHPs' biographies, as they are enacted and located in the intersubjective professional realities of everyday life, contribute sociologically to broader understandings of professional hybridity and an understanding of boundary spanning as a site of (re)organisation for AMHP professional role(s) and identities. These findings could offer AMHPs a professional script from which to draw and could influence their professional role, and possibly their professional identities, through reflecting on what AMHPs are expected to do when they enter interprofessional practice.

Conclusion

AMHPs practise within contexts and organisations that are subject to change. Changes in how organisations function inevitably impact across the boundaries of professional practice through, for example, the integration agenda of the Care Act 2014, the new Bill to replace the Deprivation of Liberty Safeguards (DHSC, 2005), and the MHA White Paper (DHSC, 2021). AMHPs practise within teams, services and organisations. They interface with users of these services and in the complex environment around them. AMHP activity is political as it traverses the public and private domains of life. Understanding these influencing contexts at professional level gives insights into the AMHP role and its identities.

In conclusion, boundaries and concepts of hybridity are important because they necessarily mediate how AMHPs work with other professionals, and how they work within and between organisations. However, the professional identities of AMHPs, as hybrids, to some degree rests on AMHPs' capability to hold on to their jurisdictional and expert knowledge claims, which afford both status and specialism. Although hybridity can be embedded in professional roles and identities that straddle boundaries of professional knowledge and practice, it is a concept that confronts and problematises boundaries, although it does not erase them. As such, hybridity implies an unsettling of identities and alerts us to the difficulties of working with cultural and professional differences. This chapter has empirically explored the complicated professional entanglements and interprofessional relations of AMHP work, illustrating how it is socio-spatially distributed within multiple organisations and within people's own homes; it spans these arenas as sites of interprofessional action and highlights a profession based on interstitiality.

Note

[1]   Names of all participants, including from cited studies, are pseudonyms.

References

Abbott, A. (1988) *The systems of professions: an essay on the division of expert labor.* Chicago, IL: University of Chicago Press.

Allen, R. (2014) *The role of the social worker in adult mental health services.* London: College of Social Work.

Association of Directors of Adult Social Services (ADASS) (2018) AMHPs, Mental Health Act assessments and the mental health social care workforce. Available at: https://www.adass.org.uk/national-findings-amhps-mental-health-act-asse ssments-the-mental-health-social-care-workforce.

Bartel, C.A. (2001) Social comparisons in boundary-spanning work: effects of community outreach on members' organizational identity and identification. *Administrative Science Quarterly*, 46(3), 379–413.

Beech, N. (2011) Liminality and the practices of identity reconstruction. *Human Relations*, 64(2), 285–301.

Blomgren, M. and Waks, C. (2015) Coping with contradictions: hybrid professionals managing institutional complexity. *Journal of Professions and Organization*, 2(1), 78–102.

Bonnet, M. and Moran, N. (2020) Why do Approved Mental Health Professionals think detentions under the Mental Health Act are rising and what should be done about it? *British Journal of Social Work*, 50(2), 616 –53.

Bourdieu, P. (1986) The forms of capital (trans. R. Nice). In J.G. Richardson (ed.), *Handbook of theory and research for the sociology of education* (pp 241–58). New York: Greenwood Press.

Cooper, A. (2017) *Social work: essential to integration.* London: Department of Health.

Croft, C., Currie, G. and Lockett, A. (2015) Broken two-way windows: an exploration of professional hybrids. *Public Administration*, 93(3), 380–94.

Denis, J.-L., Ferlile, E. and Van Gestel, N. (2015) Understanding hybridity in public sector organisations. *Public Administration*, 93, 273–89.

Department of Health (DoH) (2008) *Care programme approach*. London: DoH.

Department of Health (DoH) (2015) *Mental Health Act 1983: Code of Practice*. London: DoH.

Department of Health and Social Care (DHSC) (2005) *Mental Capacity Act 2005: deprivation of liberty safeguards*. London: DHSC. Available at https://www.gov.uk/government/collections/dh-mental-capacity-act-2005-deprivation-of-liberty-safeguards.

Department of Health and Social Care (DHSC) (2018) *Modernising the Mental Health Act: increasing choice, reducing compulsion – final report of the Independent Review of the Mental Health Act 1983*. London: DHSC. Available at https://assets.publishing.service.gov.uk/government/uploads/system/uploads/attachment_data/file/778897/Modernising_the_Mental_Health_Act_-_increasing_choice__reducing_compulsion.pdf.

Department of Health and Social Care (DHSC) (2021) *Reforming the Mental Health Act: government response*. London: DHSC. Available at https://www.gov.uk/government/consultations/reforming-the-mental-health-act/outcome/reforming-the-mental-health-act-government-response#strengthening-the-patients-right-to-choose-and-refuse-treatment--advance-choice-documents.

Edwards, A. (2011) Building common knowledge at the boundaries between professional practices: relational agency and relational expertise in systems of distributed expertise. *Journal of Educational Research*, 50(1), 33–9.

Evetts, J. (2006) The sociology of professional groups: new directions. *Current Sociology*, 54, 133–43.

Evetts, J. (2013) Professionalism: value and ideology. *Current Sociology Review*, 61(5–6), 778–96.

Flynn, R. (2004) Soft bureaucracy, governmentality and clinical governance. In A. Gray and S. Harrison (eds) *Governing Medicine* (pp 11–26). Buckingham: OU Press.

Frost, N., Robinson, M. and Anning, A. (2005) Social workers in multidisciplinary teams: issues and dilemmas for professional practice. *Child and Family Social Work*, 10(3), 187–96.

Gittell, J.H., Douglas, R. and Wimbush, F. (2010) A relational model of how high performance work systems work. *Organization*, 21(2), 490–506.

Gregor, C. (2010) Unconscious aspects of statutory mental health social work: emotional labour and the Approved Mental Health Professional. *Journal of Social Work Practice*, 24(4), 429–43.

Her Majesty's Stationery Office (HMSO) (2008) *Mental Health (Approved Mental Health Professionals) (Approval) (England) Regulations 2008*. London: HMSO. Available at: https://www.legislation.gov.uk/uksi/2008/1206/contents/made.

Hood, R. (2012) A critical realist model of complexity for interprofessional working. *Journal of Interprofessional Care*, 26(1), 6–12.

Karban, K., Sparkes, T., Benson, S., Kilyon, J. and Lawrence, J. (2021) Accounting for social perspectives: an exploratory study of AMHP practice. *British Journal of Social Work*, 51(1), 187–204.

Kerson, T.S. (2004) Boundary spanning: an ecological reinterpretation of social work practice in mental health systems. *Social Work in Mental Health*, 2(2), 39–57.

Klein, J.T. (1990) *Interdisciplinary: history, theory and practice*. Detroit, MI: Wayne State University Press.

Leah, C. (2018) *Approved Mental Health Professionals: negotiating dialogic identities as hybrid professionals*. Thesis. School of Environment, Education and Development, University of Manchester.

Leah, C. (2020) Approved Mental Health Professionals: a Jack of all trades? Hybrid professional roles within a mental health occupation. *Qualitative Social Work*, 19(6), 987–1006.

Lipsky, M. (1980) *Street level bureaucracy: dilemmas of the individual in public services*. New York: Russell Sage Foundation.

Masterson, A. (2002) Cross-boundary working: a macro-political analysis of the impact on professional roles. *Journal of Clinical Nursing*, 11(3), 331–39.

McGivern, G., Currie, G., Ferlie, E., Fitzgerald, L. and Waring, J. (2015) Hybrid manager – professionals identity work: the maintenance and hybridization of medical professionalism in managerial contexts. *Public Administration*, 93, 412–32.

McNicholl, A. (2015) Mental health patients sent hundreds of miles as cuts leave little slack in the system. Available at https://www.communitycare.co.uk/2015/07/15/mental-health-patients-sent-hundreds-miles-beds-area-placements-rise-23-per-cent/.

Morriss, L. (2014) *Accomplishing social work identity in interprofessional mental health following the implementation of the Mental Health Act 2007*. Unpublished doctoral thesis. University of Salford.

Morriss, L. (2015) Doing non-seriousness: accomplishing social work identity through humour and laughter. *Qualitative Social Work*, 14(3), 307–20.

Morriss, L. (2016) AMHP work: dirty or prestigious? Dirty work designations and the approved mental health professional. *British Journal of Social Work*, 46(3), 703–18.

Morriss, L. (2017) Being seconded to a mental health trust: the (in)visibility of mental health social work. *British Journal of Social Work*, 47(5), 1344–60.

Nathan, J. and Webber, M. (2010) Mental health social work and the bureau-medicalisation of mental health care: identity in a changing world. *Journal of Social Work Practice*, 24(1), 15–28.

Nissen, L.B. (2010) Boundary spanners revisited. *Qualitative Social Work*, 9(3), 365–84.

Noordegraaf, M. (2007) From 'pure' to 'hybrid' professionalism: present-day professionalism in ambiguous public domains. *Administration and Society*, 39(6), 761–85.

Noordegraaf, M. (2015) Hybrid professionalism and beyond: (new) forms of public professionalism in changing organisational and societal contexts. *Journal of Professions and Organization*, 2(2), 187–206.

Noordegraaf, M. and Van der Meulen, M. (2008) Professional power play: organizing management in healthcare. *Public Administration*, 86(4), 1055–69.

Oliver, C. (2013) Social workers as boundary spanners: reframing our professional identity for interprofessional practice. *Social Work Education*, 32(6), 773–84.

Quirk, A., Lelliott, P. and Audini, B. (2000) *Performing the Act: a qualitative study of the process of Mental Health Act assessments*. Glasgow: MRC Social and Public Health Sciences Unit.

Rapaport, J. (2006) New roles in mental health: the creation of the Approved Mental Health Practitioner. *Journal of Integrated Care*, 14(5), 37–46.

Rapaport, J. and Manthorpe, J (2008) Putting it into practice: will the new Mental Health Act slow down or accelerate integrated working? *Journal of Social Work Practice*, 16, 22–9.

Romeo, L. (2016) *Annual report by the chief social worker for adults 2015–16*. London: Department of Health.

Schön, D. (1983) *The reflective practitioner*. New York: Basic Books.

Scott, W.R. (2008) Lords of the dance: professionals as institutional agents. *Organization Studies*, 29(2), 219–38.

Spyridonidis, D., Hendy, J. and Barlow, J. (2015) Understanding hybrid roles: the role of identity processes amongst physicians. *Public Administration*, 93(3), 395–411.

Steadman, H.J. (1992) Boundary spanners. *Law and Human Behaviour*, 16(1), 75–87.

Stevens, M., Martineau, S., Manthorpe, J., Steils, N. and Norrie, C. (2018) *Final report: who wants to be an AMHP?* London: Social Care and Social Work Research Unit, Kings College London.

Vicary, S., Young, A. and Hicks, S. (2019) 'Role over' or roll over? Dirty work, shift and Mental Health Act assessments. *British Journal of Social Work*, 49(8), 2187–206.

Waring, J. (2015) Mapping the public sector diaspora: towards a model of inter-sectoral cultural hybridity using evidence from English healthcare reforms. *Public Administration*, 93(3), 345–62.

Weick, A., Rapp, C., Sullivan, W.P. and Kishardt, W. (1989) A strengths perspective for social work practice. *Social Work*, 34(4), 350–4.

Williams, P. (2002) The competent boundary spanner. *Public Administration*, 80(1), 103–24.

12

Framing mental capacity and mental health legislation in decision making

Matthew Graham

Introduction

Issues arise in practice when professionals attempt to balance the emancipatory principles of the Mental Capacity Act 2005 (MCA) alongside the statutory provisions of the Mental Health Act 1983 (MHA), particularly when detention and compulsion under the MHA is being considered. Being assessed as lacking the mental capacity to decide on one's own care and treatment is not an element of the statutory criteria for detention under the MHA. Essentially, this means a person who is assessed as having a mental disorder but has the mental capacity to decide what is in their best interests may still be detained under the MHA. The situation in which a person is having their capacitous self-determination legally overridden by being compulsorily treated clearly presents legal, ethical and moral challenges for the decision maker, and it is this challenge that underpins this chapter.

The aim of this chapter is to support and enable one mental health decision maker, the Approved Mental Health Professional (AMHP), to reflect upon their duty to uphold the principles of the MCA when undertaking assessments under the MHA, as well as to critically appraise the significance of understanding mental capacity as a wider construct when focusing on people's rights and strengths. The chapter will include a brief overview of the spirit of the MCA and MCA Code of Practice, and the MCA/MHA interface will be explored in order to challenge myths and assumptions. Mental capacity and compulsion will be critically analysed in order to reflect upon people's rights and the AMHP's key legal duties and responsibilities. The reader will be invited to critique their own judgements as a decision maker when considering whether someone who has mental capacity ought to be detained and compulsorily treated.

> 1. The United Nations Convention on the Rights of Persons with Disabilities (2008) requires a paradigm shift from a medical model of disability to a social model that emphasises overcoming the barriers to equality created by attitudes, laws, government policies and the social, economic and political environment. The approach adopted by a social model recognises that people with psychosocial disabilities have the same right to take decisions and make choices as other people, particularly regarding treatment, and have the right to equal recognition before the law. (Sugiura et al, 2020)

The freedom to make decisions

The principles of autonomy, self-determination, choice and independence are elements of decision making that, in most circumstances, people enjoy not only the freedom to exercise but the benefits that derive from such freedoms. A central tenet of exercising freedom and choice is to be able to make decisions that directly impact on how one functions within and contributes to society. Such freedoms also enable people to be accountable for their decisions and be afforded the power and autonomy that this accountability provides. In recent years, and certainly since the enactment of the MCA, the Equality Act 2010 and the Care Act 2014, the importance of autonomy in mental health care has been increasingly reflected in an emphasis on user involvement in decision making (Wilkinson, 2001, cited in Wied et al, 2019). The culture of care is shifting towards more enabling and emancipatory practice with people who have historically had freedom of choice removed from them due to impairment, illness or disability (Graham and Cowley, 2015).

There has been an increasing dissonance between perceptions of the MCA and the MHA in relation to which piece of legislation is utilised most comprehensively within compulsory decision making in mental health practice. Some professional consideration has even led practitioners to suggest the MHA 'trumps' the MCA. In fact, in practice, the two are inseparable when it comes to supporting people who have lived experience of mental health difficulties and of being cared for and treated in hospital.

The five guiding principles of the MHA Code of Practice (DoH, 2015) are enshrined within the values of involving and enabling people to be self-determining about their mental health care and treatment. Principles one and two refer to maximising independence, and empowering and enabling involvement (DoH, 2015, para 1.1). Over the years such concepts have gradually developed and expanded to include an acknowledgement of people being experts in their own experience and illness, and thus an element of reciprocal responsibility in care planning and treatment decisions needs to be established in practice (Hickey and Kipping, 2002, cited in Bee et al, 2015).

Choice and self-determination are central tenets of contemporary adult and mental health service provision, where professionals not only have a statutory duty to support people to uphold their views and beliefs, but also a responsibility to do so as a cornerstone of person-centred good practice. This chapter will explore how framing an understanding of mental capacity within mental health legislation is essential to further develop an understanding of the contemporary legislative landscape of mental health service provision.

The establishment of the Mental Capacity Act

Prior to the enactment of the MCA and the consequent establishment of the Court of Protection in 2007, very few mechanisms existed outside of safeguarding policies and service arrangements to scrutinise the care of those deemed unable to make decisions for themselves due to impairments or disturbances of the mind or brain. In a similar thread, little existed outside of the European Convention on Human Rights (ECHR) and the Human Rights Act 1998 to ensure that all citizens were permitted to exercise control over their choices and freedoms. The MCA is supporting professional and legislative culture to shift from a place of historical draconian practice to a place of emancipation. An example of this shift is reflected in both the changing prevalence and changing perception of people living longer. Research into and awareness of dementia has begun to attain a much higher profile in recent years. Such research remains generally pessimistic about anything other than a rapid cognitive decline among those diagnosed with the disease (Hilton, 2015 and Wilson, 2017, both cited in Weston, 2020), but the inception of the MCA has enabled strengths-based approaches, research and practice not previously encountered when considering the life and circumstances of older people who are experiencing mental health difficulties.

The MCA is approaching 15 years of enactment. In 2014 the *Mental Capacity Act 2005: Post-Legislative Scrutiny* report (Select Committee on the MCA, 2014) identified that the MCA was not embedded in practice as anticipated, with risk-averse practice and the protection–imperative remaining fixed practice ideologies within services. This failure to embed, combined with the overarching philosophy of the MHA being a piece of safeguarding law, resulted in mental health professionals being challenged. The challenge is to consider how professionals support people to make decisions in relation to their mental health care and treatment while balancing this against the intrinsic power of psychiatry and legislation that mandates compulsory care and treatment when required. The MCA and MHA are not mutually exclusive when it comes to best practice, inasmuch as the principles of the MCA must be followed when supporting people within mental health services that involve compulsion.

Mental capacity, consent and compulsory treatment

In mental health services, service-user involvement requires special attention because mental health problems may affect people's abilities and motivation to be involved and participate (Tambuzer et al, 2014, cited in Laitila et al, 2018). Arguably, this special attention stems from professionals' knowledge of mental capacity, the MCA and the factors that may help or hinder people to make decisions. Section 131 of the MHA, which refers to informal admission, is a prime example of where specific knowledge of mental capacity is required to support professional decision making in relation to understanding of choice and self-determination: 'If the patient consents to the making of the arrangements, they may be made, carried out and determined on the basis of that consent even though there are one or more persons who have parental responsibility for him'.

Consent is contextualised within the meaning of the definition of mental capacity as being 'the ability to make a decision' (DCA, 2007, para 4.1). Critical consideration needs to be made between the competence to make an informed decision, or whether the person lacks the mental capacity make that decision. It is simply not the case that the person should be determined to be unable to make a decision about their admission to hospital based upon them not having the information or knowledge they need to be able to make that decision. Incompetence to make a decision may be eradicated by having the information one needs to make that decision, whereby mental incapacity to make a decision is caused by an impairment of, or a disturbance in, the function of the mind or brain (s 2(1) MCA). Further critical analysis will support the mental health professional to consider the relationship between the person's mental impairment or disturbance, and the inability to make the decision. This so-called causative nexus between the impairment/disturbance and the ability to make a decision must be considered in all professional decision making within mental health services, most notably that of the AMHP.

In the Court of Protection judgment, *Heart of England NHS Foundation Trust v JB* (2014), Justice Jackson in handing down his judgment stated that:

> The right to decide whether or not to consent to medical treatment is one of the most important rights guaranteed by law. For the doctors, it can be difficult to know what recommendation to make. For the patient, the decision about whether to accept or reject medical advice involves weighing up the risks and benefits according to the patient's own system of values against a background where diagnosis and prognosis are rarely certain, even for the doctors. Such decisions are intensely personal. They are taken in stressful circumstances. There are no right or wrong answers. The freedom to choose for oneself is a part of what it means to be a human being.

There is an apparent challenge here for professionals when supporting people to make decisions about their own mental health care and treatment. People will require all the information they need to be able to make that decision at that particular time. As the professional offers support and information for this decision making, they must remain mindful of the first of the MCA five principles, which is that 'a person must be assumed to have capacity unless it is established that he lacks capacity' (s 1(2) MCA). The primary practice issue to consider here in relation to any decision that may need to be made around a person's care and treatment is the person's ability to consent to that care and treatment. Consent cannot be considered without capacity; these are not separate themes for discussion or practice but are impenetrable allies that support the person's human rights to make their own decisions and, therefore, cannot be separated within the professional decision-making process. This is reinforced within the MHA Code of Practice (DoH, 2015, para 13.53), which states that a 'person who lacks capacity to consent to being accommodated in a hospital for care and/or treatment for mental disorder and who is likely to be deprived of their liberty should never be informally admitted to hospital (whether they are content to be admitted or not)'.

Developing understanding between the person's mental impairment and their ability or inability to make a decision will enable the mental health professional to develop a critical understanding of causative nexus within practice. The Court of Protection case *LB Redbridge v G, C & F* (2014) shows how establishing the causative nexus is especially important in cases where an individual's inability to make decisions may not just be about a particular impairment or disturbance in the mind or brain. Justice Russell in this case stressed the importance of establishing whether G's inability to make a decision was because of the impairment/disturbance, or because 'she is a vulnerable adult deprived of capacity by constraint, coercion or undue influence' (*LB Redbridge v G, C & F*, 2014).

Knowing what law requires of professionals

Legal literacy is the ability to connect relevant legal rules with professional priorities and objectives of ethical practice (Research in Practice, 2021). Within mental health practice it is necessary to remember particular legal 'rules' when focusing on how people's mental capacity is established around making care and treatment decisions. Professionals hold the burden of proof in establishing any lack of mental capacity, and this must be based on collating sufficient evidence that can only come from the strength and detail of the assessment they undertake. In his concluding remarks in *Heart of England Foundation Trust v JB* (2014), Justice Jackson stated that 'we should not ask more of people whose capacity is questioned than those of whose capacity is unfounded'. This tells a professional decision maker that the standard of proof of a *reasonable belief on the balance of probabilities* must come from a place of not asking more of the person to understand, comprehend and communicate the intricacies of their care and treatment than the 'average person' at any given time. In a similar way, people not agreeing with professionals or forming their own construction of what they need should not be viewed as non-compliant or the person lacking the mental capacity to make the decision.

Historically, the human rights movement and the 'anti-psychiatry' movement have always challenged the medical codification of non-conformity, distress or dangerousness as treatable illness as overly simplistic (Buckland, 2016), yet the propensity to pathologise people's experiences, and reactions to how those experiences are perceived, pervade contemporary psychiatric interventions. Becker (1963, p 9) defined deviance as a social creation in which 'social groups create deviance by making the rules whose infraction constitutes deviance, and by applying those rules to particular people and labelling them as outsiders'.

Even when people have the mental capacity to make their own decisions, this can be overridden by the MHA should the individual meet the criteria for detention (which lacking mental capacity does not necessarily form part of; lacking mental capacity around one's care and treatment is not part of the criteria for detention per se, even though lacking mental capacity may be evidence as to what the assessing team may constitute as the nature or degree of the person's mental disorder). This undoubtedly creates tension for professionals when seeking to practise in as least a restrictive way as possible.

The revised MHA Code of Practice (DoH, 2015) includes a new chapter where the interface between the MCA and the MHA highlights how mental capacity, choice and decision making ought to be considered and understood in compulsory decision making in mental health practice. Paragraph 13.1 states that 'a sound understanding and application of the principles and provisions of the MCA … and of the common law relating to consent, is essential to enable decision-makers to fulfil their legal responsibilities and to safeguard their patients' rights under the European Convention on Human Rights (ECHR)'. Paragraph 13.24 states that 'professionals should seek to involve those who lack capacity in decisions about their care as much as they would involve those who have capacity'. Mental health care plans should be developed in collaboration with the person as much as possible. In order to achieve such collaboration, it is suggested that professionals frame their understanding of the person's involvement by reflecting on section 4(6) of the MCA. The law clearly mandates that professionals must consider, so far as is reasonably ascertainable:

(a) the person's past and present wishes and feelings (and, in particular, any relevant written statement made by him when he had capacity);
(b) the beliefs and values that would be likely to influence his decision if he had capacity; and
(c) the other factors that he would be likely to consider if he were able to do so.

The interface between the responsibility of good practice and the duty to uphold the law merges here because this section offers a clear overview of what involving people who may lack capacity in the decisions around their mental health care and treatment ought to look like. This should, of course, also involve discussions about advance statements of wishes and preferences, as well as considering advance decisions to refuse treatment. Paragraph 13.24 of the MHA Code of Practice (DoH, 2015) continues to state that: 'where professionals and patients disagree over elements of the care plan the emphasis should be on discussion and compromise where possible. Restrictions (including restraint) and deprivation of liberty should only be considered when absolutely necessary and when all appropriate efforts at building consensus and agreement have failed.' Consultation with those important in the person's life is also a requirement within mental capacity law. Section 4 of the MCA and Chapter 5 of the MCA Code of Practice (2007) state that decision makers must consult with those who have an interest in the health and welfare of the person, if it is practicable and appropriate to do so. This is not the same duty that applies to AMHPs when they ought to specifically consult with the Nearest Relative under the MHA (s 11[4]) in relation to compulsory admission to hospital; but, of course, it does not exclude the AMHP from their obligations under the MCA to consult with others in relation to what is in the best interests of the person if they lack the mental capacity to decide for themselves. Proposed changes to the MHA will bring people's choices about who should be consulted more in line with that of the MCA, inasmuch that what is being proposed is that the person can choose a 'nominated person' to act in what is currently the Nearest Relative role.

Balancing people's wishes and feelings against a need for care or treatment

Tension exists, however, when placing the person at the centre of a decision-making process that has legislation at the heart of it which can override people's choices. Section 4(6)(a) of the MCA states that *advance statements* must be considered as far as is reasonable ascertainable. There has been a drive in recent years to support people to write advance statements about not only their wishes and preferences, but also to document what treatment the person might wish to refuse should they lack the mental capacity to make that decision for themselves. Valid and applicable advance decisions to refuse treatment have always been a contentious issue for people with lived experience of mental health relapse and detention in hospital, due to the awareness that this can be overturned by the power of the MHA. It is good practice for the Responsible Clinician (typically the doctor who has overall responsibility for care and treatment for people being assessed and treated under the MHA) to adhere to patients' expressed wishes, but this does not always result in treatment not being given to people against their will and who have refused this prior to them lacking mental capacity. For decision makers in mental health care the decision as to whether an advance decision is valid and applicable can be complex and challenging, mostly due to what is presented in the MCA not necessarily aligning with the MHA. Nevertheless, evidence from people with lived experience of mental health difficulties often speaks positively of the power of making an advance decision. As Jessup (cited in Graham and Cowley, 2015, p 128) states:

> In hospital the advance decision to refuse treatment was respected. For me, the advance decision is one of the most useful documents I have with a recurrent illness. It means that I am able to keep control of what happens to my basic needs and important things in my life even though I can be very unwell.

The proposed reforms of the MHA refer to strengthening patients' rights to choose and refuse treatment by means of introducing 'advance choice documents'. The White Paper (and draft Bill) proposes that the advance choice document should adhere to a standard format and approach, and it should include the information about the individual's preferences, as well as any other information deemed relevant by the individual (DHSC, 2021). The government's response to the White Paper (DHSC, 2021) states that advance choice documents will be a means of providing people with the opportunity to set out in advance the care and treatment they would prefer, the name of their chosen nominated person, and any treatments they wish to refuse in the event they are detained under the MHA and lack the relevant capacity (DHSC, 2021). When it comes to people making their own decisions about care, treatment and who should be consulted, bringing mental health legislation in line with the emancipatory and enabling provisions of the MCA is overdue.

Justice Hayden, in handing down his Court of Protection judgment in *LB Tower Hamlets v NB & AU* (2019), stated 'that it is not the objective of the MCA to pamper or to nursemaid the incapacitous, rather it is to provide the fullest experience of life, and with all its vicissitudes'. This is seemingly a very positive judicial comment, which suggests that risk-sensible practice is welcome in health and social care services after many years of risk-averse practice arguably brought on by high-profile homicide inquiries of the 1990s, notably that into the care and treatment of Christopher Clunis following the death of Jonathan Zito at Finsbury Park tube station in 1992 (Cold, 1994). Practitioners need to strike a balance between enabling people and sanctioning people, and that balance sits on a very fine line. The very nature of mental health practice is to support people with often complex needs to regain and sustain a sense of well-being and connection with themselves and others, and, often, the only way to have the fullest experience of life is to be exposed to it. Mental health professionals are therefore the facilitators and enablers of people developing and maintaining the agency to make their own decisions. Of course, assessment of risk and autonomous decision making must be considered by professionals within the context of what people might experience because of their symptoms of a serious mental illness.

In September 2019, 31-year-old Valeria Munoz Biggs died by suicide after jumping in front of a train. The senior coroner for the area where Valeria died said in her report to the clinical director of the relevant NHS Trust's Acute Mental Health Services, that the team who were assigned to Valeria contributed to her death. The coroner said: '[Valeria's] symptoms were not taken sufficiently seriously … If she had been adequately assessed and admitted to hospital, her death would not have occurred at this time' (Smith, 2021). The coroner's report stated that there was 'persistent underestimation of [Valeria's] suicidality, and failure to adequately engage with and listen to the family and note their concerns' (NHS England, 2021). The coroner's Regulation 28 report to prevent future deaths referred to 'a culture of risk-taking in relation to suicidality' (NHS England, 2021).

One of the most challenging issues to contemplate when considering mental capacity in relation to mental health legislation is analysing distinctions that exist between choices people may make and the outcomes of their actions; the two are not the same and should not be conflated. Gask (2021) states 'that being told that a 'person has "capacity" to decide to harm themselves' is a virus that has spread the entire length and breadth of the United Kingdom (UK). Gask's valuable insight and concern aligns with the final report of the Independent Review of the Mental Health Act 1983 (DHSC, 2018), when it discussed constructions of mental capacity when exercising MHA duties and functions. The review highlights the potential for mental capacity to be misunderstood and the term misused. The report referred to hearing anecdotal evidence that clinicians can be too quick to assume that when a patient does not agree with the treatment proposed, it is because they lack capacity. The review went on to suggest that some clinicians obstruct people who have mental capacity from accessing the services they need (by not facilitating access) because those individuals are able to ask for treatment for themselves. The review concluded that 'this could lead to tragic outcomes, for example at A&E following a suicide attempt, where a person could be turned away on the basis that the individual knows what they are doing, so they do not need assessment and/or treatment' (DHSC, 2018).

People have the right to make decisions; principle 3 of the MCA's five statutory principles tell us that a person is not to be treated as unable to make a decision merely because they make an unwise decision (s 1[4] MCA). Conversely, there should not be an automatic determination that the person does not require support, care or intervention solely on the basis that the person has the mental capacity to make decisions for themselves. It could be argued that constructions of independence and choice have metamorphosised into counterproductive poor practice, where professionals consciously or unconsciously absolve themselves of responsibility to act and fulfil their duties and responsibilities under mental health legislation. This issue has been an increasing concern when framing understandings of mental capacity within mental health legislation.

Conclusion

In conclusion, what is being suggested is that mental health professionals' understandings of mental capacity must be firmly located with the person, their experiences, and any associated risks and concerns. In addition, how the professional understands their own ability to critically comprehend the meaning behind the individual's experience is a key driver in transforming 'mental capacity' from what can become an oversimplified objective phenomena as to whether the person 'has' it or not, to a subjective one that is fluid, has meaning, and the formation and determination of which has a direct impact upon people's safety, well-being, and decisions about the individual's mental health care and treatment (Graham, 2016).

References
Becker, H. (1963) *Outsiders: studies in the sociology of deviance*. New York: Free Press.
Bee, P., Brooks, H., Fraser, C. and Lovell, K. (2015) Professional perspectives on service user and carer involvement in mental health care planning: a qualitative study. *International Journal of Nursing Studies*, 52, 1834–45.

Buckland, R. (2016) The decision by Approved Mental Health Professionals to use compulsory powers under the Mental Health Act 1983: a Foucauldian discourse analysis. *British Journal of Social Work*, 46, 46–62.

Cold, J. (1994) The Christopher Clunis enquiry. *Psychiatric Bulletin*, 18, 449–52.

Department for Constitutional Affairs (DCA) (2007) *Mental Capacity Act 2005 Code of Practice*. London: The Stationery Office. Available at https://assets.pub lishing.service.gov.uk/government/uploads/system/uploads/attachment_data/ file/921428/Mental-capacity-act-code-of-practice.pdf.

Department of Health (DoH) (2015) *Mental Health Act 1983: Code of Practice*. London: DoH. Available at https://www.gov.uk/government/publications/ code-of-practice-mental-health-act-1983.

Department of Health and Social Care (DHSC) (2018) *Modernising the Mental Health Act: increasing choice, reducing compulsion – final report of the Independent Review of the Mental Health Act 1983*. London: DHSC. Available at https://ass ets.publishing.service.gov.uk/government/uploads/system/uploads/attachme nt_data/file/778897/Modernising_the_Mental_Health_Act_-_increasing_choi ce__reducing_compulsion.pdf

Department of Health and Social Care (DHSC) (2021) *Reforming the Mental Health Act: government response*. London: DHSC. Available at https://www.gov. uk/government/consultations/reforming-the-mental-health-act/outcome/ reforming-the-mental-health-act-government-response#strengthening-the- patients-right-to-choose-and-refuse-treatment--advance-choice-documents.

Gask, L. (2021) [Twitter post], 16 November. Available at https://twitter.com/ suzypuss/status/1460590461673000963.

Graham, M. (2016) Understanding of the Mental Capacity Act in work with older adults exploring the 'unintended consequences' for service users' emotional wellbeing. *Working with Older People*, 20(3), 151–6.

Graham, M. and Cowley, J. (2015) *A practical guide to the Mental Capacity Act: putting the principles into practice*. London: Jessica Kingsley.

Heart of England NHS Foundation Trust v JB [2014] EWCOP 342. Available at http://www.bailii.org/ew/cases/EWCOP/2014/342.html.

Laitila, M., Nummelin, J., Kortteisto, T. and Pitkänen, A. (2018) Service users' views regarding user involvement in mental health services: a qualitative study. *Archives of Psychiatric Nursing*, 32, 695–701.

LB Redbridge v G, C & F [2014] EWHC 485 (COP). Available at http://www. bailii.org/ew/cases/EWCOP/2014/485.html.

LB Tower Hamlets v NB & AU [2019] EWCOP 27. Available at https://www. judiciary.uk/wp-content/uploads/2019/07/2019-ewcop2-judgment-consent- to-sex-2.final_.pdf.

NHS England (2021) *Regulation 28: report to prevent future deaths*. Available at https://www.judiciary.uk/wp-content/uploads/2021/02/Valeria-Biggs-2021- 0034-Redacted.pdf.

Research in Practice (2021) Legal literacy. Available at https://www.researchinp ractice.org.uk/all/topics/legal-literacy/.

Select Committee on the Mental Capacity Act 2005 (2014) *Mental Capacity Act 2005: post-legislative scrutiny*. London: House of Lords.

Smith, M. (2021) Coroner slams west London mental health service after woman's death. Available at https://chiswickcalendar.co.uk/coroner-slams-west-london-mental-health-service-after-womans-death/.

Sugiura, K., Mahomed, F., Saxena, S. and Patel, V. (2020) An end to coercion: rights and decision-making in mental health care. *Bulletin of the World Health Organisation*, 98, 52–8.

Weston, J. (2020) Managing mental incapacity in the 20th century: a history of the Court of Protection of England and Wales. *International Journal of Law and Psychiatry*, 68, 1–12.

Wied, T., Knebel, M., Tesky, V. and Haberstroh, J. (2019) The human right to make one's own choices: implications for supported decision-making in persons with dementia. *European Psychologist*, 24(2), 146–58.

13

Navigating communication boundaries: statutory assessments as places for shared decision making

Jill Hemmington

Introduction

In the United Kingdom (UK), those undertaking statutory assessments must embed principles requiring the participation of people who are being assessed. This suggests that assessments can be a place for shared decision making (SDM). This chapter explores ways in which this can be supported in practice. SDM in mental health settings is not well researched and is usually limited to those who are understood to have capacity to make decisions, usually in relation to medication and side effects. Within psychiatry generally, and within statutory assessments specifically, concepts such as 'insight' (and how this is interpreted), autonomy, choice and empowerment are key. These are discussed and summarised to look at how to understand and to maximise SDM techniques with a range of people. The chapter considers SDM to be part of a professional attitude and values-based practice. It concludes by considering communication techniques and the ways in which statutory assessments can be coordinated and planned around SDM.

Statutory contexts, policy contexts and principles

Within the jurisdictions of the UK, there are statutory principles relating to service users' involvement and participation. These are summarised in Box 13.1.

Box 13.1: Statutory principles for involvement

England: The empowerment and involvement principle states that people 'should be fully involved in decisions about care, support and treatment'; that a person's 'views, past and present wishes and feelings ... should be considered so far as they are reasonably ascertainable'; that people 'should be enabled to participate in decision-making as far as they are capable'; that 'consideration should be given to what assistance or support a person may need ... and [this] should be provided, to ensure maximum involvement' (DoH, 2015, paras 1.8–1.10)

Wales: 'Empowerment: the person should be involved in the planning and delivery of care and treatment' (Welsh Government, 2016)

Northern Ireland: 'People suffering from mental disorder should: have their needs fully taken into account, notwithstanding that resource restrictions may render it impracticable to meet them; be treated in a way that promotes self-determination and encourages personal responsibility where possible' (DHSS (Northern Ireland), 1992, para 1.8)

Scotland: 'Decisions must take into account: the present and past wishes and feelings of the person' and 'the importance of the person participating as fully as possible and providing information to help with this' (Scottish Executive, 2005, p 10)

More broadly, there are policy trends and organisational rhetoric based on aspirations of collaboration, co-production and SDM with people who use (or are subject to) mental health services. The guidelines for psychosis from the National Institute for Health and Care Excellence (NICE) in England and Wales include 'working in partnership' with service users (NICE, 2014, p 10).

SDM is enshrined as a principle in England's National Health Service (NHS) constitution, with principle four stating that 'patients ... will be involved in and consulted on all decisions about their care and treatment' (DHSC, 2021a). The General Medical Council's (GMC, 2020) guidance on decision making and consent says that 'shared decision making and consent are fundamental to good medical practice'.

Part of the qualifying criteria for AMHPs in England and Wales rests on the professional's 'ability to promote the rights, dignity and self-determination of persons consistent with their own needs and wishes, to enable them to contribute to the decisions made affecting their quality of life and liberty' (HMSO, 2008, Schedule 2, para 1[c]).

Shared decision making

Shared decision making (SDM) is a relatively well-developed practice within non-mental health settings. The emphasis is on systematic, interactive participation from both person and professional in the decision-making process and agreement on the decision. Using formal stages, both person and professional share information and bring preferences that they discuss and deliberate, in order to reach a joint decision. In the absence of initial agreement, 'a process of negotiation is likely to occur' (Charles et al, 1999, p 656). NICE (2021) suggests that it is an empowering process enabling people to understand the risks, benefits and possible consequences of different options – including choosing to have no treatment or not changing what they are currently receiving. It means 'communicating with people in a way they can understand, using clear language, avoiding jargon and explaining technical terms and making sure [people] understand the choices available to them' (NICE, 2021, p 1). NICE (2021) also recommends evidence-based models such as the Teach Back method, where the professional seeks confirmation that the information provided is being understood by getting people to 'teach back' what has been discussed, which is therefore more than just asking, "Do you understand?"

In mental health settings, however, evidence suggests that professionals have difficulties predicting what the person's priorities are and that professionals' preferences tend to dominate, with decisions often being made without any negotiation. Further, professionals often use inaccessible technical language and service users report being 'seen but not heard' (Johansson and Lundman, 2002). Interestingly, clinicians may not automatically enable participation, but instead intuitively 'feel' if a person wants to be involved or not (Goossensen et al, 2007) – which may be the case, but how do we articulate this in records and reports around guiding principles? Further, issues around capacity within mental health settings have highlighted barriers to SDM, where a lack of cognitive capacity has been seen to affect a person's 'insight' and communication. According to NICE (2021), professionals believe that people only had limited interest in their treatment. In the words of one practitioner: 'I attempt to discuss the issues with the person but … if it's clear that they're insight-less, or that they're not going to agree … I don't think there is much point, at that moment in time, to get into a conflict' (Shepherd et al, 2011). This invites an evaluation of the problem of 'insight'.

The problem of 'insight'

People's rights as citizens are denied, by virtue of a diagnosis of mental illness, on the presumption that they 'lack insight' into their own experiences (Beresford, 2002). Professionals acting in a person's perceived best interests have overridden basic rights on the basis of that diagnosis (Holland, 2007). Survivor and activist Judi Chamberlin (1998, p 406) believes that 'people in power are always saying that they know what is best for those they rule over, even if those poor unfortunate individuals think they know best what they want. The powerful seldom cast their own motives in anything but benevolent terms'. 'Insight' is often a primary consideration in mental health settings, and yet its interpretations are inconsistent. Given the complex power asymmetries between professionals and service users, a perceived lack of insight can highlight the ways in which service users are not always trusted as 'knowers' (Guidry-Grimes, 2019).

'Insight' may be classed as a type of self-knowledge, but it usually relates to whether the person has the *right type* of awareness. It is sometimes considered an all-or-nothing, unidimensional phenomenon; or it can be described as 'poor', 'fair', 'limited', 'improving' – all nonspecific terms reflecting its limited meaning (Casher and Bess, 2012). Treatment or medication 'adherence' is implicated (David, 1990). Here there is a circularity problem: 'awareness of illness' is construed as willingness to accept treatment, so only those who are fully compliant 'have' insight. 'Poor insight' – perceived as a refusal to acknowledge or agree with 'symptoms' and the likely success of treatments – is received negatively by professionals (they are 'non-concordant' or 'non-engaging') and trust is lost. Fricker (2007) describes forms of epistemic injustice including testimonial injustice, where a person's credibility, authority or ability to know is challenged, and their own testimony is either not believed or not trusted. Prejudice around mental 'illness' causes the hearer to minimise the credibility of the speaker's words and this is particularly bound up within notions of capacity, 'insight' and judgements around what someone says, how they make decisions, construe problems, and express choices and preferences (Lakeman, 2010).

Lack of insight, then, is substantially a 'judgment of discrepancy between the perspective of a clinician and that of a service user' (McGorry and McConville, 1999). Of further concern, it can also be a form of social acquiescence whereby people are required to accept the predominant cultural norms and theories about what their experiences mean. This may even be the case when their differing views about their 'mental state' and behaviour arise from their cultural background and alternative interpretations about mental distress. This would certainly be borne out within the evidence of assessment biases and the ways in which privileged ethnic, racial and socio-economic groups tend to be given higher insight scores (Guidry-Grimes, 2019).

Perceptions of poor or partial insight, and consequent distrust, can lead to 'insight' shortfalls being viewed as a recalcitrance problem (Guidry-Grimes, 2019). Similarly, McKeown (2016) suggests that those who resist diagnostic labelling and medication, especially more coercive forms, take on the identity of recalcitrant, difficult or presenting 'challenging behaviour', and who then struggle to assert their own agency (Breeze and Repper, 1998).

Overall, when people are obliged to account for their experiences in an artificial or unfamiliar framework and language, they are denied opportunities for sharing what they actually believe and feel, which in turn undermines their position as a partner in the therapeutic relationship (Marková and Berrios, 1992). This is compounded by aspects of jargon.

The problem of jargon

Psychiatrist Philip Timms developed a 'Devil's Dictionary for Mental Health' (2017), based on observations of difficulties in day-to-day communication where jargon words were involved. Timms believes that these carry a covert meaning and an 'intimidating facade', whereby those inside a profession use language in an idiosyncratic way to preserve professional authority and power. Yet clearly, 'if you cannot understand a discussion, you cannot participate' (Timms, 2017, p 244). Examples of problematic phrases are:

- *Adherence*: for professionals a mainstay of treatment; for service users a reason for reluctance to reveal their disinterest and create disharmony.
- *Behavioural*: a term used to describe behaviour of which we disapprove. Commonly combined with 'just': 'It's just behavioural', where 'just' is a way to deny complexity.
- *Inappropriate* (behaviour): rational behaviour of which we disapprove (Timms, 2017, p 246).

Jargon can help professionals feel more comfortable with difficult truths, but using it means we will then not be communicating or thinking as clearly as we should. For Timms (2017), an awareness of jargon words serves us as the canary once served the coal miner: a sign that something may not be quite right, and that we need to keep our wits about us. Paying attention to how we talk (and write) helps us to think and communicate more clearly and more meaningfully, and it means we are better able to engage with everyone's reality. Otherwise, the professional takes over and the person's accounts of their own experiences, needs, values and interests become less valid: the professional is adopting a paternalistic position.

Paternalism, values and attitudes in mental health services

The idea of healthcare decision making as paternalistic originated in the Hippocratic Oath, where the physician (and today the nurse or other staff) makes decisions about treatment and care, ostensibly acting in the best interest of the person. Decisions might not involve the person, or be contrary to their wishes, or ignore their perspective in other ways, as long as they are benefited. The person is not seen as autonomous and/or rational and paternalism therefore involves knowingly and willingly going against their wishes for their own sake (Sandman and Munthe, 2010). Decisions are made and simply communicated to the person who, in turn, is expected to comply despite the fact that their specific needs and preferences may not have been fully taken into account (Sandman et al, 2011). The power imbalance within mental health settings often means that full 'patient choice' models are limited – if they ever happen (Sandman and Munthe, 2010).

Pelto-Piri et al's (2013) research identified three dominant ethical perspectives concerning the ways in which doctors and other staff members frame interactions with service users:

- *paternalism*: promoting and restoring the health of the person, providing good care and assuming responsibility;
- *autonomy*: respecting the person's right to self-determination and information, respecting the person's integrity and protecting human rights;
- *reciprocity*: involving people in the planning and implementation of their care and building trust.

The majority of approaches appeared to indicate paternalism, several represented autonomy, but only a small number were attributed to reciprocity. Yet, as highlighted earlier, the literature and mental health legislation stress that reciprocity, even in coercive care, should be seen as a core value (Pelto-Piri et al, 2013). In practice, however, it appears that shifting from paternalism seems difficult.

Some mental health professionals believe that SDM is difficult due to a lack of health literacy in the person ('information asymmetry'), and decisions are made alone. Service users may be reluctant to contradict the professional, who they view as the arbiter of a final decision. There is evidence that service users need to be seen as being a 'good patient', who is 'doing as [they are] told', and not wanting to be 'someone causing trouble' or telling professionals how to do their job (NICE, 2021). SDM inevitably needs to incorporate and work with these perspectives.

What is important to service users?

Statutory mental health assessments and their broader contexts are often deeply unequal and experienced as such, which is inconsistent with policy aspirations around collaboration (Buckland, 2020). Priorities also differ and for those being assessed for detention good interpersonal relationships are vital. Good communication is viewed as highly important, particularly with regard to being listened to, 'being believed' and 'being understood' (Akther et al, 2019). Being treated with respect is important (Olofsson and Norberg, 2001; Sheehan and Burns, 2011).

Coercion can be both objective (people *are* subjected to force) and subjective (interventions *feel* coercive). Paradoxically, objective experiences of coercion (including restraint or forced medication) are not necessarily attributed to the use of statute itself, but to the relationship with the staff who are enforcing it (Gilburt et al, 2008, p 10). Although coercive interventions are typically experienced negatively, their impact could be mitigated by kind and caring staff (Katsakou and Priebe, 2007; Wyder et al, 2015). People who have not *felt* coerced believed they were actively involved in their admission and treatment process, and were given information about the reasons, offered alternatives, and given time to consider their options and to make decisions accordingly (Katsakou et al, 2011; Akther et al, 2019).

A lack of participation in decision making has been highlighted as being a problematic aspect of coercion (Katsakou and Priebe, 2007; Jankovic et al, 2011; McGuinness et al, 2013; Smyth et al, 2017). The importance of professionals genuinely caring and listening, and of having an opportunity to participate, makes the person feel like a valued and normal human being, while lack of participation damages self-esteem (Van de Veer, 1992). Some research (Wirtz et al, 2006) suggests that people who appreciated staff's commitment rarely perceived that they were subject to coercion, in comparison with those who did not consider staff members to be committed. Talking to the person may not necessarily change the nature of the coercive intervention, but it may make them feel respected as a human being (Katsakou and Priebe, 2007; Widdershoven and Van der Scheer, 2008). Overall, mental health service users have different priorities from professionals. They are more likely to value empathy, a focus on the relationship, emotional aspects of decision making, and an emphasis on the trust and partnership aspect of decision making (Akther et al, 2019; Woltmann and Whitley, 2010).

Developing and enabling reciprocity and decision sharing in practice

Despite this, service users have described a lack of person centeredness, to the extent that the assessment is 'like it's deliberately secretive … and Kafkaesque' (Blakley et al, 2021, p 216). A recurring theme is apparent where people have spoken about their lack of involvement and influence, retrospectively being told the outcome only, and that the assessment encounter is in effect a fait accompli: 'There's no point saying anything when it's not going to have much difference. I was the subject of it but it didn't feel like a two-way process' (Blakley et al, 2021, p 215). In this same research by Blakley et al (2021), people recognise their lack of power in this process and want to have more of a voice: 'I want to change the process by being more assertive … Why didn't I just say to them, "I don't know what you mean, can you repeat the question? Can you rephrase it?" … have more input' (Blakley et al, 2021, p 216). How, then, do we create an attitude and techniques to better embed reciprocity?

Paternalism and full patient choice (or autonomy) models have been characterised as competitors of SDM, however Sandeman and Munthe (2010) suggest that this need not be the case. They use a sliding scale analogy, the end points of which are extreme versions of paternalism and full person choice, respectively. Either end has a professional monologue (involving only one person) and neither extreme is of itself compatible with SDM, but the variations in between them may be. For Emanuel and Emanuel (1992), an essential quality of the professional relationship is that of caring *in the very moment of interaction* – something that is missing in a strictly monological paternalist decisional approach. Here, the person can be enabled to share in different and developing ways:

1. *Sharing as venting*: the professional talks with the person and listens to their thoughts and concerns.
2. *Sharing as affirmation*: the professional talks and listens, and then does their best to affirm and endorse the person's thoughts and concerns.
3. *Sharing as caring*: the professional talks and listens, does their best to affirm and endorse the person's thoughts and concerns and, at the same time, tries to comfort and reassure them.

These sharing models connect to the values underlying paternalism in that the professional acts for therapeutic reasons around well-being – but there are deliberate steps to actively incorporate aspects of person choice. This is a similar approach to Sandeman and Munthe's (2010) person-adapted paternalism, which invites the person to talk about their life, what is important to them and the way they have experienced problems. What has been heard is then incorporated into the decisional process and the decision is adapted to suit the person's circumstances. Here, the professional still acts paternalistically, but the information communicated by the person is treated as an instrument for arriving at an optimal decision within the professional's own standards.

As long as the 'sharing' involved in SDM does not imply handing over decisional authority to the person, SDM in this sense can be accommodated within paternalistic healthcare – and, crucially, could be a first step toward attitude change. A further way to develop reciprocity in practice may be to consider it as active value-based practice with the following features:

- Always start with the person's perspective, but also seek a balance between legitimately different perspectives.
- Ensure that communication skills play a substantial role in decision making (Emanuel and Emanuel, 1992).

There is evidence that practitioners use a paternalistic style because they are acting, automatically, from their own or their institution's values and methods (NICE, 2021). It may not always be possible to achieve reciprocity in decision making; however, there can be an aim to reach a compromise that is acceptable to the person, as well as adequate enough from a professional perspective. Only after such a strategy has failed should we consider paternalistic decision making (Sandman and Munthe, 2010).

Communication: attitudes, styles and skills

Service users have described feeling like the practitioner's word was final, when they should actually be facilitating participation by being open to questions and challenges (NICE, 2021). Mental health professionals have also acknowledged the need for an attitude shift.

> It's about having a relationship where [patients] don't feel talked down to, where it's not punitive and you're not behaving in a parental role but you're trying to work with them on an equal – as equal as you can – relationship … it is not an easy thing to articulate … but if you're really going to have genuine partnership and not tokenistic attempts you have to shift your whole orientation towards how you work with people and how you see yourself. (Mental health nurse cited in Chong et al, 2013)

Attitudes are significant. Good communication is vital for engagement and eliciting people's preferences. Good interpersonal skills help practitioners' awareness of the person's life, social context and potential cultural differences (particularly in mental health), and a poor professional communication style is a barrier to SDM. Listening to each other is a basic rule for communication (NICE, 2021) and yet communication skills are not always learned during training. As one practitioner (cited in Giacco et al, 2018) reports: 'Any sort of training in communication and helping with choices … is helpful. 'Cause … in psychiatry you learn how to ask questions, I don't know if you really learn how to negotiate that much.'

Within psychiatry, particularly with psychosis, models of good communication are underdeveloped. McCabe and Healey's (2018) research highlights the apparent miscommunication within the doctor–patient relationship. An experience of psychosis can mean that the boundaries between the self and the external world are threatened, and the person may have some difficulties understanding both their own thoughts and those arising from the external world. Interactional trouble arises when, in practice, the meaning of the experience is disputed: for the person the experience is real, but clinicians will attribute them to a psychiatric illness. This leaves the person feeling poorly understood. There is a lack of shared understanding about the problem and its causes.

In a study by McCabe and Healey (2018), people experiencing psychosis attempted to described their experiences and discuss their meaning and emotional consequences (feeling embarrassed or afraid), asking repeated questions about the causes of their distress ("Why does everyone think I'm Jesus?"). In response, doctors hesitated, responded with a question rather than with an answer, and smiled or laughed (particularly when informal carers were present). Overall, they were reluctant to engage and thereby created disagreement. They reported difficulties in knowing how to respond: whether to go along (or collude) with, or challenge: 'It's difficult to find the middle ground. Do you confirm the patient's delusions or do you confront and challenge them?' (McCabe and Healey, 2018, p 414).

There are some immediately practical ways of enabling participation and involvement. For example, Thompson and McCabe (2016) explored aspects of 'good' communication with people with a diagnosis of schizophrenia, considering the ways in which questions are used as the primary method for developing therapeutic relationships. Unsurprisingly, neutral 'survey' questions convey indifference and represent a bureaucratic or 'anonymous' relationship, which represents a case to undertake statutory assessments without a checklist or proforma, and to conduct it in a relational way, focusing on the space between two people. Effective communicators will tailor their questions to a particular individual, which conveys a caring relationship (Heritage, 2010). Fundamentally, people who feel understood will divert less. Simply considering the types of questioning used might be helpful. Thompson and McCabe's (2016) different types of questions included the following:

- *Yes/no or interrogative*: 'closed' questions, for example: "Do you go to a day centre?"

- *Wh- questions*: 'open' questions that elicit information – who, what, when, why or how.
- *Declarative questions*: questions prefaced with 'so', for example: "So you feel a bit anxious?" "So you're quite happy being on your own?" "So you're lethargic, you just couldn't be bothered to do these things?" "So you feel okay about it?" "So that's something you want to switch off from?"

It appears that 'wh-' questions invite more extensive responses and are associated with more symptoms and poorer communication with psychosis. The only type of question associated with engagement and relationship satisfaction were declarative questions: they are used to convey mutual understanding and closer working, and indicate connection; they are heard as displays of empathy and convey a clearer 'knowing' stance than other types of question; they are associated with better perceptions of the therapeutic alliance and joint work; and they indicate empathy, which entails the mental health professional being able to 'give an account of the person's experience that the person recognizes as his own' (Oyebode, 2018, p 37).

Repair

The concept of repair, taken from conversation analysis, incorporates a further practical layer here. When people talk, they frequently encounter problems of hearing, speaking and understanding. Examples include the speaker using the wrong word, not being able to find the exact word they want or, alternatively, when a hearer cannot make out what the speaker has said. When we encounter such problems we have recourse to a 'repair mechanism': we ask for clarity and the speaker can repair the reference either by repeating the original word(s) or by substituting another word. It is an organised set of practices through which participants in conversation are able to address and potentially resolve such problems of speaking, hearing or understanding (Sidnell, 2010). AMHPs, by carefully focusing on the conversational patterns, understanding and aiming for advocacy, are also considering paragraph 14.42 of the Mental Health Act 1983 (MHA) Code of Practice, where, 'given the importance of good communication, it is essential that those professionals who assess patients are able to communicate with the patient effectively and reliably to prevent potential misunderstandings. AMHPs should establish, as far as possible, whether patients have particular communication needs' (DoH, 2015, p 120).

Barriers to SDM

While attitudes and skills can be developed at any point in practice, perhaps unsurprisingly time pressures and constraints, resource limits and high staff stress and fatigue are a consistently cited barrier to SDM. Practitioners are already pressured to finish appointments quickly and SDM is an added burden and rarely the path of least resistance (NICE, 2021). Service users recognise this and can defer decision-making responsibility due to concerns about professionals' busy schedules (NICE, 2021). This is supported by research in relation to statutory assessments in England where AMHPs' workloads prevented time for meaningful, holistic and relational assessments (Hemmington et al, 2021, p 51):

> The AMHP forgot to mention the outcome of it when he left he was that rushed. He had to get to the next appointment. He failed to tell me what was happening. I had to ask the police officers what was going on.
> [...]
> The AMHPs [are] there for five minutes to ask questions and gain the information from you ... They get the information and then go and make their decision elsewhere ... Or just not having the time ... because they are pushed and rushed and [say,] "Later, but today I have loads of people to see."

The impact on this same issue is highlighted elsewhere (Blakley et al, 2021, p 214): 'Information's thrown at you, you don't have time to think'. AMHPs frequently stress the lack of time they have to do the work, feeling rushed and the fact that 'everyone is swamped' by the volume of work and number of referrals to process. They want to be able to 'slow things down' and prevent oppressive outcomes, but they very often feel under pressure around their decision making. This limits person and family involvement and there is a recognition that being rushed into decision making is at the expense of a good outcome for the person (Hemmington et al, 2021, p 61).

Multidisciplinary team settings can bring contradictory models that prevent convergence and undermine SDM. As one practitioner (cited in Légaré and Witteman, 2013, p 279) reports: 'Currently there is much, much work in silos. We have nursing services that are the concern of nurses. There are the social workers who have psychosocial concerns ... there is nothing that brings all these people together.'

Finally, language barriers can undermine SDM, which impacts already disadvantaged and marginalised groups of people. This is compounded by people from minority ethnic groups already perceiving reduced practitioner trust. Other cultural barriers included gender, sexuality and socio-economic status. All these can intensify a lack of advocacy and empowerment in statutory assessments.

Taking the power elsewhere? The kitchen conversation

Here, I turn to my own research, which is based on observing and audio-recording statutory mental health assessments with a focus on power, communication and SDM. A developing area of contemplation is based on observation of a habitual characteristic of the assessment. There is often an invisible line whereby both doctor and (in this case) AMHP believe that they have gathered enough information to make a decision; there is a knowing nod or an explicit acknowledgement that they have heard enough, and they then retire elsewhere (a kitchen, a garden, but crucially somewhere else) to make their decision. Elsewhere (Hemmington et al, 2021, p 49), this has been experienced in different ways:

> They always asked me lots of questions and stuff and then they always go off to have a conversation, so I'm rarely involved in the actual discussion.
>
> [...]
>
> I can remember a few times where my parents have wanted to be involved in the discussion, but they've been told to wait outside or vice versa ... they've [the professionals] all gone into my garden.

The consequences of this and the negative effect of the assessors leaving the room to make their decision has been described powerfully as 'waiting for the verdict. ... So you're sat there for like half an hour worried, knowing that they're making this choice' (Blakley et al, 2021, p 214). At times, due to sensitivity or perceptions of risk for a variety of reasons, it might absolutely be the right thing to do to have this discussion elsewhere. There is, however, a need to ask ourselves whether this is *always* the right thing to do, or do we act instinctively, habitually, from a paternalistic perspective? This is where we could turn to the principles of Open Dialogue to look at reframing our approach and attitude to statutory assessment.

Incorporating principles of Open Dialogue

Seikkula and Olson (2003, p 403) describe Open Dialogue as 'a network-based, language approach to psychiatric care'. With an emphasis on the 'poetics of the interview room', it considers the language and communication practices in face-to-face encounters (Hoffman, 2007). Rather than being seen as an object of treatment, service users are 'competent or potentially competent partners in the recovery process' (Gleeson et al, 1999, p 390). The team develop a 'trustworthy context' that specifically and deliberately legitimises each person by explicitly hearing and responding to their voice and to their point of view. This enables the 'dialogical' resources of participants, as they become agents who are supported to use their own language to express their experiences. As described earlier, psychosis is understood to be a radical, sometimes terrifying alienation from shared, communicative practices: a 'no-man's land' where the experience might have no words to describe it, leaving the person with no voice and no genuine agency (Holma, 1999; Seikkula, 2002). A shared verbal language to explain these experiences is used to enable the person to articulate their psychotic speech and private, inner voices and hallucinatory signs as effectively as they can (Olson et al, 2014).

A 'polyphonic conversation' means that there is space for each voice. Boundaries between so-called sick and well are removed and the collaborative exchange brings about new, shared understandings and language, and a common experience that is 'without rank' (Bahktin, 1984; Olson et al, 2014). Crucially, listening has greater importance than a formulaic process of interviewing and, at least at the start, questions are as open as possible to invite participants to talk about whatever issues are most relevant to them at that moment. As summarised above, it is dialogical rather than monological (which would be a speaker without a contributing listener).

Differences may arise, but all voices have room to exist, and participants listen and exchange, rather than bringing polarised, right-or-wrong thinking. Not everyone has to accept all points of view, and people can disagree based on a premise that helpful changes can be made simply from the airing of different perspectives in a safe climate. Joint understanding, rather than the need for consensus, is key.

Overall, there is attentiveness to responding and reflecting (hearing, understanding and acknowledging *in an explicit way*), and an open, participatory, transparent, jargon-free conversation (Rober, 2005). From this perspective, then, the approach is not a model that is applied, but more a set of practices that are established throughout the system. It is, fundamentally, an attitude and a shift in orientation. Decisions, including on treatment and hospitalisation, are discussed and made while everyone is present. There are no separate staff meetings for treatment planning (Seikkula and Olson, 2003, p 407). There are no kitchen conversations.

Conclusion

As highlighted at the start of this chapter, those undertaking statutory assessments have a responsibility to apply principles based on empowerment, involvement, inclusion and participation. This chapter has reviewed ways in which this can be done (and recorded as such). The MHA Code of Practice in England asserts that 'AMHPs who assess patients for possible detention under the [Mental Health] Act have overall responsibility for co-ordinating the process of assessment' (DoH, 2015, para 14.41). It is strongly contended that this co-ordination is not merely setting the assessment up in practical terms (transport, planned and timely arrival of other assessors); it is also something that can and should be pulled through to, and throughout, the assessment itself.

In England, the MHA is currently being debated and reformed, with rhetoric consistent with the opening paragraphs of this chapter (DHSC, 2018; 2021b). The guiding principles are being revised and there are frequent references to 'choice and autonomy', which is the new iteration of 'empowerment and involvement' where mental health professionals should ensure service users' views and choices are respected. Similarly, there are references to 'the person as an individual' and the new Act is set to go further as the principles will become embedded and 'up front in the Act' (DHSC, 2021b), rather than just policy within the Code of Practice as they are currently.

There is also, interestingly, a recommendation that SDM between clinicians and patients should be used to develop care and treatment plans and all treatment decisions, as far as is practicable, and there are planned training requirements around the application of the guiding principles (DHSC, 2021b).

Overall, the evidence suggests that what people want from the process of SDM can vary. Service users prioritise trust, empathy and being listened to, whereas practitioners prioritise explaining options and focusing on ensuring joint decisions are made. Arguably, service users see it as a process, whereas practitioners see it more as a decision point. There are clear ways in which those engaged with statutory assessments can reflect on attitudes, values and practice changes, which will enable an approach based on advocacy, empowerment and collaboration. It is important to consider the locus of power when considering a person's ability to participate. Recognising the power and information hierarchy, along with the potential for reinforcing existing oppression, invites commitment on the part of professionals to apply epistemic humility that recognises the boundary of their own expert domain and the potential contribution of patients. Epistemic humility is a disposition and a commitment to appraise both what we know and don't know, and to understand our claims to knowledge accordingly (Ho, 2017). Any reading around Open Dialogue will also highlight a significant theme: that the 'micropolitics', or the larger institutional practices, need to support this way of working as a matter of practice orientation (Seikkula and Olson, 2003). Again, this summarises the emerging attitude shifts that need to continue into the practice of statutory assessments.

References

Akther, S.F., Molyneaux, E., Stuart, R., Johnson, S., Simpson, A. and Oram, S. (2019) Patients' experiences of assessment and detention under mental health legislation: systematic review and qualitative meta-synthesis. *BJPsych Open*, 5(3), E37.

Bakhtin, M. (1984) *Problems of Dostoevsky's poetics: theory and history of literature volume 8*. Manchester: Manchester University Press.

Beresford, P. (2002) User involvement in research and evaluation: liberation or regulation? *Social Policy and Society*, 1, 95–105.

Blakley, L., Asher, C., Etherington, A., Maher, J., Wadey, E., Walsh, V. et al (2021) 'Waiting for the verdict': the experience of being assessed under the Mental Health Act. *Journal of Mental Health*, 31(2), 212–19.

Breeze, J. and Repper, J. (1998) Struggling for control: the care experiences of 'difficult' patients in mental health services. *Journal of Advanced Nursing*, 28(6), 1301–11.

Buckland, R. (2020) Power as perceived in MHA assessment contexts: a scoping review of the literature. *Practice*, 32(4), 253–67.

Casher, M.I. and Bess, J.D. (2012) Determination and documentation of insight in psychiatric inpatients. *Psychiatric Times*, 3 April. Available at http://www.psychiatrictimes.com/articles/determination-and-documentation-insight-psyc hiatric-inpatients.

Chamberlin, J. (1998) Citizenship rights and psychiatric disability. *Psychiatric Rehabilitation Journal*, 21(4), 405–8.

Charles, C., Gafni. A. and Whelan, T. (1999) Decision-making in the physician-patient encounter: revisiting the shared decision-making model. *Social Science and Medicine*, 49(5), 651–61.

Chong, W.W., Aslani, P. and Chen, T.F. (2013) Shared decision-making and interprofessional collaboration in mental healthcare: a qualitative study exploring perceptions of barriers and facilitators. *Journal of Interprofessional Care*, 27(5), 373–9.

David, A.S. (1990) Insight and psychosis. *British Journal of Psychiatry*, 156, 798–808.

Department of Health (DoH) (2015) *Mental Health Act 1983: Code of Practice*. London: DoH.

Department of Health and Social Care (DHSC) (2018) *Modernising the Mental Health Act: increasing choice, reducing compulsion – final report of the Independent Review of the Mental Health Act 1983*. London: DHSC. Available at https://ass ets.publishing.service.gov.uk/government/uploads/system/uploads/attachme nt_data/file/778897/Modernising_the_Mental_Health_Act_-_increasing_choi ce__reducing_compulsion.pdf.

Department of Health and Social Care (DHSC) (2021a) *The NHS constitution for England*. London: DHSC.

Department of Health and Social Care (DHSC) (2021b) *Reforming the Mental Health Act: government response*. London: DHSC. Available at https://www.gov. uk/government/consultations/reforming-the-mental-health-act/outcome/ reforming-the-mental-health-act-government-response#strengthening-the-patients-rights-to-choose-and-refuse-treatment—advance-choice-documents.

Department of Health and Social Services (DHSS) (Northern Ireland) (1992) *Mental Health (Northern Ireland) Order 1986 Code of Practice*. Belfast: Her Majesty's Stationery Office.

Emanuel, E.J. and Emanuel, L.L. (1992) Four models of the physician–patient relationship. *Journal of the American Medical Association*, 267(16), 2221–6.

Fricker, M. (2007) *Epistemic injustice: power and the ethics of knowing*. Oxford: Oxford University Press.

General Medical Council (GMC) (2020) *Decision making and consent: guidance on professional standards and ethics for doctors*. Manchester: GMC.

Giacco, D., Mavromara, L., Gamblen, J., Conneely, M. and Priebe, S. (2018) Shared decision-making with involuntary hospital patients: a qualitative study of barriers and facilitators. *BJPsych Open*, 4(3), 113–18.

Gilburt, H., Rose, D. and Slade, M. (2008) The importance of relationships in mental health care: a qualitative study of service users' experiences of psychiatric hospital admission in the UK. *BMC Health Services Research*, 8(92), 92–12.

Gleeson, J., Jackson, H., Stavely, H. and Burnett, P. (1999) Family intervention in early psychosis. In P. McGorry and H. Jackson (eds), *The recognition and management of early psychosis* (pp 380–415). Cambridge. Cambridge University Press.

Goossensen, A., Zijlstra, P. and Koopmanschap, M. (2007) Measuring shared decision-making processes in psychiatry: skills versus patient satisfaction. *Patient Education and Counseling*, 67(1–2), 50–6.

Guidry-Grimes, L. (2019) Ethical complexities in assessing patients' insight. *Journal of Medical Ethics*, 45(3), 178–82.

Hemmington, J., Graham, M., Marshall, A., Brammer, A., Stone, K. and Vicary, S. (2021) *Approved Mental Health Professionals, Best Interests Assessors and people with lived experience: an exploration of professional identities and practice a report prepared for Social Work England*. Sheffield: Social Work England.

Heritage, J. (2010) Questioning in medicine. In A.F. Freed and S. Ehrlich (eds), *Why do you ask? The function of questions in institutional discourse* (pp 42–68). Oxford: Oxford University Press.

Her Majesty's Stationery Office (HMSO) (2008) *Mental Health (Approved Mental Health Professional) (Approval) (England) Regulations*. London: HMSO.

Ho, A. (2017) Reconciling patient safety and epistemic humility: an ethical use of opioid treatment plans. *Hastings Center Report*, 47(3), 34–5.

Hoffman, L. (2007) The art of 'withness'. In H. Andersen and D. Gehart (eds), *Collaborative therapy: relationships and conversations that make a difference* (pp 63–80). New York: Routledge.

Holland, K. (2007) The epistemological bias of ethics review: constraining mental health research. *Qualitative Inquiry*, 13(6) 895–913.

Holma, J. (1999) The search for a narrative: investigating acute psychosis and the need-adapted treatment model from the narrative viewpoint. *Jjvyldi Studies in Education, Psychology and Social Research*, 150.

Jankovic, J., Yeeles, K. and Katsakou, C. (2011) Family caregivers' experiences of involuntary psychiatric hospital admissions of their relatives – a qualitative study. *PloS One*, 6(10), e25425.

Johansson, I.M. and Lundman, B. (2002) Patients' experience of involuntary psychiatric care: good opportunities and great losses. *Journal of Psychiatric and Mental Health Nursing*, 9(6), 639–47.

Katsakou, C. and Priebe, S. (2007) Patient's experiences of involuntary hospital admission and treatment: a review of qualitative studies. *Epidemiologia e Psichiatria Sociale*, 16(2), 172–8.

Katsakou, C., Marougka, S., Garabette, J., Rost, F., Yeeles, K. and Priebe, S. (2011) Why do some voluntary patients feel coerced into hospitalisation? A mixed-methods study. *Psychiatry Research*, 187(1–2), 275–82.

Lakeman, R. (2010) Epistemic injustice and the mental health service user. *International Journal of Mental Health Nursing*, 19, 151–3.

Légaré, F. and Witteman, H.O. (2013) Shared decision making: examining key elements and barriers to adoption into routine clinical practice. *Health Affairs (Millwood)*, 32(2), 276–84.

Marková, I.S. and Berrios, G.E. (1992) The meaning of insight in clinical psychiatry. *British Journal of Psychiatry*, 160, 850–60.

McCabe, R. and Healey, P.G.T. (2018) Miscommunication in doctor–patient communication. *Topics in Cognitive Science*, 10(2), 409–24.

McGorry, P.D. and McConville, S.B. (1999) Insight in psychosis: an elusive target. *Comprehensive Psychiatry*, 40, 131–42.

McGuinness, D., Dowling, M. and Trimble, T. (2013) Experiences of involuntary admission in an approved mental health centre. *Journal of Psychiatric and Mental Health Nursing*, 20(8), 726–34.

McKeown, M. (2016) Stand up for recalcitrance! Editorial. *International Journal of Mental Health Nursing*, 25, 481–3.

National Institute for Health and Care Excellence (NICE) (2014) *Psychosis and schizophrenia in adults: prevention and management.* London: NICE.

National Institute for Health and Care Excellence (NICE) (2021) *Shared decision making: evidence review for effectiveness of approaches and activities to increase engagement in shared decision making and the barriers and facilitators to engagement (NG197).* London: NICE.

Olofsson, B. and Norberg, A. (2001) Experiences of coercion in psychiatric care as narrated by patients, nurses and physicians. *Journal of Advanced Nursing*, 33, 89–97.

Olson, M., Seikkula, J. and Ziedonis, D. (2014) *The key elements of dialogic practice in Open Dialogue.* Worcester, MA: University of Massachusetts Medical School.

Oyebode, F. (2018) *Sims' symptoms in the mind: textbook of descriptive psychopathology.* London: Elsevier.

Pelto-Piri, V., Engström, K. and Engström, I. (2013) Paternalism, autonomy and reciprocity: ethical perspectives in encounters with patients in psychiatric in-patient care. *BMC Medical Ethics*, 14, 49.

Rober, P. (2005) The therapist's self in dialogical family therapy. *Family Process*, 44, 479–97.

Sandman, L. and Munthe, C. (2010) Shared decision making, paternalism and patient choice. *Health Care Analysis*, 18(1), 60–84.

Sandman, L., Granger, B.B., Ekman, I. and Munthe, C. (2011) Adherence, shared decision-making and patient autonomy. *Medical Health Care Philosophy*, 15(2), 115–27.

Scottish Executive (2005) *Mental Health (Care and Treatment) (Scotland) Act 1983 Code of Practice: volume 1.* Edinburgh: Scottish Executive.

Seikkula, J. (2002) Open dialogue with good and poor outcomes for psychotic crises. Examples from families with violence. *Journal of Marital and Family Therapy*, 28, 263–74.

Seikkula, J. and Olson, M.E. (2003) The open dialogue approach to acute psychosis: Its poetics and micropolitics. *Family Process*, 42(3), 403–18.

Sheehan, K.A. and Burns, T. (2011) Perceived coercion and the therapeutic relationship: a neglected association? *Psychiatric Services*, 62(5), 471–6.

Shepherd, H.L., Barratt, A., Trevena, L.J., McGeechan, K., Carey, K., Epstein, R.M. et al (2011) Three questions that patients can ask to improve the quality of information physicians give about treatment options: a cross-over trial. *Patient Education and Counseling*, 84(3), 379–85.

Sidnell, J. (2010) *Conversation analysis: an introduction.* London: Wiley-Blackwell.

Smyth, S., Casey, D., Cooney, A., Higgins, A., McGuinness, D., Bainbridge, E. et al (2017) Qualitative exploration of stakeholders' perspectives of involuntary admission under the Mental Health Act 2001 in Ireland. *International Journal of Mental Health Nursing*, 26(6), 554–69.

Thompson, L. and McCabe, R. (2016) 'Good' communication in schizophrenia: a conversation analytic definition. In M. O'Reilly and J.N. Lester (eds), *The Palgrave handbook of adult mental health.* London: Palgrave Macmillan.

Timms, P. (2017) A devil's dictionary for mental health. *BJPsych Bulletin*, 41(5), 244–6.

Van de Veer, D. (1992) *Paternalistic intervention: the moral bounds on benevolence.* Princeton, NJ: Princeton University Press

Welsh Government (2016) *Mental Health Act 1983 Code of Practice for Wales.* Cardiff: Welsh Government.

Widdershoven, G. and Van Der Scheer, L. (2008) Theory and methodology of empirical ethics: a pragmatic hermeneutic perspective. In G. Widdershoven, T. Hope, J. McMillan and L. Van Der Scheer (eds), *Empirical ethics in psychiatry* (pp 23–36). Oxford: Oxford University Press.

Wirtz, V., Cribb, A. and Barber, N. (2006) Patient–doctor decision-making about treatment within the consultation and critical analysis of models. *Social Science and Medicine*, 62(1), 116–24.

Woltmann, E.M. and Whitley, R. (2010) Shared decision making in public mental health care: perspectives from consumers living with severe mental illness. *Psychiatric Rehabilitation Journal*, 34(1), 29–36.

Wyder, M., Bland, R., Blythe, A., Matarasso, B. and Crompton, D. (2015) Therapeutic relationships and involuntary treatment orders: service users' interactions with health-care professionals on the ward. *International Journal of Mental Health Nursing*, 24(2), 181–9.

14

Compulsory mental health work: framing the future

Jill Hemmington and Sarah Vicary

The introductory chapter outlined the ways in which this book has a wide lens, focusing on compulsion and coercion within mental health settings, as well as a more specific, narrow frame on the process of assessment and decision making that can result in detention. Individual chapters, with breadth and depth, evaluated the variables surrounding compulsory mental health work and detention, and the impact this type of intervention has on both practitioners and people with lived experience. Having explored decision making around compulsion in detail, we ask all those involved to pause, reflect and begin to reframe assessments and interpersonal exchanges as micro-encounters (Staley, 2009).

For decades, research exploring the Approved Mental Health Professional (AMHP) role in England and Wales has highlighted low morale, high stress and burnout, high emotional exhaustion, vulnerability to physical and common mental health problems, and experiences of fear and vulnerability. There are difficulties attached to the challenges of being responsible for the overall coordination of the mental health assessment, the use of coercion and the lack of community alternatives to hospital, with the consequent stress from people's needs not being met. AMHPs have reported feeling unsupported, with limited opportunities for formal supervision and debriefing (Evans et al, 2005; Huxley, 2005; Evans et al, 2006; CQC, 2018; Skills for Care, 2018; Stevens et al, 2018; Hemmington et al, 2021). All these have an impact on decision making.

Compulsory mental health work is inevitably going to be informed by the prevailing social policy orientation. This book's contents sit alongside the first national workforce plan for AMHPs in England and Wales (DHSC, 2019), which acknowledges the aforementioned challenges as well as the 'national drivers' affecting the AMHP role and workforce requirements. Consistent with calls for reflection contained here, AMHP services should be seen as 'open-learning environments' and 'supervision should be viewed as the cornerstone of quality AMHP practice' (DHSC, 2019, p 33). Further, it recognises that AMHPs should explore the impact of trauma arising from compulsory detention and recognise that this affects both service users and AMHPs themselves. Several chapters within this book engaged with these agendas and offered support and suggestions for practice.

The presence of power – both formal and statutory as well as hidden and implicit – was discussed in several chapters. Yet this power is at times experienced as illusory, particularly where mental health professionals experience anxiety from being unable to access the asylum a hospital bed can provide (Nathan and Webber, 2010). AMHPs seek social justice but are now 'oppressing people' and perceiving a 'moral injury ... and sense of guilt about the role [they are] pushed into pursuing' (Hemmington et al, 2021, p 65). Similarly, AMHPs experience 'morally dubious situations' (Hemmington et al, 2021, p 65), where it is hard to enact justice and avoid using detention and coercion too frequently, particularly for people from racialised backgrounds, as is also explored in this book. We know too that outcomes of statutory assessments are understood to be disproportionate and variable and subject to biases (DoH, 2015), and to address this means re-evaluating and reframing our micro-encounters with other people.

Moral distress arises when we know the right thing to do, but constraints make it almost impossible. It happens where professionals perpetrate, fail to prevent or witness events that contradict their deeply held moral beliefs and expectations (Jameton, 1984). Ethical dilemmas, moral conflicts and the inability to prevent suffering are among the most commonly identified stressors precipitating moral injury (Farnsworth et al, 2014), and compulsory mental health work can contradict our personal moral beliefs, causing dissonance and inner conflict (Litz et al, 2009). Yet there is no right answer and, as we saw from the view of a person with lived experience of detention in Chapter 1, hospital might not actually *be* a good outcome and asylum in the true sense of the word. Readers were invited to take a fresh look at decisions and consider ways in which conventional approaches are always in people's interests or whether hospital is always the best place for people to be. A different frame might enable more creative ways of deciding on outcomes.

Some chapters within this book have acknowledged the role and purpose of supervision and urged the reader to consider their organisational culture. We could reflect on whether expressing emotions at work is seen as a personal failure to cope or a mark of professionalism (Rajan-Rankin, 2014). Within some organisational cultures, 'reason' can be valued more highly, with emotion being seen as 'interference' (Fineman, 2000) rather than a sign of an emotionally intelligent culture that supports emotional awareness and expression (Rajan-Rankin, 2014). Further, if the emotional backcloth of organisational culture is one that views high stress levels as an innate aspect of the work (and, as mentioned earlier, this has been consistent in the realm of statutory mental health work in England and Wales), there is a risk of tolerance to it remaining unchallenged (Rose and Palattiyil, 2020).

In addition to frames considering people with lived experiences of assessment, trauma and disempowerment, the reader was also invited to consider the importance of multi-professional frames, narratives and professional identities in decision making. Some chapters take a legalistic turn, while recognising the need for both breadth (legalistic knowledge) and depth (critical evaluation and value-driven practice). In an apparent paradox given the focus on compulsion and detention, arguments were made for using statutes in a way that emphasises emancipatory, values-based practice with a focus on people's strengths and choices.

Any critical reflection, based on the above areas, will enhance creativity and thoughtfulness in compulsory mental health work, and this needs to be reinforced through practice education. Education and training methods have been seen as being functional (Thompson, 1997) and training could be less mechanistic and focus on contemplation, reflection, the discomfort attached to uncertainty and the complexity of the role, as well as competence (Parkinson and Thompson, 1998) or the therapeutic relationship – particularly at times of crisis (Thompson, 1997). Mental Health Act 1983 (MHA) assessments have been described as 'crisis, mess and muddle' occurring in situations where there is 'panic and confusion', and training could address students' reflective capacities as well as acquiring and demonstrating the necessary competencies (Parkinson and Thompson, 1998).

The chapters in this book summarise the ways in which different frames connect across practice and personal boundaries. They make the case that there are alternatives to rigid thinking – a middle ground and blurring of the boundaries – and adopting this approach is a form of practice wisdom in keeping with policy and statutory reforms. The ability of AMHPs as compulsory decision makers involves active use of their own emotions and their use, even when these are in conflict (Vicary, 2021).

Having an awareness of the potential for biases – whether around race, gender or by particular diagnosis – and reframing a scenario, might enable the decision maker to avoid being complicit. Further, we may question whether mental health professionals can be better allies or advocates even within (or *especially* within) a context of statutory assessment and decision making on compulsion. With a technical knowledge of the law, an awareness of the personal and professional value base, an ability to hear service users' experiences and choices, and an ability to critically reflect on the many practical and philosophical issues, it is likely that practice wisdom will develop. It is these themes that underpin the chapters in this book.

At the beginning of this book, we invited the reader to adopt Schön and Rein's (1994) 'double vision', or the ability to act from one perspective while in the back of our minds holding awareness of other possible perspectives. Understanding framing is understanding how we give events particular, subjective meaning and the impact these have on our decisions. People who work within – or experience – compulsory mental health work can enhance their understanding of their own and others' critical frames of reference. This is critical reflection on and in practice. It is a call for continual conceptual reframing.

A consistent theme, and indeed a motivation for developing this book, is to promote dialogical communication, creative thinking and careful consideration. In some respects, we go further and add that it is reconciling those other perspectives into our own decision making. As the title of this concluding chapter suggests, it is about framing the future orientation of decision making in compulsory mental health work. This book returns to and concludes with this fundamental point: statutory assessments and decisions about compulsory detention have a much wider frame than a narrow, legalistic one.

References

Care Quality Commission (CQC) (2018) *Mental Health Act: Approved Mental Health Professional services*. London: CQC.

Department of Health (DoH) (2015) *Reform of the Mental Health Act: summary of consultation responses*. London: DoH.

Department of Health and Social Care (DHSC) (2019) *National workforce plan for Approved Mental Health Professionals (AMHPs)*. London: DHSC.

Evans, S., Huxley, P., Webber, M., Katona, C., Gately, C., Mears, A. et al (2005) The impact of 'statutory duties' on mental health social workers in the UK. *Health and Social Care in the Community*, 13(2), 145–54.

Evans, S., Huxley, P., Gately, C., Webber, M., Mears, A., Pajak. S. et al (2006) Mental health burnout and job satisfaction among mental health social workers in England and Wales. *British Journal of Psychiatry*, 188, 75–80.

Farnsworth, J.K., Drescher, K.D., Nieuwsma, J.A., Walser, R.B. and Currier, J.M. (2014) The role of moral emotions in military trauma: implications for the study and treatment of moral injury. *Review of General Psychology*, 18(4), 249–62.

Fineman, S. (ed.) (2000) *Emotion in organizations*. London: Sage.

Hemmington, J., Graham, M., Marshall, A., Brammer, A., Stone, K. and Vicary, S. (2021) *Approved Mental Health Professionals, Best Interests Assessors and people with lived experience: an exploration of professional identities and practice – a report prepared for Social Work England*. Sheffield: Social Work England.

Huxley, P., Evans, S., Webber, M. and Gately, C. (2005) Staff shortages in the mental health workforce: the case of the disappearing Approved Social Worker. *Health and Social Care in the Community*, 13(6), 504–13.

Jameton, A. (1984) *Nursing practice: the ethical issues*. Englewood Cliffs, NJ: Prentice Hall.

Litz, B.T., Stein, N., Delaney, E., Lebowitz, L., Nash, W.P., Silva, C. et al (2009) Moral injury and moral repair in war veterans: a preliminary model and intervention strategy. *Clinical Psychology Review*, 29(8), 695–706.

Nathan, J. and Webber, M. (2010) Mental health social work and the bureau-medicalisation of mental health care: identity in a changing world. *Journal of Social Work Practice*, 24(1), 15–28.

Parkinson, C. and Thompson, P. (1998) Uncertainties, mysteries, doubts and Approved Social Worker training. *Journal of Social Work Practice*, 12(1), 57–64.

Rajan-Rankin, S. (2014) Self-identity, embodiment and the development of emotional resilience. *British Journal of Social Work*, 44(8), 2426–42.

Rose, S. and Palattiyil, G. (2020) Surviving or thriving? Enhancing the emotional resilience of social workers in their organisational settings. *Journal of Social Work*, 20(1), 23–42.

Schön, D. and Rein, M. (1994) *Frame reflection: toward the resolution of intractable policy controversies*. New York: Basic Books.

Skills for Care (2018) *The Approved Mental Health Professional workforce.* London: Skills for Care.

Staley, T.W. (2009) Keeping philosophy in 'mind': Shadworth H. Hodgson's articulation of the boundaries of philosophy and science. *Journal of the History of Ideas*, 70(2), 289–315.

Stevens, M., Manthorpe, J., Martineau, S., Steils, N. and Norrie, C. (2018) An exploration of why health professionals seek to hold statutory powers in mental health services in England: considerations of the Approved Mental Health Professional role. *Journal of Mental Health*, 30(5), 571–7.

Thompson, P. (1997) Approved social work and psychotherapy. *Practice*, 9(2), 35–46.

Vicary, S. (2021) 'Pull': the active use of dissonance – an IPA pearl to show emotion management in action. *Practice*, 33(4), 253–70.

Index

A

accountability 87–90
activity analysis 121
'acts not done' 87
adaptability skills 153
advance statements and decisions 166, 167
agents of change 151, 153
aggression 42, 48
Aitken, G. 43
alienation 62–3, 64
allied health professionals 115–29
All-Party Parliamentary Group on Social
    Work 125
allyship 35
alternatives to detention 119
anger
    AMHP's 62
    gender 42, 47–8
    and powerlessness 49
anti-oppressive practices 104–5
anti-psychiatry movement 165
antipsychotics 16–17, 34
anti-racist practices 30, 32, 33, 35, 36
anxiety, professionals' 72, 73–4, 106
Approved Clinician/ Responsible Clinician
    role 85, 146
Approved Mental Health Professional
    (AMHP)
    allied health professionals 115–16
    complex, hybrid role 84–6, 103, 122
    history of role 1
    mental health nurses 131–43
    national register 123
    occupational therapy 115–29
    personal liability 83
    professionalisation of role 147
    Workforce Development Plans 2
Approved Social Worker (ASW) 1
audits 74
autonomy, protection of 60, 162, 168, 173,
    177, 185
availability heuristic 26, 34

B

'bad faith' acts 87, 88
balance of probability thresholds 58, 165
Balint groups 68, 69–70
Banaji, M. 31, 33

Bannigan, K. 122–3
Barnett, P. 33
Becker, D. 46
Becker, H. 165
bed managers 148, 150, 155
behaviour management 46, 48
Best Interests Assessors (BIAs) 123, 146
Bibby, P.F. 117
Biggs, J. 100
biopsychosocial model 145
Blakley, L. 104, 179, 183, 184
blame cultures 60, 62, 73, 89–90
Blomgren, M. 148
Bonilla-Silva, E. 28
borderline personality disorder (BPD) 43
boundaries
    professional 4–5, 13–24, 148–50
    reflective supervision 69, 70
boundary spanning 145–60
Bourdieu, P. 153
Bower, M. 69, 76
Bracken, P. 32, 35
Brammer, A.D. 59, 62
breakaway techniques 48
British Association of Social Work
    (BASW) 125
burnout 2, 67, 106, 191
Burton J, Stanley 87

C

capability frameworks 97
capacity 17, 59, 123, 161–71, 176
Care Act (2014) 121, 156, 162
care coordinators 146
Care Programme Approach 146
Care Quality Commission 83–4, 115
Carpenter, W.T. 46
Carr, J. 123
case study methods 70
Casement, P. 72
category fallacy 26
Chamberlin, J. 175
childhood abuse histories 43
civil actions following decisions 87
Clunis, Christopher 168
Code of Practice
    accountability 88
    capacity 161, 162, 166

communication skills 182
consent 164
occupational therapy 116, 117, 119
risk assessment 58–9
shared decision making (SDM) 185–6
working with families 20
codes of ethics 123
coercion
 lived experience 18–19
 objective versus subjective 178
 resistance to 176
 women in locked wards 41–2
Coffey, M. 122
College of Social Work 89
Commission on Race and Ethnic
 Disparities (CRED) 28
communication boundaries,
 navigating 173–90
communication skills 151, 180–2
Community Mental Health Team
 (CMHT) 14
Community Treatment Order
 (CTO) 18–19, 28
competence, stages of 92, 98
competency frameworks 106, 107, 193
confidentiality 82
consent 21, 163–5
Cooper, A. 76
coproduction 2, 63, 174
cornerstones model 116
Corston Report (2007) 41
counter-narratives 36
Court of Protection 162, 164, 165, 168
COVID-19 99
Craik, C. 119
Creek, J. 119
crisis cafes 63
crisis support plans 63
crisis team 14–15, 17
critical psychiatry 37
critical reflection skills 3, 5, 102, 193
Croisdale-Appleby, D. 105
cultural backgrounds 176
Culverhouse, J. 117
curious questioning 32
cycles of admissions 59

D
Dabiri, E. 35
'damaged' individuals 46
death of patients 58, 60, 62

Debt Respite Scheme (Breathing Space)
 Mental Health Crisis Moratorium 85
deep learning 100
de-escalation 48
defensible accounts, recording 91
defensive practices 69
deliberative democracy 49
'Delivering Race Equality in Mental Health
 Care' 25
dementia 163
Deprivation of Liberty Safeguards 156
Diagnostic Statistical Manual (DSM) 56
dialectical behaviour therapy 14
DiAngelo, R. 35
difference, working with 151
direct observation 102–3
'dirty work' 132, 134, 136, 137, 140–1
disability 108, 120, 161
dissonance 81
doctors' role in assessment processes
 boundary spanning 150, 154
 and capacity 167
 communication skills 181
 and nurses 131, 132, 138, 141
 personality disorder 61
 practice education 104
'doing to' 17, 43, 104
double hermeneutic 132
double vision 5, 193
Draft Mental Health Bill (DHSC and
 Ministry of Justice, 2022) 2
Du Feu, M. 118, 120, 121, 123
duty of candour 84
duty to protect life 60–1
Dwyer, S. 61

E
Earle, F. 83, 90
Early Intervention Team (EIT) 14, 16
economy 68, 148
efficiency 68, 148
Emanuel, E.J. 179
Emanuel, L.L. 179
embodied work 30, 36
emotional containment
 (professionals') 67–79, 192
emotional intelligence 105, 107, 192
emotionally unstable personality disorder
 (EUPD) 43
empowerment 118, 123, 162, 173–4
England
 roles 1

service user involvement
    principles 173–4
epistemic injustice 176
Equality Act (2010) 120, 162
ethical dilemmas 68, 192
ethnicity
    defining 27
    frames and boundaries 25–40
    see also race
Evans, S. 106
Evetts, J. 150
exclusion from decision-making 44, 47

F
failure, perceptions of 62
Fairclough, A. 108
false negatives, avoiding 58
false positives 58
families, working with 19–21, 49, 121
feminist scholarship 42, 106–7
Ferguson, H. 81
Ferguson, I. 62
Fernando, S. 28, 34
fictitious vignettes, in supervisions 91
Field, P. 101
five dimensions of influence in decision-
    making 3–4
flattening hierarchies 48–50, 86, 151
Forrester, J. 70
four stages of learning 98
framing 5, 193–4
free association narrative interviews 67, 70
freedom, right to 60, 162
    see also liberty, right to
Fricker, M. 176
Frost, N. 151
Furness, S. 107, 108

G
Gajwani, R. 28
Garner, S. 29
gender 31, 41–53
General Medical Council (GMC) 174
Gilligan, P. 107, 108
Gilmore, S. 60
Goffman, E. 44
Grant, L. 106
Greenwald, A. 31, 33
Gregor, C. 61
group supervision 91
guided body-work 30
guiding principles of MHA 57

H
habeas corpus writs 88
Halton, W. 74
Hannigan, B. 122
Harkness, D. 105–6
hate figures, professionals as 103
hats, multiple 134–5, 149
    see also hybrid professionals
Healey, P.G.T. 181
Health and Care Bill 83–4
Health and Care Professions Council
    (HCPC) 117
health enabling approaches 117–19
health literacy 178
Heart of England NHS Foundation Trust v JB
    (2014) 164, 165
Heaving Voices Groups 22
Hemmington, J. 61, 83, 104, 117, 122,
    123, 183, 184, 192
Henkel, M. 68
hierarchies of power, flattening 48–50,
    86, 151
Hoggett, P. 73–4
holistic practice 68, 116, 124
Hollway, W. 67, 70
honesty/'truth-telling' 82, 83
Horowitz, M. 17
Hughes, E. 132
human rights 2, 84, 97, 146, 166, 174
Human Rights Act (1998) 59–61, 88, 123,
    135, 163
Hybrid Identities Project 152–6
hybrid professionals 84–6, 103, 122,
    145–60

I
iatrogenic harm 34–5, 57
immunity for decision-making 87
imposter syndrome 102–3, 108
independence, maximisation of 57, 118,
    119–20, 162, 169
Independent Review of the Mental Health
    Act (DHSC, 2018) 2, 169
individualisation of problems 34–5, 42
information, control of 44, 47, 49,
    177, 183
informed choice 13
    see also consent
insight 173, 175–6
inspections 83
institutional racism 27–9, 33
interdisciplinary knowledge 147

International Classification of Diseases
(ICD) 56
interpersonal skills 151
interpretative phenomenological analysis
(IPA) 132
interprofessional collaboration 145, 149,
153, 156
see also multi-disciplinary teams
intersectionality 47
isolation, professional 89

J
Jaconelli, A. 89
Jaconelli, J. 89
jargon 42, 175, 176–7
Jeffcote, N. 42
Jefferson, T. 67, 70
job satisfaction 106
'joined-up working' 152
jurisdictional boundaries 149, 152

K
Kadushin, A. 105–6
Kahneman, D. 31, 33, 34
Karban, K. 116
Kendi, I.X. 29, 32, 35
Kettle, M. 106
Kielhofner, G. 117
Kinman, G. 106
Klein, J.T. 151–2
Knott, G. 122–3
Koprowska, J. 105
Kraemer, S. 76
Kristiansen, K. 43

L
language barriers 183
Lavalette, M. 62
Law Society of Scotland 99
LB Redbridge v G, C & F (2014) 165
LB Tower Hamlets v NB & AU (2019) 168
lead AMHPs 89
Leah, C. 86, 103, 122, 149, 150, 156
learning processes 100–1
Leason, K. 122
least restrictive alternative 17–18, 20,
57, 118
Leedham, M. 102
legal literacy 165
legal protections for AMHP decisions 87–8
liability 81, 82, 83–4, 87–8, 89
liberty, right to 60, 84, 97
liminal spaces 145, 149, 154

Linnaeus, C. 27
listening 103, 120, 178, 179–80, 181, 185
litigation, fear of 84
lived experience 13–24, 192
living with difference 151
local authorities 69, 70, 74, 82–4, 89, 125
locations of work 150, 153
Lynch, M. 102

M
MacPherson, W. 28
magistrates 152
malignant alienation 62, 63
management cultures 67–8, 69,
74–5, 147–8
Markham, S. 34
Mattingly, C. 120
May, Rufus 22
McCabe, R. 181–2
McKeown, A. 49
McKeown, M. 49, 176
McQuire v Western Morning News (1903) 87
mediation 17, 154
medical model
and capacity 165
disability 161
hybrid professionals 146, 151
lived experience 17
occupational therapy 122, 123
personality disorder 55, 57–8,
59, 63
women 46
medication
adherence to 176
lived experience 16–17
nurses 133
and risk 34
withdrawal effects 16–17
memorisation/rote learning 100
Menakem, R. 30, 36
Mental Capacity Act (2005) 123, 161,
162–3, 164, 166, 168–9
Mental Health Acts
and capacity 161, 162, 163, 166, 167
families, working with 19–20
history of 1, 2
personality disorder 57
practice education 104
reform of 2, 131, 145, 156
White Paper MHA (DHSC, 2021) 145,
156, 167–8
Mental Health Minimum Data Set 35

Mental Health Officer (MHO) 1
'mental illness' as construct 15–16
Menzies Lyth, I. 74–5, 76
micro-encounters, assessments
     as 3–4, 191–2
misfeasance in public office 88
model of human occupation (MOHO) 117
modelling good practice 99, 101–2
moral injury 192
moral panics 74
Morgan, C. 28, 34, 35
Morgan, G. 62, 63
Morrison, T. 35
Morriss, L. 149
Mortiboys, A. 98
motivations for becoming an AMHP 101
multi-agency agreements 56
multi-disciplinary teams 118, 146, 183
Munoz Biggs, Valeria 168
Munthe, C. 179, 180

N
narratives in records 35
Nathan, J. 146
National Institute for Health and Care
     Excellence (NICE) 174, 175, 178,
     180, 181, 183
National Strategy on Policing and Mental
     Health 56
National Workforce Plan 122, 125, 191
Nearest Relative 19, 166–7
Neistadt, M.E. 120
networks 151
New Ways of Working in Mental Health
     (DoH, 2007) 131, 140, 141
next of kin, working with 19
'nominated person' role 167
non-oppressive practices 104
non-validation 37
Noordegraaf, M. 147, 148, 150
Northern Ireland
     assessment criteria 107
     roles 1
     service user involvement principles 174
nurses 131–43

O
Obholzer, A. 73
observed, being 102–3
occupational therapy 115–29
ODDESSI trials 20
Olson, M. 184, 185, 186
ongoing personal development 29–30

Open Dialogue (OD) 20–1, 184–5, 186
organisational defences 73, 74–5
O'Sullivan, T. 92
Owen, S. 43

P
Parsloe, E. 102
participant observation 68
paternalism 43, 177–8, 179–80
peer supervision 90–1
peer support 61, 83, 86, 99
Pelto-Piri, V. 177
performance measurement 147–8
personal liability 88
personal safety 139–40
personalised plans 46
personality disorder 55–65
Pieterse, J. 27
Pilgrim, D. 58
police powers 56, 153, 155
polyphonic conversations 185
Powell, J. 46–7, 48
power asymmetries
     AMHPs feeling powerless 62
     experienced as illusory 191–2
     flattening hierarchies 48–50, 86, 151
     and 'insight' 175
     need for trainee supervision 106
     paternalism 177
     shared decision making (SDM) 186
     staff-patient power imbalances 41, 44,
          48–50
     women in locked wards 41, 43, 44, 46–7
practice education 97–113, 193
practice placements 98
pragmatic reasoning 120
presence of a mental disorder,
     establishing 58–9
pressure on decision-makers 61
primary care, working with 119
Prins, H. 34
private and family life, right to 60, 84, 97
probabilistic decision-making 58
professional identity 132, 135, 137, 139,
          141, 146, 148, 156
progression 46, 47, 49
projective identification 72–3
proportionate action 57
psychiatric models 32, 55–6, 58, 151, 181
psychoanalytic theory 68
psychosis 14, 16–18, 28, 184
psycho-social spaces 73–4, 90
punishments 44–6

Q

questions, asking good 32, 181–2
Quinn, A. 45, 48–9
Quirk, A. 85, 103

R

race
    Community Treatment Order
        (CTO) 28
    defining 26–7
    detention rates by race 2, 25, 28, 104
    frames and boundaries 25–40
    institutional racism 27–9, 33
    professionals' 103, 108
    racial justice 30
    racisms 29
    racist processing 25–6
Ravalier, J. 106
reasonable adjustments 119
reasonable care, duty to take 87, 88
recalcitrance 176
reciprocity 177, 178, 179–80
recording practices 35–6, 91, 175
Reed Report (1992) 41
referrals 31–3
reflection-in-action 92
reflective practice 81–95
reflective practice groups 67, 68, 69, 71–7
reflective supervision 67–79, 82–3
reframing 5, 193–5
regulation of AMHPs 83–4, 107
Reid, W. 30
Rein, M. 5, 193
relational agency 153
relationships, developing 101, 102, 151,
        153, 178
remote working 99–100
repair 182
restrictive interventions 41–2, 44–6, 47–8
retention 106
risk
    balancing with rights 59–61
    and capacity 163, 168
    history of abuse 43
    MH legislation 104–5
    occupational therapy 118
    personality disorder 55–65
    racialised patients 33–5
    suicidal ideas 168–9
    trade-offs 148
    use of medication 34
Roberts, Z.R. 73
Robinson, G. 69

Royal College of Occupational Therapists
        (RCOT) 117, 118, 119, 123–4

S

safety 139–40
Sainsbury Centre for Mental Health
        (SCMH) 34
Sandman, L. 179, 180
Schön, D. 5, 92, 147, 193
Scotland
    assessment criteria 107
    roles 1
    service user involvement principles 174
seclusion 42, 44–6, 47
section 3 orders 18
section 135 152
section 136 56, 57, 155
section 139 87–9
Seikkula, J. 184, 185, 186
self-determination 162, 174, 177
self-harm 44, 55, 57–8, 60–1, 168–9
senior managers 75–6
service-user-led safe spaces 63
Sewell, H. 28, 30, 32, 35
shared decision making (SDM) 173–90
Sit, H. 100
Skills for Care 115
Smith, J.A. 132
Smith, M. 168
Social Care Wales 107
social intelligence 106
social justice 146, 149, 192
social learning theory 101–2
social model of care 134
social model of disability 161
social perspectives 55
Social Work England 83, 107
Soteria Houses 21
Spandler, H. 49
staff shortages 47
staff-patient power imbalances 41, 44,
        48–50
statutory roles 1–2
stereotypes
    gender 42
    professionals 108
    race and ethnicity 31, 32, 33
    racisms 29, 30
    unconscious bias 26
Stevens, M.J. 117, 121
Stone, K. 122
street triage services 56
strengths-based approaches 63, 163

stress 2, 81, 106, 191, 192
Sue, D.W. 29, 35
suicidal ideas 55, 57–8, 60–1, 168
supervision
    lack of 82–3
    legal requirements for 90–1
    occupational therapy 123
    open-learning environments 191
    reflective supervision 67–79, 82–3
    remote 99
    of trainees 105–7
surface-level learning 100
symbolic violence 46–7

T
Tang, C. 100
Taylor, P.J. 46–7
Teach Back method 175
Tew, J. 116
therapeutic relationship 48, 62, 121–2,
    132, 193
thinking in cases 67, 70
Thomas, P. 32, 35
Thompson, L. 181–2
time pressures 61, 183
Timms, P. 176, 177
tort law 87
toxic interaction theory 26, 32–3, 35
trade-offs 148
training
    assessment criteria 107
    practice education 97–113
    race and ethnicity 29–30
    role of senior managers 76
    supervision 105–7
transparent decision-making 59, 84,
    104, 120
trauma
    from the assessment process
        itself 191
    embodied 30
    gender 41–2
    history of abuse 46, 56
    racial trauma 36
    women in locked wards 42, 43
trauma-informed practice 26, 36, 49
Travers, R. 42

U
unconditional support 48
unconscious bias 26, 28–9, 31, 32, 37, 193
unconscious competence 92
United Nations Convention on the
    Rights of Persons with Disabilities
    (2008) 161

V
Van der Kolk, B. 30, 36
Vernon, P. 34
vicarious liability 89
Vicary, S. 61, 81, 122, 132, 193
Vinkers, D. 104

W
W, R (on the application of W) v Doncaster
    Metropolitan Borough Council
    (2003) 87
Wadeson, H. 46
Waks, C. 148
Wales
    assessment criteria 107
    roles 1
    service user involvement principles 174
Walker, J. 107–8
Walker, S. 28
Warner, S. 43
Watson, D. 122
Watts, D. 62, 63
Webber, M. 146
well-being of AMHPs 61, 81
    see also burnout; stress
Whitaker, R. 34
White Paper MHA (DHSC, 2021) 145,
    156, 167–8
Whittle, M. 62
Wilkins, T. 43, 69
Williams, J. 42
women 41–53
Wong, C.J. 5
Work Discussion groups 68
Workforce Development Plans 2, 69–70
working from home 99

Y
Yelloly, M. 68